KNOWLEDGE OF THE GODS
By A. M. Muhammad

April 1982

Copyright 2015 © by A. M. Muhammad

All rights reserved. This book, or parts thereof, may not be reproduced in any form without permission.

Published by:
New World Nation of Islam Publications
PO Box 8466
Newark, New Jersey 07108

www.newworldnationislam.com

Library of Congress Cataloging1 In1 Publication Data:
Knowledge of The Gods
ISBN 13-digit 978-01-98904251-21-9 (Paper)
ISBN 10-digit 0989042529
ISBN 13digit 978-1-944992-04-0 (Hardback)
ISBN 10-digit 1944992049
ISBN 13-digit 9781-01-98904251-31-6 (e-Book)
LCCN: 2015938956
1.
Nation of Islam1   3. Elijah Muhammad1   4. Messenger of Allah1   5. Malcolm X1   6. Minister Farrakhan1   7. Newark, NJ1   8. Fruit of Islam1   9. New World Nation of Islam1   10. Minister James Shabazz1   11. Belton X1   12. Fard Saviour1   13. Saviour's Day1   14. Allah in Muhammad Speaks1   15. Prophet Muhammad ibn Abdullah1   16. Master Fard Muhammad

Cover design and layout by Nuance Art
Book design by NuanceArt order@aCreativeNuance.com
Edited by F.C. Mutadirah W. Ali
Proofreaders/Transcribers Samataha Ali, Captain Nobel Ali

Printed in USA

DEDICATION

Thanks, thanks to our Father, the Most Honorable Mr. Elijah Muhammad, Who taught us to be good Muslims and to believe in God, in the Person of Master Fard Muhammad.

KNOWLEDGE OF THE GODS
Introduction

In the Name of Allah, Our God and Saviour, in the Person of Master Fard Muhammad, the Beneficent, the Merciful. To Him alone do we submit and seek refuge.

We are living in a time when a higher knowledge is necessary if we are to survive. The light of the old world is extinguished and Allah is making Himself known. The highest knowledge and greatest light, is of God from God. This labor of love by the Mahdi exposes us to this light.

"I, Allah am the Seer. A Book which We have revealed to thee that thou mayest bring forth men by their Lord's permission, from darkness into light, to the way of the Mighty, the Praised One." (Holy Qur'an 14:1). This KNOWLEDGE OF THE GODS gives us a New Way of thinking.

This Godly Knowledge enables us to rise above the darkness and decadence of this decaying world. Muhammad, the Divine Spokesman of Allah, in the Person of Master Fard Muhammad, brings us face to face with the reality of Allah and what we must know today.

For thousands of years the KNOWLEDGE OF THE GODS has been absent in the people, except for a few. Now this Wisdom is flowing like water. The Mahdi displays profound insight in this long awaited KNOWLEDGE OF THE GODS.

We have known the author all of our awakened life, and his actions have been nothing short of uprightness. His uprightness serves as a model for us all.

KNOWLEDGE OF THE GODS

He brings with this effort his experiences from the battlefield to having a Nation on His shoulders. We wish to thank Him for this Guiding Light.

For many years He has suffered, struggled and searched for these truths in order to present these truths. We benefit directly from His labor through this timely little book KNOWLEDGE OF THE GODS.

Creative awareness is what we need, which is why we should all value this work. The Honorable Mr. Elijah Muhammad said, "You should remember that the time of Wisdom, now, is coming to you. And creative thoughts, now, are coming to you."

Look carefully into the words of this book. Nothing is said without reason or meaning. We are children of the Creator and will make unlimited progress under the Guidance of Allah, in the Person of Master Fard Muhammad.

The Honorable Mr. Elijah Muhammad prepared us for this. The Wisdom, Idea, and way of thinking of Master Fard Muhammad, to Whom Praises are due forever, is Superior to any way of believing today. There is no one to hinder His Image or Thought for that which has not yet been conceived in our brain.

This Wisdom has the effect of directing us to the root of things, awakening us to the knowledge of self. The KNOWLEDGE OF THE GODS is designed to put us on the top.

Muhammad, with his words of Guidance, teaches us the nature of life and the law of life. In an Ant Colony the Action Centered Ants awake first and make noise with their antennae to awaken the others. To do what? To serve the Queen! She is the essence of the Colony. We know, as KNOWLEDGE OF THE GODS, that we can serve our Originator better by knowing more about Him. All the ants know who the Queen is, and their relationship to Her.

A. M. Muhammad

As basic KNOWLEDGE OF THE GODS, shouldn't we know the essence of our lives? At the center of our lives is THE SUPREME BEING, and what we are about to read teaches us to think in the way of Gods and behave in a Godly manner. New Thoughts produce new actions. Muhammad offers these keys to turn those rusty locks. We are in need of what is written here. Knowledge is just to know, and we must move on what we know.

Our moving on what we understand of this truth, will demonstrate that our spiritual sight hasn't become locks too rusty to open. Only those with a high spiritual sight can see God as He Is.

This work is in the true light of his previous book, UNCLE YAH YAH, wherein he says, "I am Uncle Yah Yah and I have something to say to you. I must have my say. Whether the fools accept these small truths or not - I could care less. This message is for my kinfolk. The Wise Ones, who have awaited for me to trumpet this call to higher consciousness for more than 400 years."

We agree that he indeed has something to say, and, we are the richer for it.

This book is food for the Gods. Satisfying, informative and fulfilling. "Man shall not live by bread alone, but by every word that comes from the mouth of God."

Some books are to be tasted, others chewed and swallowed. This Divine work should be carefully chewed and digested and made a part of our being. Since we are what we eat, let us feast on THE KNOWLEDGE OF THE GODS.

Written by,
The Mighty F.O.I.

KNOWLEDGE OF THE GODS

A. M. Muhammad

Introduction 1

Chapter One Black Woman The Queen Mother of The Planet 7

Chapter Two First Light 22

Chapter Three Operation Clean-Up And Get The Mosque 26

Chapter Four Respect For Our Leader And Prophet Of Islam 31

Chapter Five Fight The Devil..34

Chapter Six Pass Over 36

Chapter Seven Knowledge Of The Gods...................................38

Chapter Eight The Will of Allah..56

Chapter Nine The Time 71

Chapter Ten Prayer 83

Chapter Eleven Our History...96

Chapter Twelve The Event...117

Chapter Thirteen Saviour's Day 131

Chapter Fourteen..

You Can't Accept One Without Accepting The Other And The Difference In Fard Of Today From Fard Of 1930 148

Chapter Fifteen Ramadan 162

Chapter Sixteen A Brief Talk...175

Chapter Seventeen Brief Talk II 203

Chapter Eighteen Home Coming...223

Chapter Nineteen Counsel To The Household of Brother Ali ...238

KNOWLEDGE OF THE GODS

Chapter One
Black Woman
The Queen Mother
Of The Planet Earth

The Holy Tribe of Shabazz (Shabazz means Perfection) are the original family that came with this part of the planet. The other part called moon is the coffin of an old enemy of Allah, who thought he could destroy civilization with high explosives. He succeeded only in blowing away that piece called moon and changing the orbit and the atmosphere of this part, which is now called Earth. At that time the planet was called Blue Ether.

We, the black Gods and Goddesses came to this part 66 trillion years ago. Our Scientists took an expedition which traversed the earth 2 1/2 times looking for the best part. We decided to establish our new civilization at the sight now known as Mecca, Arabia. We marked that sight with a Black Stone, also known as the Sacred Kaaba of the Muslims.

It is because of that portion of our history that the speculation concerning the creation of our Black Woman came about.

It is most important that we remember what our Father the Honorable Mr. Elijah Muhammad (the Last God, of the Old World and the First God, of the New World) taught us. He said, "Don't try to teach any history past 66 trillion years, because anything past 66 trillion years is considered dream history." And concerning our women He said, "If you want to know when they were created, they

KNOWLEDGE OF THE GODS

came with the Blackman." Whenever he came she came also, and there was never a time when she wasn't with him.

We thank Allah for such truth and divine guidance regarding this science of the past and future of our Beautiful Black Woman. Our women have always been with us. She remains the most loyal and the most loving and dedicated to her Black Man regardless to the hard trials of history, she is still with us.

For example, look at 1555 Jamestown, Virginia, when the slave ship named Jesus brought the first Shabazzians, 21 in number (11 women and 10 men) to North America. The Queen-Mother of the planet earth, was kidnapped and forced into shackles and chains and sold into slavery. The Black Man suffered the inhuman breeding camps and she suffered too. He suffered the beastly auction block and she too went to the highest bid. He labored long and hard under the sun and the whip in the devils cotton fields, she was beaten and forced to work at his side. The lynch, rape and murder of him was also of her. She never deserted us.

It is a historical reality that the women goes with the spoils of war. But our Black Queen would not leave us. No. They could not be forced to leave us no matter what they suffered. We thank Allah forever and ever for our great and strong Black Goddess.

Rejoice my beautiful black sister, wipe your weeping eyes. Your suffering is over. Your Saviour has arrived in the person of Master Fard Muhammad. He has declared that He will force the world to respect you and His angels will fight and kill those who mistreat you. No more will your head hang low. Be proud and happy because this is your Day.

Allah loves you Black Woman, Queen Mother of the Planet Earth.

Our Saviour, Master Fard Muhammad, continues to teach every

day that we must love, honor, respect and protect our beautiful Black Woman. She is the Black Goddess, the Queen Mother of the planet earth and the hand that rocked the cradle of every civilization known. It is through our Black Goddess that we will reproduce the Gods of the NEW WORLD (Kingdom of Heaven, or Gods).

Our Saviour seeks only to please Allah and is dedicated to let our Father's (The Honorable Mr. Elijah Muhammad's) will be done. He told me that of all the divine supreme wisdom taught to Him by Our Father, there are but three things we must do to make Our Father proud and maintain His love for us. They are:

1. Be good Muslims; Muslim means complete submission to Allah and Muhammad.
2. Respect, Honor, and Protect our Women.
3. Do good and righteousness regardless to whom or what.

The Saviour told me that men are created a degree above women and all Muslim men are responsible for upholding and protecting Muslim women's rights. He said that in His Kingdom (New World Nation of Islam) there will be a stiff penalty for any Muslim brother who allows a Muslim woman's rights to be violated in His presence. It is better to die fighting than to let that happen Brothers. The greatness of our civilization depends on the right treatment of our women.

You must remember that we are the Gods and Goddesses of the universe. We came from other planets before making the planet earth the home of Islam. The Lord (Master Fard) said we are on our way back to reunite with our neighbors on the seven inhabited planets in our solar system. They are waiting for us. Flying saucers ain't no joke.

We are the fathers and mothers of civilization. Every civilization ever created is recorded in the genes of the aboriginal Black man

KNOWLEDGE OF THE GODS

and woman. Genes are the transmitter of heredity and character. When a people live or act in a certain way for a long period of time their actions form a pattern and become characteristic of those people. Those developed characteristics are passed on to the offspring in what is called heredity. Therefore, heredity is the book or record of a people. In the genes of the aboriginal blackman and woman is the Encyclopedia of Civilization.

Scientist call this substance (record) in the genes DNA (deoxyribonucleic acid). DNA is the essential component of all living matter and the basic chromosomal material transmitting the hereditary pattern. A chromosome is any of the microscopic rod shaped bodies bearing genes.

The devil Scientists are now trying to break down the code of the DNA. They believe that this code (knowledge) will give them the power to create life (clones) also know our ancient past and our future. The future Hereafter is not for the devils to see.

Prophet Muhammad Ibn Abdullah (peace be unto him) gave us a description of heaven (our future) that we could relate to in this life in the writings of the Holy Qur'an. But these descriptions are only a sample of the future heaven that none have seen yet, but Master Fard Muhammad. As it was in the beginning so shall it be in the end. We came from heaven (space), and we must return to our father in heaven. The devils are now seeking out the heavens (starry space). He will find a divine flame waiting on him. However, if the idea of a heaven had not been recorded in our genes we could not have any concept of God and heaven. We could not have had faith in a day the Angels of the Lord would come in fiery chariots, coming to carry us back where we came from, heaven, over Jordan, and after studying the higher sciences for twenty years in Egypt, on into space travel. Without the Black Woman we could not reproduce the Encyclopedia of Civilization Record.

A. M. Muhammad

Things on earth shall be as it is in heaven. The Holy Quran says that paradise is a garden of joy where you are among pure and beautiful companions and we would hear no vain or sinful talk, but only the saying of Peace, Peace, and Praise be to Allah. The true believers being well pleased with his Lord, and the Lord being well pleased with them. He would never want to leave such a happy and peaceful condition and company.

The heavenly garden can and should apply to our beautiful Black Woman, Queen Mother of the universe. The Black Woman is one of the blessed gardens promised to the true believers. Just one good woman, or good land, and you will produce enough growth and development to satisfy any man. Your garden is the land in which you plant your seed to reproduce good fruit, the future angels of the Lord. (This also refers to the individual brain).

If you have wives who are true companions and love you and trust you and only wish you peace in this world and peace in the hereafter, then you have your heaven right now. Man's home is his castle. Also, man's body is the house of or temple of God. And a wife who is pleasing to her husband in all she does, and smells of perfume, and is a true believer in Allah and Muhammad . . . that is heaven.

It takes gods to reproduce gods. A Black Queen married to a fool or some other dumb animal will not reproduce a god. Our Father said that we must stop our women from sweethearting with the devil and marrying them. That goes for the brothers too, this act is becoming the greatest of crimes. We must separate not integrate. We must have mates of the same kind. The word mate is best described exactly by Allah and the nature world.

The Holy Qur'an says that Allah created man and of man he created his mate. God did not create a new life in his making woman. He fashioned her out of the same material he used in the creation of man. Out of man He made woman. Allah is the Greatest.

Everything is created in pairs. Snakes marry snakes, birds marry birds, fish marry fish and cows marry cows. Do you get the message? Do not marry other than your own kind. Our Black Queen is the most beautiful and with her 16 original shades of black, brown, red, and yellow, she is a true flower garden.

Before going any further let me direct a few words to the devils, hypocrites and enemies of Islam. Your perception of us does not disturb no one or nothing. When you go your perception will go with you. We are at peace. We are not imitating any philosophy or culture that you can judge. We are not of this world. We have a New World. Truth and Numbers are our science. Leave us alone, or Allah will cause you great suffering.

Now, as we return to our subject, I would like to quote Sister Tynetta Muhammad, from her book titled, THE WOMAN IN ISLAM EDUCATIONAL SERIES.

"After God, makes a Messenger, then He makes for the Messenger a family or families to back up the Messenger in His Divine Work and Mission to give life to the dead. This is not a voluntary act on the part of the messenger, but it is by the Command of God, and by His Divine Will to order into the Creation His pattern and design of a New Heaven and a New Earth. Thus, He teaches the woman through the Messenger some of the wisdom that He has designed in the making up of a New World Order in the Latter Creation."

THE SUN, MOON AND STARS AND THE NINE PLANETS

The study of the Messenger's domestic life corresponds to the study of our universe of the Sun, Moon and Stars and the Sun's family of nine planets. Everywhere one reads in the Holy Qur'an of a revealed law to govern the people, one reads of a corresponding sign in nature to match that law in the divine creation of the heavens and the earth. This bears witness to their divine origin coming from the originator Himself, the grantor and sustainer of all life on earth and in our universe. After God created Himself by His Own divine power and will, He causes everything to pattern itself after the nature of His Own creation which is Islam, meaning entire submission to the will of God.

The activation of light and heat energy from the sun causes all life of the nine planets to rotate around her, at approximately the same rate of speed of 1,037 1/3rd miles per hour. So it is in the life of a chosen Messenger of Allah. God sets His messenger in motion by His Own divine light and calls all spiritual forms of life into being so that He serves their spiritual growth and development as a light giving sun.

Thus, the Messenger's life pattern on earth and that of His Nation corresponds to the signs of our universe. This is in our Holy Flag of Islam. The Sun, the Moon and the Stars which actually include the planets that we are given to study in our lessons.

In THE THEOLOGY OF TIME, the Honorable Elijah Muhammad speaks on this subject of our women in relation to the nature of things in our earth and in our universe.

"The lower heavens that the Scientist refer to as our heavens, the sun family they call it, contain nine planets. That red sun rules the nine planets. The nine planets are the Kingdom of God which also represents the God-like Wisdom and Power.

The Black Woman was made by the God who made Himself. God makes woman to imitate our nine planets. So, Brothers, don't take her for nothing. She is something too. Treat her good if she's producing men and women for you and I. She should be honored and respected for having this kind of power. I studied our women,

KNOWLEDGE OF THE GODS

their actions, and the creation of them in regard to the knowledge of the Man and what he had in mind. I say brother, I am with the Holy Qur'an. The Holy Qur'an teaches us that she is to be respected as we. The only thing that is different is that we are a little better than her in the power of our creation. We have more powerful brains than she because we were made to rule. She is a helpmate. She helps the man wherever she can. It's wonderful to know thyself. The greatest thing you lack is that you don't know yourself. We must treat them right and honor them. Then they will learn to honor you and they will produce you a little baby who will honor you."

All praises are forever due to Allah in the person of Master Fard Muhammad, for our Black Woman. Allah said Be, and the planets came, found their orbits and submitted. We are like stars, none of us are the same, scattered and separated by vast space. But the one law of the universe governs us all. Each planets rotation is a private relation with his creator.

Our Black Woman is our mate and friend and the Queen Mother of the planet earth.

The Lord taught me that the number nine is the number of completion. The science of the sun and its nine planets refer to the perfect universal order by which the Black man and woman must aspire to.

This is an old science and the original man has practiced polygamy throughout history. Most black, brown, red and yellow civilization still do today. The European has always been out of accord with nature and the universal order of things. Polygamy calls for exceptional character in the man and woman who are practicing it.

The sun gives freely of its life, light and warmth to its family of planets. Their life depends on that suns ability to keep on shining. If it goes out, the planets go out too. Polygamy is not an easy way of life. You must have a strong knowledge of God and self before you can even begin to choose a mate.

The world steps aside for the man who knows where he is going. He must have that strong character that can only come from knowledge of God, and self. Only then can he generate enough energy to produce life in abundance. Such an abundance above and beyond his needs should be shared. A wealthy individual, mentally and physically, can support several families. Polygamy is not for the average man. Such a way of life calls for superior men and women whose goals and wisdom are above petty selfishness and jealousy. Polygamous societies are generally free from the social ills of Western Civilization. Polygamy builds strong character.

The man must have above average health if he is to satisfy more than one wife. His virility must be stronger than average. His ability to govern several families must be great or the women will not accept his leadership and his household will fall into complete chaos.

In all Muslim Nations polygamy is for the exceptional (unusually good) and not the rule for everybody. To impose such a weighty lifestyle on the average man would be unjust to say the least. Everyone does not develop in higher understanding at the same rate of speed. Also, to be responsible for marital choices one must know what constitutes a pair. He cannot have this knowledge unless he has a thorough knowledge of God and self.

Mates are the same mentally and physically. Proper mating produces true friendship. Friendship allows them to be themselves with each other and supportive in everything they do. As a result, their pursuit of peace and happiness is complete. All praises are forever due to Allah and Muhammad.

KNOWLEDGE OF THE GODS

WIFE BEATING

Our Father, the Most Honorable Mr. Elijah Muhammad said, "If you have a disagreement with your wife, take her behind closed doors and when you come out have the problem solved. Not that I'm telling you to do her physical harm, but just solve the problem."

Master Fard (our Saviour) told me that physically abusing our women is against the law of the New World Nation of Islam.

Prophet Muhammad says, we must treat our women with kindness and to be gentle with them. GENTLE means: Of the upper class; refined; courteous; generous; kind; tame; patient; not harsh or hard or rough. Never strike them in the face, nor our children, nor should we strike even our domestic animals in the face.

However, the head of the household is the boss and must be as sharp with teaching his wisdom as he is in administering the sword of discipline. Discipline and regimentation are the signs of a great society. Regimen means: A system of diet and exercise for improving health, standard of living, etc. . . .

We must put our women back on top where they belong and keep them there.

Our Black Woman, Queen Mother of the planet earth, is the most important part of our lives, next to God. Next to the life-giving Sun on this planet, as we know it, could not exist if it was not for the power of the moon over our waters and our growth. That little piece of dried up planet, called moon, is very powerful. And when you understand the significance of that power of hers to influence its very magnetic atmosphere, as well as our brain, you will love, honor, respect and protect her.

Exceptional means: UNUSUALLY GOOD. You should study the words *unusual* and *good*. Look these two words up in the dictionary and learn all about yourself.

It is our day to be the best Muslims on this earth. We must lead the world in righteousness.

Holy Qur'an, chapter 3, verse 109 says: "YOU ARE THE BEST NATION RAISED UP FOR MEN: You enjoin good and forbid evil and you believe in Allah. And if the people of the Book (old world) had believed, it would had been better for them. Some of them are Believers (in the teachings of our Father the Honorable Mr. Elijah Muhammad) but most of them are transgressors."

Footnote 475 says: "Not only are the Muslims the chosen people of God, who are now called upon to be the standard-bearers of Truth in the world, but they are at the same time declared to be the best of the people that had ever been chosen for this purpose. This was no doubt due to the Excellence of that Great Teacher who thoroughly purified them of the worst vices and made perfect the light within them. No prophet ever found a people in a worse condition, and none ever raised His people to such eminence. Note that the Excellence of the Muslim people lies in their enjoining Good and forbidding evil and in their great faith in Allah. If they lose these characteristics, they lose their EXCELLENCE as well."

In closing this subject, I would like to speak briefly on Children and Prayer, Food and Fasting and Cleanliness.

Brother Fard Saviour, taught me that there will be many New Worlds succeeding each other as we grow through higher civilizations. We will never be stagnate. Our government will be under the person of God Himself, and based on progress, excellence and humility, doing good regardless to whom or what. Of all the New Worlds coming and the many changes brought about by such new ways of living, He said, the one thing that will not change is prayer. He said that prayer is here forever and ever. There will

KNOWLEDGE OF THE GODS

always be prayer to Allah, The Lord of all the Worlds.

You, my Beautiful Black Sister, are the hand that rocks the cradle of civilization. The first teacher of our tomorrow, our children. All that they need to know in life, they have the ability to learn in the first five years of their lives. Their minds are sharp and more advanced than us because they are made of the best that is in you and your mate.

All the good that is in you make up the heredity of your child. He is your future. You give the child life as he passes through you then that child provides a life for you. Teaching that child and giving the best you can to send them forward with the best survival tools to take the family to distant horizons or higher aspirations.

You must, my sister, realize that the greatest work of yours is to teach our children the most important lessons of survival. The greatest of these lessons are to submit to Allah and Prayer. Teach the children to pray as early as they are able to imitate you. If you sisters don't teach our children to pray by your example Allah will not bless you or your non-praying children. And Allah would not care for us at all, if it were not for our prayers. The old angels know what I'm talking about, because all they survive on is prayer. Sisters, please don't take what I'm saying to you, concerning our good Muslim children of the New World Nation of Islam, lightly. I am ordering you to do your job.

You must teach them to pray but not by telling them. Each of you must be an example. If you don't pray, they won't pray. Do it Black Goddess and Allah will bless your great Genius (genes) to shine today, tomorrow and in the future like the brilliant and illuminating New Moon that you are. Shine on Black Woman, Queen Mother of the Planet Earth. Our Father said, "If they are 14 years old and do not pray, beat them."

Teach the children to have love and unity of black-self and kind and to protect each other against the loss of life and property of our own. Teach them Word Is Bond and to fight the devil's suggestions of laziness, envy, hatred, selfishness, pride, jealousy, fighting and killing each other. Teach them children to help each other and to be brave and to die the death of a Muslim, taking the devils off our planet, as you have learned to do.

Our future is in your hands Queen Mother of everything. Is it any wonder that Our Saviour demands that we learn to love, honor, respect and protect you before we (the Black Man) can be recognized? Nothing is more important to us today then our Beautiful Black Woman. Do your job right, sisters. It is a must that you teach our children to pray. Muslims can't survive without prayer.

FOOD & FASTING

Our Father taught us HOW TO EAT TO LIVE but some of us Live to Eat. He said it is what we eat that takes us away or keeps us here. If we make ourselves sick from eating the wrong foods we should be ashamed to go to the doctor. He taught us that we don't need all the different foods we are eating. We consume too much sugar and salt and many other things that are poison to our systems.

NEVER EAT THE FILTHY HOG

We are what we eat. Our Father (the Honorable Mr. Elijah Muhammad) taught that whole wheat bread, navy beans, fruit, whole milk and butter is all that we need to eat. Stop eating all day and all night. One meal a day will keep you healthy. Study the HOW TO EAT TO LIVE, Part One and Two and live by it.

Some of you may say, I get tired of eating beans all the time.

KNOWLEDGE OF THE GODS

Beans can be prepared in many different ways. Some of our older sisters, such as Sister Lanna Shabazz (the Champ's cook), Sister Hilda (of the Nile restaurant, Elizabeth, NJ) Sister Tynetta Muhammad, and many more who would love to pass on these bean recipes to you, once they see that you respect the teachings. These sisters will show you how to prepare these Divine Recipes in a sacred manner respecting the fact that these are the foods prescribed especially for us by God, Himself.

Brother Field Supreme Minister Fard Saviour, told me that after seven years of following the strict regimentation of HOW TO EAT TO LIVE, one meal a day, one meal every other day, one meal every three days and one meal a week, we will grow into a completely new people (A New Growth). We will be New mentally and New physically. Fasting is our New Way of Life. Remember: One of the things that aggravates our Father the most, is to see a fat Muslim. Eat to live. Don't live to eat.

CLEANLINESS is next to Godliness. Take a bath at least once a day. Keep your house clean. If you have one suit of clothes, keep it clean. The Saviour does not like to see our women and children filthy and shabby dressed. We believe in our women and children being clean and smelling good. Don't try to hide the dirt with strong deodorants, which is a common practice of this evil society. Be clean. Take a bath. Muslims love water.

To complain because you are always giving, is to deny Allah's blessing you to have that which you give.

These are the names of Our Father's wives, seven of whom worked for the Nation of Islam as secretaries: Sister Clara Muhammad, Sister Lucille Karriem Muhammad, Sister June Muhammad, Sister Evelyn Muhammad, Sister Tynetta Muhammad, Sister Ola Hughes Karriem Muhammad, Sister Bernque Cushmeer, and Sister Lovlita Clayborne. Of these eight wives Our Father has

21 children. They are our family that is those who hold on to Our Father's teachings.

Today is your day Black Woman. Rise and Shine, Queen Mother of the Planet Earth and give all praises to Allah in the person of the Honorable Mr. Elijah Muhammad, Who raised from amongst us our Beloved Saviour, Master Fard Muhammad.

UNUSUALLY GOOD

UNUSUAL: Remarkable, rare, extraordinary, strange, outstanding, great, uncommon, special, distinguished, prominent, noteworthy, awe-inspiring, unique, fine, unheard of, unexpected, seldom met with, surprising, superior, astonishing, amazing, prodigious, incredible, inconceivable, atypical, conspicuous, exceptional, eminent, significant, memorable, renowned, refreshing, singular, fabulous, wonderful.

GOOD: Moral, upright, just, honest, worthy, respectable, noble, ethical, fair, guiltless, blameless, pure, truthful, decent, kind, conscientious, honorable, charitable, kind, considerate, tolerant, generous.

Chapter Two
First Light

The teachings of the Most Honorable Mr. Elijah Muhammad, is now being taught by Master Fard Muhammad, our Saviour from a high spiritual plane.

You thought that you understood His teachings before, but you had only understood that Elijah was the Messenger of Allah.

Brother Fard taught me that if you accept Our Father, Elijah Muhammad as an apostle, then your reward is that of an apostle. But if you accept Him as God, you will receive a God's reward.

This is the Supreme Wisdom as taught to us by our Saviour, the Son of Man. You may ask, "What man is He the Son of?" He is the son of the only Fearless and Supremely wise black God in the Wilderness of North America, the Most Honorable Mr. Elijah Muhammad.

Not a physical Son, but a spiritual Son who honors the father as the father honored and prepared the path for the Son. Elijah prepared the way. He never let us forget that Allah is in the Person of Master Fard Muhammad, who came in 1930. We will crush the wicked after the resurrection of our people, the so-called American Negroes.

He, Elijah (like John the Baptist) came to His own, but His own knew Him not. He accepted His own but His own accepted Him not. You have begged white America to remember Martin L. King, but to forget about Elijah. You were blind to the true identity (spiritual sight) of Elijah and you were not to know His true identity until the Saviour taught it to you.

And as many that will accept Him and the teaching of Him,

Elijah, shall be as sons and daughters of God. It takes a God, to recognize a God.

Fard Saviour brings in the New World Nation of Islam. He reveals the high secrets that bears witness that Our Father, Elijah, is the last God of the Old World and the first God of the New World. The Great Master with the crown of the universe upon His head. He was dead, but is alive forever more.

The Saviour taught me that Our Father told Him that in the time that He, the Saviour would reveal the secrets to the general nation the nine planets would line up to show that the heavens bear witness that the Son of Man is now gathering His people.

The icy cold from the north would be a sign to the enemy devils that they cannot win in a fight against Him because He commands the forces of nature and the Third World War called Armageddon will start. At that time we will not have to teach you that the white man is the devil because the time would be so hard, the white man will show you how much of a devil he can be. No more jobs! No more welfare and handouts! Conditions are so bad economically, the white man must put the black slave out in order to help his own white self. If you don't know that he is the devil now, then nothing we can tell you will wake you up to that fact.

The teachings of the Saviour Master Fard Muhammad brings you face to face with God, Himself. You must come out of that slavery teaching that God, is a spook up in the sky that you can't see until you die. It is foolish Black men and Black women, for you to accept such teaching as the truth.

If you went to heaven after you die, don't you think that the heads of the Christian Church would be just dying all over the place trying to hurry and get to heaven? But you don't see that. Instead, you see the best doctors in the world being called to try to keep those leaders (the pope) from dying. They want to stay here on this planet as long as they can. Wake up Black brothers and sisters! Don't go for that old slavery trick anymore.

THE BLACK MAN IS GOD, AND THE WHITE MAN IS THE DEVIL

If you can bear witness that evil is spread far and wide over the planet because of man's hands, then common sense tells you that if the devils can influence people all over the planet to do evil, then should not God, have power to influence the world? Some men ought to be susceptible to God's power and influence. Such a man would teach righteousness, want for your brother what you want for yourself, pray, fast, respect the prophets and the books they brought and say He Allah God, is one God the ever living and independent God.

These are the teachings of Our Father the Most Honorable Mr. Elijah Muhammad. He is the mouth of God, the hands of God, the feet of God, raised up from amongst us as all men of God in the past. Or would you rather believe the white man who says, "God, won't lower Himself to speak to no nigger?" Think about that.

Wake up Black men and women and reclaim your own the kingdom of Islam, heaven right now while you live under a wise king, Master Fard Muhammad, the Mahdi, our Divine Saviour. Saviour means *one who saves*. If Fard Saviour did not hold on to Our Father's teachings in order to preserve them and to teach us a higher understanding of the true identity of Our Father the Most Honorable Mr. Elijah Muhammad; you and I, the so-called negro who are the original tribe of Shabazz (the God tribe) who came with the planet earth 66 trillion years ago, would be lost forever. The Saviour saves us from the wicked and evil satan.

The Saviour is the proof that the promise of Elijah is true.

Our Father taught us that what He was giving us would only prepare us for the Saviour and that when the Saviour came He would give us all the truth, a higher Islam or Supreme Wisdom.

Many of you with knowledge (brothers and sisters with an X) are wondering why the majority of the nation is scattered about and many are in the mud after standing so tall in the temples throughout the country.

The Saviour says to you to come on back home. It is time. The Kingdom could not come until there was a falling away first.

The teachings of Our Father gives us life and brings us face to face with Allah God, in the Person of Master Fard Muhammad. Not a spook, spirit or ghost but a man raised by the hand of God, to lead us Eastward back into our own Holy Nation of Islam.

Master Fard is our Leader and Prophet of Islam to you and I and He will soon be recognized by the Muslim nations all over the planet earth.

Chapter Three
Operation Clean-Up And Get The Mosque

All praises are forever due to Allah.

What is that thing that tells the Robin Red Breast that his struggle is over, that his seemingly endless flight is over and that he has arrived?

His awareness, that he has reached his goal, makes him want to cheer and cry at the same time. Like the new born. How happy he is to be alive but sad for his helplessness.

We feel this thing in us that says, "By God, we've done it! It is all over now. Job very well done. Victory!"

To an old and good Soldier nothing sounds better, feels better, tastes better, smells or looks better than Victory. We have arrived.

Our Father, the Most Honorable Mr. Elijah Muhammad has turned the hearts of the father back to the children and the hearts of the children back to the father (Shabazz). Elijah made us Muslims. It is because of Him that we are now alive and not mentally dead.

The power of this truth that resurrects our people is His power. We are only the bearers of His seed, His children. He, it is, who said to Brother Fard Saviour, "You are the Official Representative of my Model Mosque #25. You are the Field Supreme Minister of the Nation of Islam, in charge of all the Muslims wherever you may go. You must now raise your own Field Staff."

Master Fard, being a true believer, could only say, "Yes Sir. I hear and I obey."

A. M. Muhammad

It is Our Father's work we are doing and we must be good examples and perfect servants to do our Father's will. Not our will, but Elijah Muhammad's will. Not our teachings, but Elijah Muhammad's teachings. We must be humble as He taught us. We must dress as He taught us and we must eat as He has taught us or we cannot claim to be His followers. This is the New World Nation of Islam as He has taught us.

The world's universe is 360°. Everything in motion travels towards its opposite. What goes around, comes around or you reap what you sow. We must travel through these worlds of life, aware or unaware, willing or unwilling. The key is not remaining in one place and becoming stagnant, inertia. If you are not attached to anything, nothing can hold you down. You must travel through these spheres accumulating knowledge, the power which makes us Gods. Here is where the problem begins: Getting into and out of life's spheres or worlds without making a fatal mistake. You must have guidance. All prophets of the past were guides and Muhammad is our guide today. Master Fard Saviour said to me: "You (Brother Ali) are my Field Supreme Captain in charge of raising, teaching and training my staff." I said, "Yes Sir."

Muhammad guides you into peace and heaven. Only those in it can see it. The closer you are to Muhammad, the closer you are to Allah. You have no fear or grief because what Muhammad has taught you comes from the mouth of God, Allah in person. You have peace and you see a long, happy and busy life ahead of you.

As our Father says in **How to Eat to Live, Book No. 1 Pages 57-58**

"Obey and do all that He Allah bids us for life in This Life, the way He lives. Think the way He thinks; the thoughts of good. Seek to be like Him, both physically and mentally. As the Holy Qur'an teaches us, when we have submitted ourselves entirely to the will of

KNOWLEDGE OF THE GODS

God, He then guides us into His path, His way of life. And then guides us into life in these words of the Holy Qur'an: 'O soul that is at rest, Enter into My Gardens, into My Paradise among Servants well pleased and well pleasing."

This is what man has sought: the heaven within and the heaven without. If heaven does not begin within, we will never enjoy it on the outside. We do not go to a certain place for heaven. Nearly all of my followers and I are already in heaven (a peace of mind and contentment for the necessities of life, such as food, clothing, shelter, and without the enemy of fear and grief). And with the protection of Almighty God, Allah, what more do we want?

If we went into another place, we still would not enjoy it more. Oh, certainly, we would be happy to live in a place where there was nothing but people like ourselves, thinking as we think and trying to obey the law of God.

But still within ourselves, we are happy because this evil world does not attract us anymore. We do not desire this kind of life that the wicked live. Our thoughts or mind feast upon the spirit of goodness. Therefore, the spirit of evil cannot find a place among us to dwell.

Remember life is what we make it. Stay away from hog (the swine), the stinking tobacco weed, the hot, fiery alcohol, wine, beer, drugs, foolishness, ignorance, madness, drunkenness, gambling, murdering, robbery, deceitfulness, lying, mockery and seeking to take advantage of your brother and sister, and believe in the presence of God in the person of Master Fard Muhammad, to whom praises are due forever."

You did not know how Muhammad would teach and train you out of such life-destroying habits. Many have left in a state of shock and confusion because they judged Muhammad to be wrong. But

A. M. Muhammad

Allah and Muhammad are never wrong and none disputes the Messenger but the disbelievers. Allah sealed their hearts so they understood nothing.

Those few of you still standing are the strongest of the strong. The family and the Staff. We are all that is left because everyone else wanted something already made for them, so they wouldn't have to work or suffer. We are those who sacrificed home, husband, wife, children and all that we have and are glad to suffer in the name of Allah and Muhammad. We say, "0 Lord, surely we were nothing before you gave us life, we now give this life to Thy service all our days and our offspring too." Muhammad has taught you and trained you. Now you are the chosen. You will not let anything come between you and your duty to Allah and Muhammad.

You are made great and your hearts are high with the love of Allah and our poor lost but now found people The Holy Tribe of Shabazz. You are now made fit by Muhammad to be the pure leadership for Muhammad's Model Mosque #25. You have kept the faith even when times were dark and you couldn't see or know what was going on or what would happen next. But you held on. Look at you now. You are someone to be proud of. Even the devil had to bear witness that in all his years he has never saw a stronger and more faithful followers as you. He said you act like you are hypnotized. You just hear and obey.

No one knew how Hiram Mcbiff, the Master Builder, would fashion the cornerstone for the Kings Temple.

You did not know that you were the human blocks to be used to lay the foundation for the Model Mosque. You did not know what methods Muhammad would use to teach and train you into such a high state of consciousness. But whatever His secret method is, you are the proof that it brought about the right results. All praises are forever due to Allah in the person of Master Fard Muhammad our

KNOWLEDGE OF THE GODS

beloved Saviour, and Muhammad His Slave.

We are not finished working. We are just finished with one sphere of activity. We have overcome many wicked habits but we still have a few left; Pride, Jealousy, Envy and Selfishness. We must knock those devils out of us. Those devils killed the old world officials. Most of us are far ahead in fighting those beasts but a few of us must be trained to fight a little harder.

So let us clean up what we have left to clean up. Let us open our Mosque with the song of victory over the wicked and evil Satan.

Remember Our Father, the Honorable Mr. Elijah Muhammad said, "They are watching to see if you will be good Muslims." Read Holy Qur'an Chapter 59: Verse 8, 9 and 10.

May Allah continue to bless us with success. I remain your brother telling you that which God, has told me to tell you.

Chapter Four
Respect For Our Leader
And Prophet Of Islam

It is a serious sin to disrespect the Prophet of Allah. When you show disrespect to the Prophet you are showing that same disrespect to Allah.

You can't accept one without accepting the other and you can't respect one without respecting the other.

Holy Qur'an Chapter 33 verse 1: "0 you who believe, be not forward in the Presence of Allah and His Messenger, and keep your duty to Allah. Surely Allah is Hearing, Knowing."

Our Saviour Has Arrived, not to come, He is Present and has been amongst us doing His work and gathering His people now for 22 years. Our Father, the Most Honorable Mr. Elijah Muhammad sent a message to Mosque #25 in the year 1959 that "Master Fard was visiting our city and that we should be very careful of the way we talked to strangers because we might be talking to Allah in Person."

The Presence of Allah in the Person of Master Fard Muhammad is rarely advertised and only a select few can recognize Him in or out of disguise. You who are blessed with the Presence of Allah must not let yourself forget the proper respect. The Saviour is so humble and respectful to everyone, you forget that you are face to face with God. He makes you feel important and He acts like He is your servant. Don't be caught with your guard down brothers and sisters who have been blessed to know Him. Respect His Presence. The Saviour makes us feel like we have known Him all our lives and

KNOWLEDGE OF THE GODS

we begin to speak and call out to Him as we speak and call out to each other. You must not do that. Lower your voice in His Presence.

It is reported to me that at one of our recent meetings Brother Fard Saviour was discussing some Islamic science with some of the Fruit of Islam and the Lord's sister-in-law walked in and called out, "Brother Fard will you give two sisters and myself a ride home? We are ready to go." The Lord looked up and said, "Yes ma'am. I'll be right with you." Never interrupt or call out to the Saviour or speak in a loud voice in His presence. It is hateful and you will lose your blessing. Never talk to Him like you talk to each other.

Brothers, you sound and look like a braying jackass when you stand in the Saviour's presence boasting and trying to show Him how smart you are. A Brother's attitude in Allah's presence should be: *Lord, I'm your servant and I want whatever you want for me.*

Sisters! Our Father, the Most Honorable Mr. Elijah Muhammad told us that when He made pilgrimage to Mecca, He was invited into the homes of very important people of the Muslim World. He said that one of the things that impressed Him the most was the obvious absence of women in these homes. The women kept out of the men's presence and out of sight, but if anything was needed like food or drink it miraculously appeared.

Take a lesson from this sisters. Stay out of the way. Don't be like the sisters who spoil their blessings by imposing themselves on the Saviours presence. Not long ago the Saviour came into the city from a distant trip. He elected to spend the night at one of the believer's homes. As soon as His presence was known the sisters of the household began to follow Him through the house asking all manner of questions and kept Him up all night teaching them Islam.

These sisters showed no respect for His privacy or that He needed His rest. Some even had the nerve to be in His presence with their night clothes on. Sisters, you must be respectful. Stay out of His way. He will request whatever he needs. Cover yourself and put your head coverings on in His presence. Cast your eyes down and speak softly. This is better for you.

Remember, we are blessed to be the first people of God, in this Day of Judgment. Also the Jesus warned us that the Prophets are respected more by foreigners than in their own house.

Study Chapter 33 of the Holy Qur'an. May Allah forgive us if we forget and make a mistake for surely we are full of shortcomings.

Chapter Five
Fight The Devil

We can't remind you enough to watch the devil and to fight him on every level.

Picture this situation in your mind. A brother waiting for his wife to return home from her visit to her mother and father. It is getting late so he calls mom's house, but no answer. The devil says to the brother, "You know she's out in the street with some of her old friends. She lied to you about going to her mother's. That is the oldest line in the book and here you are sitting there like a big fool while she's out partying." So says the devil. The brother listens to the devil and gets madder and madder. The devil's suggestions get worst. The brother starts to think of his wife as if she's the worst person in the world.

Meanwhile, the truth of the matter is that the sister, her mother and father are on their way home right now and the reason for them being a little bit late is because they stopped to shop for him a coat for the winter. When the brother finds this out he feels sick at the stomach for listening to the devil's suggestions.

Remember, when you are with Allah and Muhammad everything is alright. Allah and Muhammad can't do no wrong and only the devil will suggest any such thing. Remember that right guidance always makes you peaceful and happy. The devil's voice always breaks your peace and makes you sick with grief. Fight the devil on all planes of existence. Teach yourself to think right at all times.

Muhammad ibn Abdullah (Peace and Mercy of Allah be with Him) taught his followers 1400 years ago to mount your camel from the right side, put on the right shoe first, eat with the right hand and many other things he ordered them to do to keep them aware of the doing and thinking right at all times.

Muhammad taught them that we have a devil sitting on one shoulder and an angel on the other shoulder, both suggest to us all the time. We must learn to be wise enough to recognize the voices and follow the Angel. This is the difference of heaven and hell. You must get to the heaven inside you first and that can only come from right guidance from Allah, the Lord of all the Worlds.

Fight the devil hard and soon there will not be one devil left amongst us. May Allah forever bless us with His Divine Protection.

Chapter Six
Pass Over

My beloved Black Brothers and Sisters. May Allah's richest blessings forever be upon you.

We are living in the End of time. The devil's time to rule is over as of now (Armageddon, the third World War). Life as we have known it is passing us by.

As the devil's power passes, he, the devil, tries to influence you to turn back from Allah and Muhammad and the Heaven you are promised. He wants to take as many of us with him that he can. You must understand that the devil is as real as Allah, God.

The devil suggests evil, wicked and negative things in your mind to get you to go against your salvation. He uses tricks on your mind. The devil knows the things that you are attached to and hold dear. He uses these things to make you curse God. He comes to you in every form. He will appear as your wife, brother, sister, husband, child or friends, even your house pets and cars, jewelry, and anything and everything.

The devil will always take the thing that you love and place it between you and Allah, then the devil tries to influence you to choose *something* instead of Allah and Muhammad.

You must be on your guard against such evil suggestions. You must be alert because the devil is sneaky.

This passing of this world is real. It is like a baby being born. He changes his form of life, from the dark sea of its mother. As the baby is born he comes into a new world of light and object lessons.

We must get as close to Allah and Muhammad as we can and

constantly remind each other to fight the devils.

We must clean up and be good examples of the Officials of Muhammad's Mosque #25, the Headquarters Mosque for the New World Nation of Islam.

We must now come out of the mud and the streets (wilderness) and we must lead our folks out of it and show them how to clean up.

We are entering the world of Allah. He is now ready to teach you how New World Muslims live. All of our attention and efforts should be on establishing our Mosque.

As we come out of this devil's world and enter the Mosque of the New World, be conscious of Satan's passing over us. Keep to Prayer and the remembrance of Allah and Muhammad. Know that the devil will make you fight God, if you let him.

Join with our Lord and Saviour, as we continue to recite;

> *"0 Allah, make us to enter a truthful entering.*
> *And make us go forth a truthful going forth.*
> *And grant us an authority to help us do Thy Will."*

May Allah continue to bless us. We thank our Father, the Most Honorable Mr. Elijah Muhammad, for giving to us our Saviour, Master Fard Muhammad.

Peace! Peace!

Chapter Seven
Knowledge Of The Gods

I thank Allah, in the person of Master Fard Muhammad for blessing me to be able to speak with you. I am proud and it is a privilege to be speaking with you today. You, my beautiful black brothers and sisters of the New World of Islam are blessed. You are blessed to be wise enough to be present here today. To be awake spiritually, to see and to hear, to know and to act upon truth. You are blessed my beautiful black brothers and sisters. This is the day of our deliverance. Master Fard Muhammad, Almighty God in Person is in our midst. I am your Poor Brother Ali. I am Muhammad Ali, the Spokesman for Master Fard Muhammad. I am here to teach you some of that which Master Fard Muhammad has taught me. This teaching is the Knowledge of the Gods.

We are the Shabazzians, the God Tribe. You are all familiar with your lessons. You are now being prepared for the presence of Master Fard Muhammad, that is, to be in direct contact and directly taught by our God and Saviour, Master Fard Muhammad. It is my job to teach you that which will make you worthy of His presence. This is the Knowledge of the Gods that we must know and now conform to. Our Father, the Honorable Mr. Elijah Muhammad has given us all we need to bear witness to the presence of Master Fard Muhammad in our midst.

There should be no confusion as to who we are. Some say, "But the Nation of Islam was under Elijah Muhammad and this New World of Islam, who is this under?" We want you to know that the Nation of Islam and the New World of Islam are one and the same. Throughout Our Father's teachings he always proclaimed that we was the Nation of Islam here in America and that Master Fard Muhammad would establish the New World of Islam when He came among us. Well, alright. Master Fard Muhammad is among us and He has proclaimed that the Nation of Islam is now the New World of Islam, just as the Honorable Mr. Elijah Muhammad has taught us for years. So there should be no confusion on that point.

I am your Brother. I grew up among you. For 20 years you've known me to teach you Islam. My history is clear. I have been called everything under the sun, but there is a few facts that has remained with me throughout my history. For 20 years no one has ever doubted the fact that I am with Master Fard Muhammad and do represent Him, and that Brother Ali has never been charged with telling a lie. That is a great acclaim and no one can make you great, save Allah. And if Allah intends to bring you down, there is none who can uphold you. I am the Spokesman there is no doubt about this. But you must remember the Knowledge of the Gods today.

Get out of that spookiness and stop looking in the clouds. Get away from the spirits, the idea that Angels are flying around with wings. Realize that God is a Man and the Angels are men. You can understand that the white man is the devil; you know that. Then you should understand that Angels are men and that God is Man, and that we are all Gods. We are teaching you the Knowledge of the Gods so that you will be ready for Master Fard Muhammad, for He is close at hand. I'm telling you that you are almost ready for Him. I know that some of you get in a hurry. You think that you might be ready now, but let me remind you, nobody is more in a hurry for you to be ready than Almighty God Allah, Himself. Don't think that you are being held back. No! In fact you're being brought up as quickly as you can be brought up and you've got to remember it takes someone who loves you to have patience to wait for you to learn a lesson.

KNOWLEDGE OF THE GODS

You've got to remember, it takes a God who has a love for you with no limitations, to let you develop slowly and properly. You've got to remember only God could love us to the extent that Master Fard Muhammad loves us. No, you're not ready for direct contact with Master Fard Muhammad. But the year is almost "78" and you brothers and sisters present right now, yes, you are the model, the mold, the Man of Action, which means we can now start creating our people. That Space of Time that Yakub saw, that gave him an opportunity to do what he did; this is the point of time in which we are blessed to be in.

It is the Knowledge of the Gods that blesses us, that gives us the power to step off into a New World of Heaven (Paradise). It is the Knowledge of knowing the time and seeing the space, the opportunity to do a particular thing, or to say, "Be," as God declared and then move in on it - being a man of action. This is the point of time that we are blessed to be in. So you must now be taught the Knowledge of the Gods, so that you will be prepared for direct contact with Almighty God Allah, in the Person of Master Fard Muhammad.

We are teaching you the Knowledge of the Gods. What makes man a God? How is it that we determine that a man is a God? Well first, brothers and sisters, we must understand that nothing is impossible to God. Therefore, man must be God because man has not been able to find anything that he could not do. Anything that a man's mind can conceive he is able to produce. There is no man outside of God. Alright. Man is God, now what? He must have the power to say "Be" and it is.

That is, to decide upon a particular action, to resolve to do it, and then do it. It is as simple as that. It is as plain as day. Why do you think our Father taught us in His last Sermon, and in the Theology of Time, "Give you nothing. Get up and get it yourself." You remember? Those are famous words. I know all of the True Believers have stacks of Our Father's columns and they must have Theology of the Time. Isn't that right? Is that what He said? Well then, if no one is to give you anything and He directs us that we will have to get it ourselves-then that is the Knowledge of the Gods. Do you understand? It is clear to me.

Let us look at a little history here. I thank Almighty Allah for blessing me to be here at this time, to teach you some of the Divine Supreme Wisdom that Almighty (God) Allah gave to me, in the Person of Master Fard Muhammad. I want you to understand, brothers and sisters, that you are the first to receive this Supreme Wisdom, and you are only getting a token. You are just prepared now to receive some of the Truth that Master Fard Muhammad gave to me to give to you. You are not ready for Him. You are hardly ready for me. Just a few weeks ago the slanderers wanted to call me everything in the book, but Allah blessed us. He said, tell the believers to read chapter 33:58-66 and they will see how the hypocrites today are the same as they were thousands of years ago.

Where did Brother Ali get the Guidance to tell you that? And when you opened the Holy Qur'an and read and saw the guidance, did not the slanderers words bounce off you like water off a duck's back? Knowing in your heart that this is the Truth you are receiving from Brother Ali, causes you to follow the Guidance and resolve that nothing else matters. You would not believe a lie - the Truth bears witness to itself! Anything else concerning Brother Ali's family, and who washed the laundry, or whether or not the baby's diapers were changed, that is Brother Ali's personal business.

The President could tell you it is the end of the world and to pack up your things and to be at the docks; and all of you sitting here today would say, "Pay that no mind brother, pay that no mind sisters, you know the devils are liars, let us check with Brother Ali." Do you

KNOWLEDGE OF THE GODS

understand what I am saying here? I am saying that in 20 years of teaching, and everybody knows that Brother Ali has been running his mouth about this Islam for 20 years, and has been called everything, yet no one has ever been able to say that Brother Ali is a liar. Those of you who are here today know that this is the Truth. If Brother All tells you, "Look brother, look sister, pack up, this is it, this is the Judgment." No questions are asked. You would say, "Yes Sir." When you tell another believer they will ask you who said that? And when you say Brother All said it - then it is alright.

I am not setting myself up trying to get credit or praise from you. I am trying to show you a sign of wisdom. I am trying to show you that if Allah elevates you to a point where all men must recognize your integrity and honesty, then no one can bring you down. If we have taught the Truth, and we have, then the True Believers, who are the only ones we are interested in (Shabazzians), are the only ones who will recognize this Truth.

When a Shabazzian hears the slander they say, "Praise be to Allah, we do not have time to listen to that stuff. Come on, let us go to the Fruit meeting, or M.G.T. Meeting." Only Allah could put me in that kind of position, and keep me there for so long. Brother Ali did not just start to teach. This is the first time the teachings have been heard. You are the first men and women of Action to bring this about. Do you understand?

Let me give you a little of the history to show you about this Knowledge of the Gods. When Brother Fard and myself went into the prison in the early 1960's, the atmosphere was like that of going among savage animals. Men were like the beast of the field . . . Brutality was the order of the day. Just about everybody had clubs and home-made knives, or something they figured they had to have to protect themselves. Brother Fard walked into the prison and said, "This is the first Academy of Islam." He told me this, and a few believers of that day and time.

Then he began to show us, by setting up a training schedule along with a study schedule, which turned the prison into an Islamic Academy. Before long the news media were talking about the 'Training Ground' for the Elite Corps of Black Muslims in Trenton State Prison. It wasn't easy. You read this and it sounds like Brother Fard stepped in the door and said, "Abracadabra" and everything changed. No sir, brothers and sisters, it didn't happen like that. When Brother Fard stepped into the prison, the word had already been out that he was coming. It was known that the Field Minister was coming into the prison, and that all the brothers were to respect him as the authority there because He was in charge of all Muslims wherever He went. When He got there a lot of people were professing to be believers. They knew He was there, they received Him when He got there; but they were no better than the rest of the (mentally dead - Lazarus), because they (the hypocrites) were doing the things that Lazarus did. They too were acting like savages.

Brother Fard did not carry a home-made knife or club. When He went among these wild men, these people who had terrible thoughts and were animalistic, He carried Himself in such a way that the animal would recognize that His word was His bond. As a result of Him being upright He became a status symbol. It became more important for your word to be right then the number of heads you had cracked, or people you had stabbed or cut-up. Brother Fard began to train in the yard and the animal began to recognize that here was a man who had respect for His physical body. Brother Fard had a perfect physical physique. He started off running all day long, from bell to bell, as we called it in the old school. So the animal began to recognize that here was a man who was disciplined enough to have control over His body. So they began to act like Brother Fard. They would come out and start training or get into some kind of athletics.

KNOWLEDGE OF THE GODS

Then Brother Fard began to go to school. He began to read, books. He would read and study and study and read. He was an avid reader. He has a photographic memory and read three and four books at a time. So when they began to see that He would take time and read, they too began to go back to school. I was one of them! When He talked to you He could explain things in so many ways, He talked so plain to you.

When I came to the prison to join Brother Fard, He had already made me the Field Captain, but I had offered an argument. I told Him the only reason I did not want the job was because I was illiterate. I could hardly read or write. I felt He needed someone in such an important position who could at least read and write. He just said He was going to hold onto me until He found somebody better. His going to school embarrassed and ashamed me to the point, that I had to go to school. So, in going to school I began to learn. Others seeing me go to school, people who knew I couldn't read or write, and they couldn't read or write, began to follow our example. Eventually there was a constant school program and curriculum in the prison.

Brother Fard's graduating class was the first G.E.D. (General Education Development) class in Trenton State Prison, of which I was a part. Throughout the cycle Brother Fard use to call me the Old Straggler. He use to affectionately call me that, and He still does. It was because wherever he would go I was right there. It is something like two brothers. Those of you who have brothers you know how you compete with each other. That is the kind of closeness I had with Brother Fard - and still do. Whenever He would do a thing, I would be right there. My attitude was, if He could do it, then I could do it. As a result of that, He was always first in the class and I was always second. Whether it was physical exercise or mental exercise.

However, what I am telling you is that this took years of Brother

A. M. Muhammad

Fard knowing who He was. You think the Truth sounds strange now, this was during a time when only three people knew the Reality of Allah. That was Our Father (the Most Honorable Mr. Elijah Muhammad) Master Fard Muhammad and Myself. Can you imagine how that was? Here is a Man on the scene and only a couple of people knew He was God. He made Himself do that which He knew He had to do. He knew in order to be the Representative for the Nation of Islam, and follow in our Father's footsteps, that He had to read everything He could. He knew that He had to commit to memory all of His Father's Lessons, all of His Father's columns. He must do this if He is Master Fard Muhammad. Do you understand?

He knew that He had to gain mastery over His body so that when our Father said fast, He fasted. When our Father said pray He prayed. But Brother Fard is a perfectionist; whatever our Father said do, He wouldn't just do it. He would do it and do it some more, and then try to be perfect in it. As with the training, He would run from one movement to the next. He wouldn't run one or two miles, He would run and keep on running. When it came time to pray Brother Fard would have us in the old school, First Graduation Class, praying all night for a week straight. Then we would pray all day for a couple of more weeks, fast six days dry, come down, then get off for another seven days dry. It was because Brother Fard taught us, if our Father said these were the things we must do, then that is where we develop our strength of character; that is, to make our physical bodies do the things that we must do. He taught us our body is like a machine, and when you control the machine, you can make that body do anything you want it to do. I am talking about the Knowledge of The Gods. Do you understand what I am saying?

When Our Father said, "It is time for Master Fard Muhammad to come on the scene," that's what time it was! You must remember that before the early 1950's Our Father was saying that Master Fard

KNOWLEDGE OF THE GODS

Muhammad was coming. But around 1958 He began to say that he was here - that He was present among us doing His work. This is the Truth; I am talking about the Knowledge of The Gods. That's what I am talking about.

You see there is a space in time (here is that space again that I am talking about), where if Master Fard Muhammad is among our people, and He hears the call, then He stands up and starts doing what Master Fard Muhammad is supposed to do. I am talking about the Knowledge of The Gods. I am talking about a space in time. I am talking about Our Father and teaching our people. Bringing them up to the level of meeting God face to face.

He knew that Master Fard Muhammad among us (being among us) would one day recognize the Truth and stand up and start being Master Fard Muhammad. All praise is due to Allah. So it is, as the Saviour recognized His identity and the time, He recognized what He had to do as Master Fard Muhammad. Praise be to Allah.

If He had not put into action the principles that our Father had taught Him when He came to school, He never would have become disciplined enough to do the things that He did. Not only did He become a legend Himself, from this particular training, he also made a legend of me. How do you think I feel when people come to me and say, "I have been hearing about you all my life." Don't you think I realize, and know, that this is only because of my Saviour? Now look at the space of time here. I am your brother, the last Minister of the Honorable Mr. Elijah Muhammad, the First Convert of Master Fard Muhammad. Here I am right here at this space, at this time, when the tail of the dragon has knocked down 90% of the stars. Don't you see? Here is Brother Ali with the proof - 20 years of labor.

You must bear witness to me . . . that I do teach you that Allah is God, in the Person of Master Fard Muhammad, and to hold onto Our Father's teachings - the Most Honorable Mr. Elijah Muhammad.

A. M. Muhammad

You must bear witness to this. Isn't this the truth? No one can impersonate me. It took 20 years of work of making myself do what I must do. I learned this from God Himself. He said that is all there is to it. There is absolutely nothing that you can't do. He learned it from the Honorable Mr. Elijah Muhammad. The Honorable Mr. Elijah Muhammad learned it from Master Fard Muhammad, or received the keys (received the rebirth - the resurrection), so that now, through Him, we all are resurrected. We now have that knowledge coming back to us, so that now we are illuminated with the Knowledge of The Gods. It is so plain. It is just so simple.

Our Father said, "Up you mighty race, you can accomplish what you will." Don't you see? If we study, if we educate ourselves, knowledge is power. If we have the will power, the desire and the love that you and I demonstrate for Allah, then you can do anything that you want to do. This is the Knowledge of The Gods, and the Knowledge of the One among us, who is always with His people (The Tribe of Shabazz); Who is a most Perfect example of our Father and all the wisdom before Him and all the prophets before Him.

We believe in all the scriptures and we make no distinction between any of the prophets. That cannot be taken from us. We now have our history. Nothing can stop us now. The only thing that was holding us back was the Man of Action. This is you and I. I am here to activate this knowledge; to program you in such a way that you will be ready for Brother Fard. You are just waking up. We are giving you the knowledge that pulls you out of the grave. This is the Bible, the scriptures which are going to eventually be spread far and wide, once you step into the Divine Truth, the Knowledge of the Gods. Once you understand that the scriptures of the past are only history, just like any other book of history. Once you are into the New World, the Knowledge of The Gods, all scriptures come to an

KNOWLEDGE OF THE GODS

end.

The Truth that Master Fard Muhammad has for us, the New Wisdom that He has for us can only be described as things that you would imagine. Like things you see in Star Wars or Star Trek, it is Universal Knowledge. He says that the planet is now off its course. It is not in its proper axis. He says that it will take a thousand years to clean the planet up and bring it back to its proper axis. He explained that the reason it will take so long is because we must progress in society to the point that we understand enough about the Earth to begin to move it (the Earth) back to its natural ability to rejuvenate itself.

He is hard at work and is preparing for us the Superior Wisdom that takes us into an advanced society. What you now know makes you the greatest Black People, the greatest organization of Black People in the world. This is you right now with the Wisdom that you have. But this is only the beginning of establishing a Society of Gods. A people who understand the Perfect Wisdom of self-control, right intent, and doing things right. A Society of Righteousness where your word is your bond. When you are given a duty, regardless to where you have been vacationing or lounging, when your turn comes to keep your duty, you are ready, willing and able to do your job perfectly. If a man of this attitude and posture, if his society is of this attitude and posture, then you have a society of righteousness. You have no time to bicker about mistakes or misfortune, as long as you are worrying about your particular duty being right and exact. If someone comes up short that is their business, but mines is going to be right. Such a society is more interested in the duty of the individual than what he does behind locked doors.

A man's home is his castle. Brother Fard taught us to trust nobody. That a brother's best home, and best castle, is with Allah

A. M. Muhammad

and Muhammad. We should not trust no brother, we should not trust no sister. We should trust Allah and Muhammad. Master Fard Muhammad was teaching us this years ago, long before the general Nation ever knew what a hypocrite was. Master Fard Muhammad was teaching us about Wallace and Malcolm being chief hypocrites. And one of the things that I remember He told us about was the police attack on the brothers and sisters in Los Angeles. Our Father said, "Those brothers should have fought." He said that, "Time and again I have told you that we are never to be the aggressor, but when we are attacked we must fight." He said, "We should fight to the last man." Those brothers did not do this. So as a result of what our Father said, (and this is not a direct quote), He said, there was no need in us collecting a whole lot of money to defend those brothers against the very people who did them wrong. So don't collect money for a defense fund, because there is no justice in the court.

Brother Fard showed us newspaper clippings where Our Father said He did not want anyone to collect money for a defense fund to defend those brothers in Los Angeles. He said, "Now read this!" And there was an article of Malcolm holding a rally in a church to raise funds to defend those brothers. So Brother Fard was showing us how, even then, that the man (Malcolm) was a hypocrite. At the time He was teaching us this, there were a lot of people who were still in sympathy with Malcolm, and they began to say that Brother Fard was misinterpreting what was said. So, in the paper, MUHAMMAD SPEAKS, they were trying to uphold Malcolm.

A few weeks later, we found out that the brothers did not have any money for their defense. Brother Fard said, "See how Allah makes manifest the enemy." There were many things of this nature which Brother Fard was revealing to us long before they came about.

We thank Allah much! We want the sisters to know that we are very proud of their progress; and that the Knowledge of the Gods is tailor-made for the sisters. A mother is the first teacher of the children. If the mother has self-discipline, which gives her strength of character, that is the strength which makes her word her bond. Whatever she says she is going to do, she will then set out to accomplish that; and will do it and will do it right. If the mother is of that attitude, then her children are born with it. Her teaching that child is like second nature to that child. It is like when a duck hatches her ducklings. She knows that every one of them is going right into the water like they are supposed to. So this is how your children come up in your character; and in your teachings sisters, you must mold your children.

Our children are our future Gods. Brother Fard said that we are now preparing the best of everything, in the way of education, educational aids and good teaching tools, to make our children the most advanced in the world. In fact, in the universe! He will make us the head, not the tail. We are going, to lead new inventions. We are going to lead in the production of new materials. These are the things we are going to do because we have the power to do it. So sister, be self-disciplined. You are going to demonstrate to the world just what the New World Muslim represents. You carry the Judgment of us, your brothers.

I have told you often that Brother Fard said, He does not want to see my face until we have placed our sisters back on top. Sisters we love you and see your progress, but you are getting the Knowledge of The Gods now. You can become any kind of woman you desire to make of yourself, right now! You are the fashioner. If you want our women to be known for their word being bond, then each one of you has to practice that. You must do that sisters. If you want our sisters to be known for their cleanliness, their love for their children, their dedication to their husbands and for their strong faith in their men, it is up to you sisters. Don't you see? How could our Father, the Most Honorable Mr. Elijah Muhammad, become the Honorable Mr. Elijah Muhammad if He did not make Himself get out of the bed in the morning? You know how that is. He would tell Himself, "Well it is time to get up," and He got up! Some of your sisters just lay there and think, "Well, I guess I'll get me another hour of sleep." Then your conscience would say, "Now you know that ain't right. You know that if you lay there you are going to get more than another hour; it will be twelve o'clock before you get up, just like you have been doing every day for a week or more." So you see, that is the fight against the devil, against evil suggestions, that which keeps you away from the remembrance of action towards Allah's Will.

Keeping your duty, that is the fight that you sisters must fight, in order to be who you are supposed to be. That is the key! God does everything right. He does not want anybody to help Him. He will do this Himself. This is what He has taught us. While He was teaching us what we should do, Master Fard Muhammad was doing it Himself. He will not sell us short. He would ask a brother if he had missed his salats (prayers) that day, and if the brother would say yes, Brother Fard would then act in such a way that His attitude would let the brother know he had done something very bad. You can imagine, brothers did not miss too many salats, after one or two experiences with Brother Fard. Then He made us learn these lessons, this is the Knowledge of the Gods. Give you nothing. Give you what?

Look at you, we are a body now. We are now taking the first steps, now that we are united in heart, like Brother Fard taught us. We love nobody but Allah and Muhammad. Then your duty is all that you should be interested in. So if everybody feels like that, which is how the Believers are supposed to feel, then you should be able to look around you and see WORKERS. And that, we are! Who

KNOWLEDGE OF THE GODS

has been doing this! Who brought this about? You would not be sitting there if work was not being done.

So this is the space of time. This is the time when the sisters can mold themselves, into the women who are supposed to represent the New World of Islam. This is your day! It is the work that you are doing today which makes the history, so that brothers and sisters, years from now, can look back and say, "Those brothers and sisters, they were the first Gods. They were disciplined enough to do what they knew they had to do." You see how everything is resting on you, right now? This is your time to act. That is the Knowledge of The Gods. The Gods see what has to be done and then do it! We will be successful every time.

Every one of you represents the body. Now we are able to give instructions to men and women of action; and in giving them instructions, they go right ahead and do it. That is where we are at, right now! We are not interested in everybody, we are only interested in those who are of our family. Allah is getting ready to give us a pay day brothers and sisters; and we are, all of us right here, we are like family. We are the only ones who can control a large amount of money if we receive it at this time. So it behooves a brother and sister to study the lessons. Pray and fast. I am telling you, this is the way. This is the Knowledge of the Gods. There is no short cut. Every chance you get fast, pray and study your lessons.

You first brothers and sisters should not view yourselves as the head of some dress factory where you are sitting around ordering brothers and sisters about concerning the pattern of the dresses. No, no! This is not how you will spend your day. Brother Fard told me that the first brothers and sisters are the Staff of the Government. Can you see what I am saying? If you had a job which had something to do with making clothes, you would be in charge of making all the Nation's clothes. You would have people who are skilled at that, in charge of that, reporting to you. You would be responsible for the job that we give you, on how we want clothes made for our Nation. But this is what we want you to understand. You MUST have self-control. You MUST have self-discipline and you MUST make yourself follow the steps that have already been proven.

Our Father, did He not become the God? Certainly He did! And you see what He had to go through. Nobody knocked on any doors for Him. No one taught one class for Him. He did His own work. Do you see what we are saying brothers and sisters? The greatest teachings that He could give us was the Knowledge of The Gods, then force us to go for self.

What we are getting ready to do here is going to be beautiful. It is going to be something that we can be proud of and it will show the world who we are, that we are Our Father's Children. We are the only people alive with Our Father's teachings.

You may ask, "Well why did not Elijah give you the Nation before He left?" He did give us the Nation before He left, Saviour's Day 1960, but the hypocrites rejected our Commission. That is why We are called the Rejected Stone.

Our Father said, "Don't look for another Messenger to come after me, behind me comes God." What He is saying is, 'Follow in My steps, and you have got to become God.' That is the only way! Nobody else can do this. Only the God Tribe can identify with the Superior Wisdom, or the Knowledge of The Gods. Other people would be scared to death.

Brother Fard told us how we are going to look fifty and sixty years from now. The people are just not ready for some of the things that Brother Fard has taught us. But you can see, can rationalize, that if you get on the right diet you will change physically. Some of you are beginning to change now from eating a pure diet. You have

KNOWLEDGE OF THE GODS

gotten away from the hog, away from most of the impurities, and away from that junk food that we have been existing on. You can see the change. So it should not be strange for you to know that our entire physical appearance, that's right, our entire physical appearance is going to change! We will get to Brother Fard, and the Superior Wisdom He has for you, when the time comes. Right now we are taking our first steps.

We are realizing that nobody is going to give us anything, and that we are proud to be able to do this ourselves. It is truly ours when we do it ourselves. Brother you have to get out there and teach. You have to understand that our teachings are not like the teachings of the hypocrites. We do not go anywhere and try to force anyone, nor twist their arms, to accept this truth. We are only interested in those who are interested in this truth. But you must understand this, unless the disciples fulfill their history, then there are no disciples. So what you are really doing brother, when you go out in those streets, and go into those houses and teach, what you are really doing is saying, "Hey, bear witness to me, I am a believer. I am one of the disciples in this day and time that I am knocking on the doors." How else will you be known for this brother, if you do not do these things? This is the Knowledge of The Gods.

The Knowledge of The Gods. If you want to be known as a disciple, do the work of a disciple. You know that the key is that only those who are chosen will wake up. There can be no, 'This brother teaches better than me, so he is able to wake up more than me.' No sir. That is not the case. No one raises from the dead except that Allah has ordained it. So you and I can only deliver this truth. What makes one brother more successful, in teaching than another, is that one brother is meeting and teaching more people than the other; and, the only ones who are going to wake up are the ones already numbered. You have to get out there and teach every chance you get, in order to fulfill the history of the disciples.

THAT IS THE KNOWLEDGE OF THE GODS!

May Allah forever bless you, as I close in the Name of Our Father The Honorable Mr. Elijah Muhammad.

Peace! Peace!

Chapter Eight
The Will of Allah

This is your Poor Brother Ali, and it gives me great pleasure to have this opportunity to speak with you again. There is a certain pleasure that we all receive from working; that is, from doing the things that we want to do. There is that certain pleasure, when you have accomplished what you said you would do. It gives you a certain pleasure.

Years ago we often thought about the time that would come when we would be able to say, "My brothers and sisters, it gives me great pleasure to speak with you today." Years ago when there were only brothers on the scene, we dreamed of the day when we would say, "My brothers and my sisters, it gives me great pleasure to speak with you today. I am happy because I know that Allah is blessing me and He is blessing you, and that you are now working. Yes, it gives me great pleasure to speak to you today. We have labored long and hard in the fields just so we can have this day, this time."

Yes, it took a lot of faith, a lot of fulfilling of history to get to this time that we are now living in. It took the realization that I had to sink or swim. Brother Fard use to say that when times get rough, we get tough.

We are thankful for today because we have been practicing our Islam all the time. We are ready to teach you today. We have lessons we have forgotten, that are stored so far back in our memory that we have forgotten that we even know them. But they are for you. We are ready to teach you. All Praises are forever due to Allah, in the Person of Master Fard Muhammad, our Brother. That's right!

A. M. Muhammad

We thank Allah. We are ready to teach you today, and that gives us a great feeling. A feeling of accomplishment that we are able to come before you and know that we are teaching our beloved, long sought after, long awaited brothers and sisters. You, who are just like us, who believe as we believe. I don't think I can even explain, or attempt to explain how good it makes me feel. So let us get on with what we are going to talk about here. Praise be to Allah.

You can tell the fruit by the tree it bears. Now just hold on. I know a whole lot of you are thinking, Poor Brother Ali, you have got it backwards, and we know you mean well. We know that you just got it a little backwards there. It is you can tell the tree by the fruit it bears. That is what you meant to say Brother Ali. No, brothers and sisters, I said what I had to say. All Praises are due to Allah.

I agree with you that sometimes I stay pretty drunk and this is because of Brother Fard. He gives you that strong drink all the time. But today I know what I am saying and I did not make a mistake. You can tell the fruit by the tree it bears. Now I am going to explain. I am going to show you that sometimes Poor Brother Ali knows what he is talking about. I am not incoherent all the time. Yes, we are going to explain it to you; so just relax for a moment.

The fruit carries the seed of the tree. The fruit has the life thought of the tree. It is the fruit which passes on the future generations, the tree's life existence. If it were not for the seed you could not have the tree. You must have the seed. The seed is what produces the tree. Now, I know that you want to hear that it is the tree that produces fruit. That is true, that is very true. But it is trees that I am trying to make of all you wise brothers and sisters out there. That is the exact point that I am trying to make here, because our Father taught, "Celebrate the Son so that the Son can celebrate the Father," or, "Celebrate the Father so that the Father can celebrate the Son." So now we have the same similarities, the same likeness, the One being

KNOWLEDGE OF THE GODS

the source of the Other.

If you take an apple seed and plant it, you will expect an apple tree to grow from that seed. You would be foolish to look for anything else. If you take a pear seed and plant it, you expect a pear tree to grow. You would not plant squash seeds and expect tomatoes to grow. The seed produces the kind of tree which it came from. Sure it does. So now what am I trying to get to? We just want you to see this - you can look at the fruit and tell its source. If I show you an apple you would know right away that it came from an apple tree. Without a shadow of a doubt, a pear comes from a pear tree and tomatoes from a tomato vine, it is so plain. It is by this same method that we are going to see who we are. We are going to see what our source is.

How do we know our source? We look at the fruit, and when we ask the fruit, "What can you do?" They say, "We hear and obey!" Is that right? That is what they say. So what does this tell us? Here is proof of that - that we celebrate our Source. We are Fard's Fruit. Why? Because that is what Our Father taught us. He said our God was Allah in the Person of Master Fard Muhammad. The Wisest God, or Wisest Scientist among us. He always has been and He always will be, because we are the Tribe of Shabazz. This is what He taught us.

So now all you have to do is examine the Fruit and you can tell the Source. We know the Tree was the Honorable Mr. Elijah Muhammad. He was the Source without a shadow of a doubt. Now you must bear witness to that. Every time the Fruit opens their mouths, they say, "All praises due to Allah, and we forever thank Our Father, the Most Honorable Mr. Elijah Muhammad." Our Father is the Source! The Fruit reflects the Tree and the nature of the Tree. That is Our Father. He is immortal. His name will always be praised and remembered among us. Our children will be taught all about Him. We will forever remember Our Father because that is our Source. How in the world can an apple tree or an apple come on the scene and then decide that it wants to be something other than what it is? It just don't happen that way.

Well now, let us look at the other people. Wallace. Does he celebrate the Source? Whose fruit is he? What tree will he bear? Our Father says we must fight for independence. Wallace says there is no fight, we must unite the world. We are all brothers and sisters; we do not carry arms, and we do not think about fighting. He further said of him and his followers, 'We want to turn in anyone we catch with a pistol.' Whose fruit is he? What tree will they bear in future generations?

Our Father, the Most Honorable Mr. Elijah Muhammad, teaches us that God is not a spook, God is not a spirit, that God is a Man among us. He walks, talks, breathes, wears clothes, goes to the market place, drives a car, and raises a family. God is a Man!

Wallace says God is a spirit, neither male nor female, cannot be seen and does not manifest in a physical form. Whose fruit is he? What tree will he bear? All praises are due to Allah. We bear witness that you can tell the tree by the fruit it bears, and you can tell the fruit by the tree it bears. To bear also means to uphold. Who is Wallace upholding? Is he upholding Our Father? Absolutely not! He tells his followers not to even read Muhammad's articles because he says, "That's old teachings." He says what he has for them now is new things, that it is higher. He says that his father was not divine, and that his father was just a plain human being. That he was a great man. This is what he says. He says he is divine though. But now, what is his source if he is a divine man? What is his source? What does he uphold? One of the Scientist, Islamic Scientist, Brother Minister Basir, told me that Wallace gets his revelations from President Ford, and, I am inclined to go along with the wise brother.

KNOWLEDGE OF THE GODS

He definitely did not get his revelations from Our Father.

His work does not uphold our Father. He upholds the devil, his father. It is the work of his father he is doing by forcing integration upon our people. Teaching them that there is a mystery God. He is putting our people further in the hole. Placing the dirt that Our Father removed, back on them. Wallace and his helpers, all the ministers that are with him, are kicking dirt back on our people. Whose work is that? Is it the work of Our Father, The Most Honorable Mr. Elijah Muhammad, the Last God of the old world and the First God of the New World? Is it His work? No sir! Those are the works of the devil, and that is the work which Wallace is doing. So he upholds his source. He bears his tree, the tree of the enemy.

We thank Allah much, because it is plain simple mathematics to us. But we are different. He claims that we want to take his wisdom. That is not so! Wallace is a liar! Always has been. He is describing his death. We do not want what he has. We want only what is our due, only that which we work for. We want only those who believe as we believe. Those who understand and see, on the plane that we see and understand, that Almighty God Allah, in the Person of Master Fard Muhammad, is our Brother, raised from among us by Our Father, the Most Honorable Mr. Elijah Muhammad. If they cannot see that, cannot accept that, cannot submit to that Wisdom and Truth, then they are not of us. No, we do not want what Wallace has. We have left the old world and shall never more return. As in the history of Lot, we will not look back. We want only those that are of us. The Tribe of Shabazz.

Wallace has even changed the name. The old world is no longer the Shabazzians, they are the Bilalians. Do you understand? What is his source? Who is he upholding? Where does this Bilalian truth come from? All praises due to Allah. We are after our people, the Tribe of Shabazz. They are those who believe as we believe, and have only to hear this Divine Truth, and they will stand up and be just like you and me. You are the proof of that. I am the proof of that. Our success can be measured by every brother and sister who is a true believer. We are in our time. Shabazz is now on the scene. That's right! Resurrected from the dead, just as Our Father promised us. We cannot make liars of the prophets.

Our Father said He was here to pave the way for the Great Mahdi, to prepare us for the Great Mahdi. This means that everything He gave us was essentially what we needed for our acceptance of the Great Mahdi. You cannot tell us that the Books of the Honorable Mr. Elijah Muhammad are insignificant. You cannot say that. His Books are of the utmost importance. They are Divine Revelations. Divine Guidance from a God showing us the way.

If it were not for the teachings of the Honorable Mr. Elijah Muhammad where do you think we would be? It is from that Great Tree that we owe our existence. How can you cut off the existence of the tree and expect to have fruit? You just cannot do that. No prophet came on the scene cutting off the history, or calling the Guidance, of the prophet before him a liar. Every prophet who came on the scene, came on the scene bearing witness to the prophet, or the God, before him. Jesus said, "I did not come to change the laws of Moses, I come to fulfill the laws of Moses." Jesus told the people of John the Baptist, that they would not understand John the Baptist, that they did not know who John the Baptist was. He told them that there was none greater in the heavens than John the Baptist.

All prophets come on the scene bearing witness to the prophet before them, and declaring that every word that came out of the prophet's mouth, who was before them, was the absolute and Divine Truth. Sure, that's right! All Praises due to Allah. Now comes Wallace, the chief hypocrite, who by his words and actions, says this is not so. He said what my father taught you was wrong.

KNOWLEDGE OF THE GODS

We thank Allah, in the Person of Master Fard Muhammad, and We forever give Praises to Our Father, the Honorable Mr. Elijah Muhammad, for if it were not for them we would really be in bad shape.

Now look at all of those who say they follow the Honorable Elijah Muhammad and do not. Such as ministers, captains and lieutenants, etc. Now look at us. Look how easy it was for them to turn their backs on the Divine Teachings of the Honorable Mr. Elijah Muhammad. Now look at how easy it is for you and I to hold onto our Father's teachings.

See how easy it is for us to celebrate the Praises of Allah, in the Person of Master Fard Muhammad? If it were not for Master Fard Muhammad we would not be holding onto our Father and recognizing Him as God; you and I would not have the power, without Him, to hold onto Allah with the firmest grip. We would be just like those fools who call themselves the Bilalians, who go against the Divine Laws of God. Who tried to put out the Divine Truth of our Father, the Honorable Mr. Elijah Muhammad, with their filthy mouths? They worked to help the devil destroy the beginning of the New World of Islam. Think about that.

Wallace hates his father, and it appears he has always hated his father. He is insane for leadership and those fools around him, who call themselves ministers, are no better. They are as bad off as he is. He is the chief hypocrite. A hypocrite is one who says that he believes with his mouth, but does not believe. He only seeks to deceive the true believers.

Our Father said there is no doubt that the white man is the devil and he must be destroyed. He said there is no way he can get out of the destruction which has been divinely appointed him. A Muslim does not love the devil regardless to how long he studies. Did not our Father teach us that? After he has studied from 35 to 50 years, trying to do and act like the original Man, even though we will do trading with him, his head would still be taken off by the sword. There is no out for him. It is a Divine Decree. You cannot reform the devil because he is a snake of the grafted type, and if he be allowed to live he will sting someone else.

He was only created so that God could show forth His Power. That He could make a devil, and give him power to rule for 6,000 years, and then rise up, and in one day destroy the devil, without falling victim to the devil's civilization. This is to show and prove that Allah is God, always has been and always will be. Now isn't that what our Father taught us? Did He ever say maybe? Did He ever say perhaps or could be? Did He ever say I am not sure? Brothers and sisters, our Father always made it perfectly clear that there was no hope for them. Where does this fool Wallace come up with the idea that they are our brothers and sisters?

You cannot make liars of the prophets. History has shown for thousands of years that the hypocrites have always been against the believers. Those who seek to put out the light of Truth with their mouths are brought to their doom. They see the Judgment Day far off, but the Believers see it near. The brothers know what I am talking about. All praise is due to Allah. I think our sisters got an idea. Praise be to Allah! Look around you. What do you see? Only Brother Fard and His Fruit are the upholders of our Father. Why is this? It is because we are the only ones from the Divine Source. We have no choice in the matter. What else can we be but children of Our Father? We know the Truth. We cannot get out of it. This is the truth. It is a rabbit's nature to wiggle its nose, to stroke its ears, and to hop. It does not have a choice in the matter. It is the same thing with us, and we thank Allah. We have no choice in the matter but to be Muslims as Our Father named us Muslims, and to give praise to Almighty God Allah, in the Person of Master Fard Muhammad,

KNOWLEDGE OF THE GODS

because our Father taught us to do so. We are happy today because in you, Fard's Fruit and M.G.T. & G.C.C., there are seeds for a whole forest of Divine trees of the Lord, planted in the field. These are our beginnings, we are the mature Fruit. We are showing signs of maturity. Our identity is now solidified. We are now ready to reproduce ourselves. You see sisters fasting and studying. You see brothers fasting and studying. Everybody is getting ready to start teaching. The city will soon be alive with a New Teaching, with a people who love Muhammad, and are dedicated to Master Fard Muhammad. People who will not let anything come between them, Allah, His Messenger, and their duty. That is going to be a sight to see.

We are the only Muslims. They have not seen Muslims before. The only Muslims on the scene today are us. People are going to come to us in companies.

Homes are going to break up, wives are going to leave their husbands, and husbands are going to leave their wives. Children are going to leave home. That is what you are getting ready to see taking place first, in the Holy City, the New Ark, the Model City.

Before you know it we will be large enough in numbers, to establish the New World of Islam's Model Mosque #25 - our Headquarters. Soon we will have our own newspaper called the ALLAH IN MUHAMMAD SPEAKS. There will be front page portraits of Our Father, centerfold articles of His teachings, repeats of all His old columns. Soon you will be able to buy Our Father's Books in one volume, on onion skin paper, and with gold bindings. Soon you will see our sisters in their long dresses, with veils, just as Our Father desired. You will see our brothers in their uniforms. It is almost here, you can just about touch it.

You know that there is fruit because we are here. You know that you have an apple tree, if you have an apple Seed. The Seed is in the fruit. All praises due to Allah. All Holy praises are forever due to Allah, in the Person of Master Fard Muhammad, the Great Mahdi, the Son of Man, the Christ, and the Crusher of the wicked. Yes, yes, all praises are due to Allah, in the Person of Master Fard Muhammad. I really feel good!

I can remember when these teachings were kept a secret. These same teachings which you brothers and sisters now discuss openly, that are now common place among you, at one time was known only to three people on the planet. This was Allah, Our Father, the Honorable Mr. Elijah Muhammad, Master Fard Muhammad, the Great Mahdi, and Myself. Praise be to Allah. That's right! It could not be told. It had to be hidden until the time was right. Now I look out there and see the brothers. I see the sisters, and my, my, my. Praise be to Allah.

Yes, the world is getting ready to see us for the first time. They are getting ready to see Muslims. The first thing they are going to see is our Unity because we are not like other people. We are the same kind. We look out for each other. When you see a couple of brothers in the street it looks like they each are employed to protect one another. You don't know which one is the most important, because each of them acts like a security agent for the other.

It is only natural because we are the same kind and species. You find this same kind of unity demonstrated in the field among the animals. You notice that the animals always have sentries around watching over the rest of the flock. With grazing animals, some graze while others are watchful for enemies. This is how we naturally take to each other. We realize that value of each brother and each sister.

They are the seed of our doctrine, the seed of our Nation, of our species and our kind. Therefore, we just naturally feel protective towards each other. We want to look out for one another's welfare.

KNOWLEDGE OF THE GODS

The first thing the people are going to recognize about us is that the brothers and sisters of the New World of Islam, has the Divine Unity. We love each other. They are going to see it. They will say, "Those brothers and sisters are some together people." They will talk about how we look out for one another. This is the truth. Brother Fard said, "The unity slogan for Muhammad's Model Mosque and the New World Nation of Islam is, *If one brother has a bowl of soup, you have a half a bowl of soup. One for all and all for one.*" This will be the order of the day. It is easy for us because we love each other. A hypocrite could never practice such a thing. When we issued the F.O.I. Training Rules, Brother Fard said it was not time for us to institute the slogan, "If one brother has a bowl of soup, you have a half a bowl of soup." At that time I did not understand what He meant, but I do now; because I can look back and see that of all the people on the scene then, none of them really believed. There were no brothers and sisters. Brother Fard is so Wise.

When it is time for you to be turned over to Almighty God Allah, in the Person of Master Fard Muhammad, I will be so happy and you will too. You think you love your God now, just wait until you can rub shoulders with Him. Wait until you can sit down and talk with Him, eat with Him, laugh and joke with Him and listen to Him. He is without doubt, the Wisest Man in the Universe. There is no doubt about it.

The next time you are standing up somewhere teaching, and your little chest is stuck out, ask yourself where the Wisdom came from? If you have just enough to make you feel a little proud, and you know you have only been around for a few minutes, then all you have is just a little bit of Wisdom from Master Fard Muhammad. Can you imagine that little thimble full of Wisdom can cause you to feel so high and mighty? Well then imagine the Power of the Great Ocean of knowledge in Our Lord and Saviour, Master Fard

Muhammad, the Great Mahdi! You will see, you will see! All praise is due to Allah.

They will recognize our Unity because it is natural. We are just like the animals in the field. All people love and respect their own, when they know their own. The animals love and respect their own. So in closing, let me share with you Chapter 26 of **OUR SAVIOUR HAS ARRIVED,** entitled The Will Of Allah Is Being Done:

"The New World of Islam is coming in - not the old world of Islam, but a New World of Islam. Behold I make all things new!" (Revelation 21:5).

We are living in the change of worlds. The old world is going out and the New World is coming in. This is something to be happy and thankful to Allah for - to bear witness to the change of worlds!

This is the first time that Allah (God) has been known in Person. The coming of Allah in Person indicates this change of worlds - signifying a permanent change, where God will set up His Kingdom of Islam without interference.

This is the end of opposition and attacks against the righteous and their righteous religion, Islam. Islam has a righteous name that corresponds with the principles and beliefs of Islam. It is a very beautiful name.

The white race worked hard for 6,000 years to try to destroy the religion of Allah (God). But the white race missed. We are still here.

The Name, Allah is a Great Name! I'd rather call Him Allah than to call Him God. God is an English name for the Supreme Being. To say God - this refers to the Supreme Being, but we have too many gods, and we would like to give credit to only One God. So we rather use the name, Allah. I want Allah to have all the credit that we can give to Him.

Allah is a Great Name for the Supreme Being. It means Allah

KNOWLEDGE OF THE GODS

everywhere, It covers everything. I like that Name, Allah!

Let Thy Will be done! The Will of Allah must be done! I want to talk with you a few minutes on the Will of Allah. Let Thy Will be done.

We want always that God do His Will, but we are not always prepared to receive His Will. While we wait for His Will, we do our own will - that is no good!

Thy Will be done! The Will of Allah must be done! We must, today, accept the Will of Allah and not our will - not the will of other than Allah.

You have too many gods in your religion, Christianity. We do not know which one you mean. You curse with the Name of God and you are always disrespectful to the honor due to that Name.

Allah says there is no God but He, Allah is the Best Knower. If you want to make a spook out of me, look at me good - I am not a spook. I stayed with Allah and we were together for three years and four months, night and day. If you think you know Allah, better, here I am - question me.

The Will of Allah must be done. Allah, through His Will, will come out Himself to be the Champion and lead the righteous to victory. His will shall not be hindered by anyone.

When a person gets righteous, God accepts him as His FRIEND. Then the Will of each other is with each other. What one wills, the other wills. It is the will of both.

The Messenger's will is in accord with the Will of Allah. The Messenger cannot will something opposed to Allah. Allah has taken over the Messenger's heart, mind, and brain and Allah is making them to react according to His Will!

This is what the Holy Qur'an teaches - that the Will of Allah is the will of the Messenger and the will of the Messenger is the Will of Allah.

Jesus himself said that he was not God. The coming of Jesus was not God. The coming of Jesus was not ever prophesied in the Old Testament of the Bible. What you read of Jesus, in the Old Testament - that is myself, the last days with a government upon his shoulder. (Isa. 9:6) Jesus did not have a government upon his shoulder, which is what he needed for a prophet that is to rule, attack, and destroy the Jews, Christians, and Greeks - authorities over religion. He needed that knowledge and power. If he had a government upon his shoulder - what government?

The Will of Allah must be done! Knowledge and belief are different. I can believe that there is an airplane out there on the doorstep, but there is no airplane out there.

There are many people who believe that angels are out in the air somewhere, but if they are out there, we cannot see them. There is no such thing as formless spirits flying around out there somewhere in space, unless it is righteous minds.

The Will of Allah must be done. Allah could not have a Will Himself until He had brains, Himself. Allah was created; self - created from an atom of life. The atom of life was not only able to create flesh and have blood from the earth that He was created on - Allah (God) was created on the very earth that we are on today. But the earth was not as it is today.

I want to come back to our subject, our text, the Will of God. The Will of Allah must be done. Allah's (God's) Will could not be done as long as He has an enemy powerful enough to force his rule against the Will of God.

Allah (God) allowed the enemy 6,000 years in which to rule. Now this is the time that the enemy cannot force his will against the Will of Allah. The white man no longer has power to force his will

KNOWLEDGE OF THE GODS

against Allah and against the representatives of Allah, the prophets!

Thy Will be done. The Will of Allah must be done. It is not the Will of Allah that His people, the Black people, be sick. When a man has no sickness in his body, we call him happy. He is happy. He does not feel any pain the body is happy.

This is just the life Allah (God) teaches you to enjoy. It is not the Will of Allah that you get sick. You make yourself sick.

Allah does not have a set time for you and me to die. We kill ourselves. We can prolong our lives by living right and eating the right food.

People who want their will to be done, let them go to Allah and obey Allah and the Messenger."

All Praise is forever due to Allah, in the Person of Master Fard Muhammad. The Truth is so plain that even a fool can understand. Our Father laid down the Truth in such a way that no one can come up with an excuse for not following the Truth.

So with that we will close in the Name of Allah, in the Person of Master Fard Muhammad, the Beneficent, the Merciful, Our Saviour of the lost but now Found, Tribe of Shabazz. I greet you my beloved brothers and sisters, and we exhort you to hold fast to Allah and His Messenger, and to let nothing come between you and Allah and His Messenger. We greet you with the New World's Greetings of Peace and Paradise.

Peace! Peace!

May Allah bless you. May Allah bless us forever.

Chapter Nine
The Time

My beautiful black brothers and sisters, we thank Allah much for this day, July 4, 1977. This day holds much significance for us. Our Father, the Honorable Mr. Elijah Muhammad, said that we must have a knowledge of the time if we hope to be successful. We are living in a very important time. We are the children of the Honorable Mr. Elijah Muhammad. There is no doubt about that.

You are all gathered here today to celebrate our Unity and Independence; and to reaffirm that there is no God besides Allah, in the Person of Master Fard Muhammad, and that Muhammad is His Slave. This makes this event very important because it is happening at a Divine Time. This is what we are going to be covering in our subject today - THE TIME!

I have a brief message for the brothers before I get into the Time. We want you brothers to realize that we have the best sisters in the world. They are the most beautiful, they are the most dedicated, they are the most loving, and they have never left us. They have been with us through thick and thin. Allah is now fashioning them my brothers. He is qualifying them to sew, cook clean the house, take care of their husbands, rear their children and how to act at home and abroad as civilized people. They are now making us very proud of them. They are now coming together, for the first time, and taking the first steps which qualifies them for all of the respect, from all of the people, all of the time. So we thank Allah for our sisters. We want you sisters to continue to strive hard. It will not be long before you are able to put on your long dresses and begin to wear the veil.

KNOWLEDGE OF THE GODS

Allah is definitely blessing you, and you are beautiful. We thank Allah for our sisters. Brothers, you protect our sisters, look after our sisters. There are none like them.

Our subject today is The Time. This event taking place today is full of signs and symbols. There are a lot of prophetic signs and symbols which show and prove what time it is. If we are not aware of the time, our actions will not coincide with the time, and we will cause great discord. We will find out that when we try to do things, they just will not come out right, because we are out of time. So, today, as we come together, the main thing that is on our minds is the verification of the time. This is important.

The Saviour taught me that the Holy City of Mecca, 1400 years ago, would coincide with the sign, or coincide with signs, of the establishment of the Kingdom of Heaven in the Time of the Judgment. He said that when Muhammad ibn Abdullah (Peace and blessings of Allah forever be upon him) began to study religion, as a young man, before he received his first revelations of the Qur'an, there were many different kinds of religions in the City of Mecca.

Allah and Islam was the old time religion. People had gotten away from the worship of Allah. They had become interested in other things. When Muhammad and His few followers began to meet together and worship Allah, they were looked upon as a people who were establishing a new religion. This is a sign of what is happening today. This event is a great event. This very day that we have come together, marks a sign. Allah said that when Muhammad began to teach, "Hold on to that old time religion, hold onto Islam," they began to persecute Him and the few followers that believed in Him. But this marks a great event. It marks the Judgment! In the Holy Qur'an, it speaks of the event when you will have three classes of men. It says that there are three classes of men, which includes, those on the right hand, and these are happy, and those on the left hand, and these are wretched and the foremost, they are the foremost.

This is to show that, as it was in Mecca 1400 years ago, when a group of people (regardless of their number) came together to teach, or to worship in a particular way, it automatically sets up those on the right hand and those on the left hand.

There are those who believe and are seeing the benefits of their belief. This refers to members of the New World of Islam. It is the City of Newark, New Jersey which is the Spiritual Center. This is where the knowledge of the Original Man (Our Father the Honorable Mr. Elijah Muhammad, proclaimed the Lord of all the Worlds, as taught by Master Fard Muhammad) first started. This is where the teachings first started.

As a few began to believe, they became strong in their faith and attracted the attention of the masses. As a result, there were those who looked to these few believers for this Truth being taught. It is a fact that Master Fard Muhammad, who came in 1930 is the Manifestation of Allah. And it is a fact, the Honorable Mr. Elijah Muhammad is the Alpha and Omega who taught us Islam that is older than the sun, moon and stars.

The Great Mahdi did not come with a New religion. He came to remind the people. He came to turn the hearts of the children back to the Father and the heart of the Father back to the children. He came on the scene saying, "You know we are Our Father's children. You know we have to do what He said do. You know that Elijah's teachings are the Truth. You know that the white man is the devil, and that the Blackman is God. So why are you talking about and doing something else? Why do you want to integrate with the enemy?"

Because of this the people on the right hand begin to stand up;

KNOWLEDGE OF THE GODS

that is, those who can see and recognize the Truth. They say, "Yes sir, brother, you right! I know that there are not many of you, but it is the Truth and I must stand up. I am with you." These are the ones who become those on the right hand, because they have enough sense to recognize the Truth when they hear it.

Then there are those on the left hand. These are they who oppose the Truth. They say, "No sir, brother, the teachings of the Honorable Mr. Elijah Muhammad are old. We do not need that anymore. He was telling a lie. He and Master Fard Muhammad were trying to trick our people out of their money, and they were false prophets." These are the ones on the left hand. They are the wretched. They are the ones who are condemned. They turned away from the Truth. They turned against Our Father.

The foremost are the foremost. This simply means that those individuals who are saying, "You better hold onto Elijah. You better do like Our Father said in order to build the House of Our Father's desire." These individuals who are saying this, and at the same time being rejected and persecuted, they are the foremost in faith. They are the first Believers.

Those on the right hand could not endure the trials of the foremost, and all the time be bearing witness to the faith. Therefore, the foremost are only described as the foremost, because they had the foresight to never lose faith in Our Father. They held on and did not allow anyone to deceive them. So as those on the right hand bear witness, they must bear witness to the foremost, who were on the scene all the time calling the people to the Truth.

We are known today, the New World of Islam, the people who believe in the Honorable Mr. Elijah Muhammad and teach that He is the God of the Universe. They teach that Master Fard Muhammad, The Mahdi is now among them, and He is qualifying them for the New World. These are the teachings of the Honorable Mr. Elijah

A. M. Muhammad

Muhammad, the old time religion. We are the foremost because we never gave up the faith. We bear witness to the first Believers, hearing this Truth we are teaching, and who came to us.

When these three classes of men have been established, then you have the judgment. Allah taught us that in Mecca, when the believers began to teach Islam, the enemy tried to destroy them with their mouths, then they tried to destroy them with force. But instead of destroying them, they just brought it to the people's attention that they were there. So the people began to stand up and bear witness. Mecca was under Judgment. Now, do not forget. We are talking about what time it is. We are not going to take up to much of your time. We just want to say a few things here. We are talking about the Time.

When Mecca comes under Judgment that is the end! Today the City of Newark, New Jersey, the Model City, the House of God, Mosque #25, this is where it all starts. The Judgment is taking place right before your very eyes. Look around you, and you see Brother Karriem. You see these brothers and sisters and you say, "Yeah, I know that brother, I know that sister! They have been around for a long time teaching Islam, hanging in there and keeping the faith." This is the Judgment. This is as it was in Mecca 1400 years ago. When people began to stand up and accept the faith, they bore witness to those who had been on the scene all the time, because these are the ones they had to come to in order to learn this truth. These are they who showed the direction. The foremost who hung in there. They kept the faith.

We are teaching about the time. We just want you to see the big picture. We want you to understand that this is the Judgment! We want to show how this event today is testimony for our time. The time when those on the right hand, are blessed for their steadfastness; and those on the left hand are going to be mad as hell,

KNOWLEDGE OF THE GODS

because they refuse to accept the Truth. We want you to understand the Time. We want to take our time and show it to you. So please be patient.

Look at it. Today the hypocrites are going around telling people that the Truth is a lie. They are doing it in such a way that they are exposing themselves. They are being exposed so fast that the Believers are not getting a chance to expose them. They are telling on themselves. Their arguments are weak. We have the truth.

People are beginning to realize that this is the Truth and that they must accept it, and they should never turn their backs on Elijah, because he is Our Father. They understand that they would not know any of this if it were not for Elijah. So, as we bear witness, we come together like today, and we socialize and are saying, "Hey brother, hey sister, how are we supposed to do this? When we come together, what are we supposed to wear? Sister, what are we supposed to do? What are we supposed to eat? Brother, how should we act?" That is what is happening today at this event.

Today, marks the first time that you have to think about setting up ways to function together. Today marks a time that we must come together as a society, and a form, means by which to live, and ways to get along with one another. A culture is now being fashioned. This event pulls out of us the guidance for existing together, as a unified whole, for the benefit of all.

Our coming together looks like a small thing, because there is just a few people. Now we are wondering, "Are the sisters going to wear their longs, and will the brothers wear suits? How are we going to conduct this affair?" In coming together you have to decide how you must act. How you should respect each other and how to dress.

You may ask, "What is this Brother Ali? How is that the Judgment? How does having a Unity Party relate to the Judgment?"

A. M. Muhammad

This is not just a Unity Party. It is an occasion to practice that which we believe in. This means that every time we come together, something new will be established in the way of custom, tradition and the way we will act towards one another in public and private. Our culture is now being formed.

As you continue to teach, more people will become aware of our society. As they visit our homes they begin to see how we live. They will see Islam being practiced. They will notice how we do not tolerate gossip. They will notice how we do not take advantage of one another because of the freedom to do so. They will see how we share with our people, unlike the hypocrites, who take advantage of our people. They will notice our love for our children, and how we have dedicated ourselves to make a better future for them. They will notice in coming among us, that we are interested in having the best women, the best homes, the best clothes, and the best of everything. This is our way. It is not the way of everybody, it is our way! As people begin to socialize with us, attend our events, they will naturally bear witness to the Truth and in bearing witness to the Truth, they bring about the Judgment.

I know you are thinking, "I am still not clear Brother Ali. I do not understand how it is the society, and our acting like Muslims, that will bring about the Judgment, or is the Judgment. It seems a little foggy." Well just hold on brother. Hold on sister. Maybe we can clear away some of the fog.

When we come together and begin to establish a culture, which is what we are doing right now, this becomes a definite way of action. This is how we act every day. We become more aware of how we are supposed to act around each other and the Lord of All the Worlds, in the Person of Master Fard Muhammad. The Truth is simple, it is so plain, but yet simple Truths are sometimes difficult to see. But you are all wise, and I am certain you will see what I am

KNOWLEDGE OF THE GODS

about to say in summing this up.

A society is people coming together for one common cause, as the lessons say. When they come together for a common cause, and begin to put certain things into action, they are called a society.

There have been a vast variety of nations on this planet. All of the Prophets, the Wise men, have predicted that there would be all kinds of societies in existence, with every kind of idea you would imagine, that would bring people together in a common cause. These societies would be about life and how people should act. There has been all kinds of nations on the earth, but the last society would be the society that would bring about the Judgment. It would be the last way of living to be tried, and it would be a Society, or Nation, of Gods. That is what the scriptures say. That is what we have been taught. That in the Judgment, God would establish a New World and in the New World everyone would be a God and Goddess. That is the Last Society.

We are the only Society which teaches the Presence of Almighty (God) Allah, and that we are all Gods. We are doing this now, that is, putting these principles into practice. As a result of this, every Shabazzian that comes into contact with one of us, from now on, will wake up. They will see our way of living and say, "Yes, that is for me. I like everything about the New World of Islam. It's just me. They did not change the teachings of Our Father, which we know is right."

The Honorable Mr. Elijah Muhammad told the Truth all the time. He meant what he said, and said what He meant. His books are scripture to us. No imposter can come to us and deceive us concerning our Father, the Honorable Mr. Elijah Muhammad. We are the only people teaching of the Society of God. We are the ones establishing the Society. When this happens, according to the history, according to the prophets (and you cannot make the prophets liars) then that is the Judgment!

Brothers and sisters it is so beautiful when you can really see and understand. That is what time it is. You either put this Islam into action or it goes for nothing.

Here you are today, only a few. The foremost drawn nigh to Allah, with no thought of turning around and you cannot understand why anyone would turn on Elijah, after hearing His Truth. You are asking yourself, "How could they be so dumb?" Look at you, look at you, you are beautiful! You are the Judgment. It is too late to stop us now. You are raised. The principles are now being fashioned. The foundation is now being laid.

Gradually the City will become brand New. As Mecca became brand New many years ago. When a few followers began to practice the old religion (Islam), and because the Truth was so powerful, in a short period of time, the whole of Arabia was converted to Islam. Because this Truth is manifested in our actions, it is only a matter of time before everyone will be trying to get to Newark. That is where this Truth will be centered and taught.

People coming from Newark will be carrying the Truth willingly and unwillingly. As we grow in numbers, and do more things, the City will gradually become a Muslim City, the Model City. When the City is in our possession, the attention of the world will be focused on us. Our Music, and all the things that we do for entertainment, will set the pattern, will set the pace. Newark will be the Spiritual Center where you can come and understand what the New Song, what Islam is all about, what the Honorable Mr. Elijah Muhammad was really teaching, and what this Superior Wisdom really is. You will hear Wisdom straight from the Mouth of God.

Newark will also be the fashion center of the world. You are doing this right now! You know how we do. We see a brother or

KNOWLEDGE OF THE GODS

sister wearing something we like, and after complimenting them on how good it looks on them, we want the pattern. Our clothing will be original. Our style of dress is now being created. As we begin to patronize the business establishments of our own people, as we begin to socialize more, our style of clothing and our original ideas will become predominant among us, and for those who are with us. So that if people outside of our community want to be up to date, and original, they will have to pattern after us. We will be the only true representation of the Original Blackman. In order for them to act in an original way, they will have to copy us. In that way, the City will become a fashion center.

When we have control of the City we will not spare any funds in our efforts towards better health, welfare and education and the police. We will make advancements that other cities will not make because of their bickering and being divided. We will make advancements in business, education, technology, and in every facet of government. We will become the trade center for black people worldwide, but for the Blackman here in America first.

Allah told me that a Black Hollywood film production, and corporation, could be enticed to come to Newark. He said when you control a large amount of money you can just about hire and fire whomever you choose. If we want a movie industry in the area all we need is the finance.

What I am trying to show you here is that this event is not just a simple event, it established the Judgment. It is just as the prophets predicted - a time of darkness. Spiritual darkness, where the Sun rises in the West, upholding all the prophets and the prophecies; bearing witness chiefly to Our Father, the Honorable Mr. Elijah Muhammad; and being the actual Salvation of our people by giving us dignity and respect for one another; and to stand up and be counted as a Righteous Nation under God. We are resurrected and fulfilling the Divine Scriptures as it has been predicted. You, the First Fruits, represent the Judgment.

We cannot go back once our eyes have been opened. We can only go forward. This Islam we are putting into practice today is the first step in the Judgment of the world. Some of us will enter heaven immediately. That is the success of our unity, the reward for our actions of doing what we know is right in following the principles, and of hearing and obeying. The fruits of those labors are now coming to us. Allah is going to bless everything we do. Our fair dealings with each other are going to prosper, because we will begin to realize how much we need each other.

We are going to see how when a brother or sister keeps their duty it helps us all. We are going to fall in love with unity, and in seeing the things we touch turn to pure gold. We are going to feel good doing the things that Our Father has laid out for us to do. We are going to feel good when we can stand up with the independent feeling that we are not Toms, Tools or Niggers! We are the children of Our Father. We are a Nation and we are building this. We have our own customs, and we have our own aims and goals. These first steps, small though they may be, are the proof of the Judgment of this world.

Our people have no choice but to accept this Truth that we are giving to them. Because we have stood fast through thick and thin. We are the first to experience the benefits of our works.

I thank Allah, and I want to thank you, for being patient with me. I want to remind you that if you do not fully understand what I am saying at this time, don't worry about it because, you will soon see believers coming to us in companies. This is the Judgment, and we are fulfilling the Scriptures. As it was 1400 years ago, in the City of Mecca, there was nothing but confusion, but Muhammad knew the Truth, and the Truth overcame falsehood, just as it will today!

KNOWLEDGE OF THE GODS

I am not going to hold you. I am not going to take up anymore of your time. I thank Allah for blessing us to be His people, His chosen, those who are resurrected first, to bear witness to a Mighty God in our midst, in the Person of Master Fard Muhammad, to be raised as leaders for our Nation, the New World of Islam.

May Allah bless us with many more successful Unity Meetings. Soon Allah will bless us to open our own Mosque, Muhammad's Mosque #25 of the New World of Islam. The Judgment is set and the end has come. We can be happy now. The doors of heaven are now open for the true believers. The gates of hell are roaring and asking for the hypocrites, disbelievers, back-biters, tools, toms, and rejectors. So with that my brothers and sisters, I pray Allah to continue to bless us to stay in the Light of Truth, to be good servants of Allah, and perfect examples for our people.

With that I close. I would like to thank the brothers and sisters for their, gifts, their dedication, and pray Allah will bring us together soon. For we have a lot of work to do.

In the Name of Allah, the Beneficent, the Merciful, in the Person of Master Fard Muhammad. And in the Name of Our Father, the Most Honorable Mr. Elijah Muhammad, Whom we love and forever praise. I greet you my beloved brothers and sisters with the New World's Greeting of Peace! Peace!

May Allah forever bless you!

Chapter Ten
Prayer

I am your Poor Brother Ali, the Spokesman for Master Fard Muhammad, Almighty God in our presence today. I am just like you. I am just a plain man, I am your Poor Brother. I was blessed to have walked and talked with Almighty God, in the Person of Master Fard Muhammad. I was blessed to have slept and ate with Master Fard Muhammad, to have fought the devil with Master Fard Muhammad and to have gone to the First Academy of Islam with Master Fard Muhammad. I am His Spokesman, the first to witness and the first to submit. I am just like you. If you would have met Him before me, and recognized and submitted to Him, you would have the job of the Spokesman for Almighty (God) Allah. That is the only difference between you and I. I cannot tell you anything other than what I have been taught by Master Fard Muhammad. I have no claim to fame other than being the first to submit to Master Fard Muhammad, Almighty God in Person among us today.

Before going any further, I would like to take this time to congratulate you, and to give you the Peace and Blessings from your God and Saviour, Master Fard Muhammad.

In the Name of Allah. Peace, Peace, to you brothers and Peace, Peace, to you sisters. Our Lord is proud of us. He told me that He is especially proud of our sisters. He said He now sees you fulfilling the history of the Qur'an, the righteous vying with one another in righteous deeds and that He is very proud of you. That the sisters are trying to outdo each other and that is good. He said this is Divine.

He said, "The brothers are moving at a very good pace and that

KNOWLEDGE OF THE GODS

everything is alright." He said, "We should keep on doing what we are doing." All Holy Praise is due to Allah. He told me not to worry about the white folks. He said, "When you are free, concentrate on teaching Islam, not to worry about anything else."

We thank Allah in the Person of Master Fard Muhammad. He suffered long before you or I. He is our very life-blood, brothers and sisters. He knows us better than we know ourselves. This Wisdom that you are receiving today, coming from the mouth of Almighty (God) Allah, this Great Truth, it stands by itself. It needs no one. You know the power of this Wisdom that you have received. Nowhere can you find anyone to bring up arguments that will condemn that which you have been taught. Only a Mighty God can produce such Great Wisdom.

We can be happy today my brothers and sisters. We are well on our way. Thanks to Almighty (God) Allah, Who is blessing us with Guidance, because if it were not for Him, we would surely be in great hell. All Holy Praise is due to Allah, in the Person of Master Fard Muhammad. And we forever thank Our Father, the Most Honorable Mr. Elijah Muhammad, for His great love for us and His great dedication. He showed us the way, so we would be able to recognize and submit to Almighty (God) Allah, in the Person of Master Fard Muhammad. We will forever praise Him. Praise be to Allah, the Lord of all the worlds.

Our subject is prayer. Prayer is as necessary as food and drink. Muslims cannot survive without prayer. You must have spiritual food to live. We are obligated to pray at least 5 times a day. And if we awaken at night, we are to pray twice at night, after 12:00. These prayers are obligations. This is the only way to stay in tune with Almighty (God) Allah. You are living in two worlds. One is material and the other is spiritual.

Look at the white man's society. He is so wrapped up in material things that he has totally neglected the spiritual side of life. Look at the sickness, the pettiness, the grief, the wars, the murder, the bloodshed, the hate, the envy and the jealousy. Look at all these things brothers and sisters. The murders, the cheating, the stealing. Look at it. These things are totally opposed to Peace.

Peace comes from a mind having proper guidance and understanding. As the mind creates an idea, it makes a firm resolve to bring that idea into action, into materialization, then the hands fashion that idea into shape. So, if the mind is not at peace, then the only thing that the hands can create is chaos, disorder, fighting and the killing of one another.

There are 360 degrees to a circle. This circle represents the entire world or universe. It is two forces, spiritual and material. You cannot be successful, unless you have a thorough knowledge of the two.

Almighty (God) Allah is Most Wise, the True Guide, and is the Source of Spiritual Energy and Guidance. All things come from Him. Therefore, if we are in touch with the Divine Supreme Being we become familiar with Right Guidance. Right Guidance allows us to move in the material world without suffering grief or loss of peace. We are able to rationalize our situation when we have Right Guidance.

Now just relax a little bit and let me teach you that which no other people have been taught. This comes from Almighty (God) Allah, in the Person of Master Fard Muhammad, who is now giving us this Supreme Wisdom to put us on top of civilization. It is plain and you will bear witness in a minute. Throughout history when a prophet or divine man came on the scene, his wisdom was the spiritual food to elevate the people. Those who received this teaching, the truth, the guidance, directly or indirectly, were elevated above the wickedness of the civilization they were living in.

KNOWLEDGE OF THE GODS

We are talking about prayer. We are saying that prayer is a must. You can't live without prayer. Prayer is as important as food and drink. A Muslim must have prayer to survive!

Throughout the history as these prophets came on the scene and taught the Truth from Almighty (God) Allah, the people would rise above the evil conditions they were living in at the time. Why? How? What was the magic of this? What can someone say to a person to make their whole life change? How does this come about and what makes it happen? I am going to explain. Just relax, I am going to show you how blessed we are to have Almighty (God) Allah in our presence today.

I know some of you might be thinking, "Why don't he get on with it? I want to get to the meat of this!" I know you are in a hurry to get this, and when I do give it all to you it will seem so plain and so simple that you are going to recognize it and say, "All Praises are due to Allah!" But I want you to remember this is a sign of the great blessing you have above all people. You have the Divine Supreme Wisdom right here, being given to you, the First of the Believers, my beautiful brothers and sisters. Do you realize how blessed we are? Well, let me get on with it.

The prophets would reveal these truths and the people would rise above the conditions. We are going to show you how that is done. All Holy Praises are due to Allah.

When a man is working and he has a friend, and his friend tells him, "Say brother, I am going to help you this morning." And they set out to work. Then the man's friend decides that he does not want to work. He changes his mind.

The other man says, "But you said you were going to help me. I depended on you coming to help me and I have set everything up, and now you have changed your mind. You are letting me down."

The friend says, "Well yeah, that's too bad, 'cause I'm gone."

Now when the friend goes, the man cannot do anything because he is very mad. And then he wonders, "Why did my friend lie to me? Why did he say he was going to help me if he knew he wasn't going to? I don't like stuff like that." He starts thinking all kinds of things, evil things that he could do to this fellow for lying to him like that. His whole day is messed up. The adrenaline in his system messes him up. He is unable to work. He is so upset he sees fire.

"That sucker came and lied to me like that," he thinks. "He just outright lied and turned on me like a snake." His whole day is messed up. I know everyone is familiar with that. All of us have been disappointed by someone making promises and failing to come through. It makes you so mad that you want to hit them in the head with something. Is that right? Sure that's right. You know this is the truth. It slows you down and you cannot work because you are so mad.

If you force yourself to do some work, you can't concentrate on doing good work because your mind is on the evil that you just experienced. All you can think about is the deceit, how you were tricked, fooled and lied to. Do you understand?

Now let us say Divine Guidance is given to this same man. He stands there all upset and along comes a Muslim and he says, "Peace, Peace, good brother, how are you feeling?" That man replies, "My friend lied to me, and I'm so mad I could kill him." The Muslim says, "Brother you ain't supposed to depend on nobody for help but Allah and Muhammad." Then he begins to explain to the man why he shouldn't trust nobody but Allah and Muhammad, and the man understands that.

The very next day the same friend can come on the scene and say, "I'm kind of sorry for messing you up yesterday but I'm going to

KNOWLEDGE OF THE GODS

help you out today." Then the man says, "You do not have to help me. It makes no difference to me because I don't depend on anyone but Allah and Muhammad anyhow." Do you see what I am saying brothers and sisters? Do you see the difference of being in tune with the Divine Supreme Being and His Divine Supreme Wisdom, and not being in tune?

Just the day before he was so messed up he couldn't work. That was before he got the wisdom, before he was in tune, before he was put in touch with Almighty (God) Allah. Now that he is in touch, he can maintain his peace because he knows now how to handle that kind of situation. Nothing can disturb or upset his plans to depend on himself and ask Allah for guidance.

He depends only on Allah, therefore his peace is not disturbed. It wouldn't matter if a hundred people came and offered him assistance, or if no one came. He has his peace in knowing that he can only depend on Allah and Muhammad. This little wisdom lifts him above all of his friends who are still fighting and killing each other because of their dependence on each other to survive. You know this is the truth.

Here is another example: You are walking down the street and you pass a funeral home. A sister is crying, "Oh my child is dead! O' Lord, why did you take my child away?" She is falling all out in the street. She is about to kill herself with grief because her child is dead. She does not know how to get above the situation, so the situation dominates her. The material world that she is living in dominates her, so she faints, cries, and moans at the loss of her child.

But then along comes a Muslim and he says, "What's the matter sister?"

And she says, "My child is dead and I want to die too."

But the Muslim says, "Wait a minute sister. Allah is God! He does not take something from you except to give you something better in return. Nothing comes into the world and nothing leaves the world, except it be with Allah's permission. You should want what Allah wants for you. God gives and God takes away."

He explains this to the sister and makes it so plain and easy for her to see it. Thereafter, whenever she sees this brother, her whole attitude changes. No more will the death of anyone in her family upset her. If someone comes to her and says, "Sister, I don't want to tell you this because I know it is going to hurt you, but your brother just died."

The sister says, "Praise be to Allah, nothing lives forever. We all must go someday. Allah gives and Allah takes away." She does not lose her peace. She rises above the situation. While everyone around her is falling out with grief, she is holding her head up. She understands that it is Allah's Will, and to get upset with Allah's Will is to show lack of understanding of the Divine Supreme Being's Will. Is that right or wrong? You know it is the truth.

When someone is given the proper guidance they are able to rise above a wicked civilization, above the wickedness of a material world. When your mind is in the right place, the things your hands create will be righteous. However, your mind won't be in the right place without prayer, which is the proper food.

Let me show you why. When a Muslim prays, he goes and he washes up. He makes an ablution. His thoughts are, "I've got to get cleaned up. I've got to get rid of all the dirt. I've got to turn to Allah, trying and showing that I want to be upright, so the evil I've done with my hands, I'm going to wash away. The evil I might have seen, heard, smelled, or tasted, I just want to get rid of it and clean up."

He thinks, "First I want to wash away my sins. I want to show the Lord that I am not playing a game. I know I am faulty. I know that

KNOWLEDGE OF THE GODS

the Lord has never given me wrong guidance. I know that all I have to do is call on Him and He will help me. I know I must first demonstrate to Him that I want to hold on. I want to put on special garments that are clean, so He can see that I have come to Him in sincerity. That I am for real and that I turn myself to Allah, and confess every fault that is in me."

That is what we Muslims do. We are not interested in no God but Allah. We are only interested in the Guidance of Almighty (God) Allah. It is the sincerity of our hearts, brothers and sisters, which opens us up for Divine Guidance. When we make our prayers, and we follow the steps that Allah wants us to make, this is the ritual that He desires us to go through to make us fit to receive the Guidance. In this sincerity our hearts are cleansed of any wickedness that may have been in us before stepping onto the prayer rug. It is so simple.

How many times in your life have you felt that you just had to come clean? That you had to be sincere? That you had to tell the truth? You may have been lying for just a few minutes, but something made you say, "I've got to come clean." And you confess. "I lied, and this is how the situation is." At that point there is no wickedness in you because your being truthful pushed it all out. The very core of your nature thrives on that kind of sincerity, that kind of truth. This is when you are closest to Allah because that is Allah's Being. He is Truth Personified.

When you step on the prayer rug in sincerity you tune up with Almighty (God) Allah. Your heart is open for revelation from the Lord of the Worlds. Do you understand? You can then begin to receive the nourishment from Wisdom, Knowledge and Understanding. The Guidance!

We believe in all the prophets. We make no distinction between any of them. We believe in the truth that every prophet brought. In the past, if you even heard of a prophet, if you read the scriptures, if somebody told you about a prophet, you were blessed. You were blessed even if you met someone who had met a prophet. Any way you could get some wisdom from a Divine Prophet, you were blessed. This was because the prophet's wisdom elevated you above the people. Think, brothers and sisters of how blessed you and I are today. We just don't have someone telling us about Almighty (God) Allah, or just someone promising us that one day God will come, we have Almighty (God) Allah with us in Person today. Brothers and sisters this is the greatest blessing known. There has been no prophet to have come up with any wisdom greater than the promise of God coming among His people in the Last Day and Time.

If prayer elevated a people above the material wickedness of their civilization thousands and thousands of years ago, whenever a prophet came, think how fast you and I can rise brothers and sisters if we pray. We have Almighty (God) Allah right here with us. You walk around here giving up wisdom like its common place. This is because you are used to it. Look around you. Look at how many gripes the people who are not Muslims have. Look at the hypocrites. See how uptight they are. Look at the white folks. See how messed up they are. You and I are learning to forgive one another. Why? Because we know that if you don't show mercy, you can't get mercy. That makes us above holding a grudge.

Think about how uptight people get about simple things. A brother takes your jacket, wears it to a party and gets a smudge on it. As a result, you want to beat him up and hold that against him for the rest of your life. You say, "I hate that nigger," and hold the grudge. But not you and I. Because we have guidance. A Believer says, "We can't receive no mercy brothers and sisters, unless we show some mercy." Who is more unclean than we are? We have a lot of faults, so how are we going to fault a brother if he forgets and makes a mistake, and then we turn around and ask Allah to forgive

KNOWLEDGE OF THE GODS

us for our faults? We say, "Forgive me Lord if I forget or make a mistake, but I'm not going to forgive anyone if they forget and make a mistake." We learn to forgive our brothers and sisters.

The spiritual guidance that we receive tells us, "Forgive your brother, forgive your sister. We all make mistakes. Don't hold grudges." If a brother makes a mistake, or a sister makes a mistake, none of us will lose our peace. Is that right? We say, "Well, praise be to Allah. We all learn through our mistakes." A sister will say, "Get the lesson." And a brother says, "Well we got a lesson from that." Do you realize the wisdom you brothers and sisters are blessed with? Do you realize how blessed you are to be directly in touch with Divine Guidance?

People thousands of years ago only knew of the promise that there would be brothers and sisters in the Last Day and Time with Allah in Person. They used to pray and wish that they could be here today with Almighty (God) Allah, the Manifestation of all Truth, for all Time.

You can't ask Master Fard Muhammad a question He can't answer. And whatever He gives you no one can condemn it. That is Guidance brothers and sisters. Something you can only get through the sincerity of your heart through prayer, through supplication and submitting to this Divine Teacher, this Divine Guide. In this day and time brothers and sisters, I will not attempt to go into the finer science of prayer. But suffice to say, you must pray! This is the quickest way for us to be successful.

When a Muslim rises in the morning, at 5 o'clock, to make the Dawn prayer it is a sign. The Scientists among you know that it is a sign of what time it is for you and I, right now. This is the start of our day at 5 o'clock in the morning. And we, my beautiful brothers and sisters, have risen. Aren't you awake? Look at you. Everybody's eyes are open. What's the first thing on the agenda? The first thing on the agenda is getting guidance. Getting ready to ask the Lord what he wants us to do.

You are the manifestation of the first people of Almighty (God) Allah, who are above this civilization, already awake and seeing it and knowing it. You are sincere and taking the first necessary steps. This is what is happening to us right now, throughout this darkness, this spiritual darkness of night.

You and I, my beautiful Black brothers and sisters, we were up all the spiritual night, praying. Everyone else fell asleep on our Father's teaching. We are trying to do the work, looking for guidance and helping each other. We are the first people to rise up this morning proclaiming Almighty (God) Allah, in the Person of Master Fard Muhammad as our Lord and Saviour, and Muhammad as His Slave.

We are the only ones up. You know how it is at 5 o'clock in the morning. You know how it was 5 o'clock this morning. What usually happens? The Sun comes up. It gets real bright and hardly anything is moving. But then, in a little while, you look around and everybody is busy. Some are trying to get themselves together for the day, for the day's activities. They start waking up around 7:30, getting ready to go to work.

You are getting ready to experience the great awakening of the general population. You will see. You can see it now. We are the first few people given to God, Master Fard Muhammad. All of you are of the Family of Ali, the Greatest People, the Greatest Tribe of Master Fard Muhammad. You are numbered in the first 12,000 of the Tribe of Ali, the Family of Amran. In the history of the Bible, in the Book of Numbers, you are the Family of Aaron. In the Holy Qur'an, in the history of Abraham, you are the Family of Ishmael.

You are that people. The first to rise up and do the first duty of a

KNOWLEDGE OF THE GODS

Muslim. And the first duty of a Muslim is to pray! You must understand the necessity of prayer and that you should pray brothers and sisters, all the time. Always say, "Praise be to Allah," that is, "Al Hum-du-illah." That is the shortest prayer. When you say, "Praise be to Allah," it is a prayer. When you are walking say, "Praise be to Allah." Think of Allah when you recite your lessons, when you rise, and when you sit. Anytime that you can think of it (prayer) keep constantly aware of Allah.

There is no greater teaching that we can receive today than that of the necessity of prayer. We must pray Brothers and Sisters. I thank Allah so much for blessing us to be His people. For blessing us to understand this Great Supreme Wisdom which He has given to us and this Great Guidance. Master Fard Muhammad loves you brothers and sisters and He is gradually elevating you to shine like Morning Stars. Not only for our own Holy Nation Tribe of Shabazz, the New World Nation of Islam, but for the entire world.

You are already leaders in spiritual wisdom, knowledge, understanding, and the material things will follow. While we are on material things, I want to mention briefly that we are not attracted to the material world. We don't want the things of this world. We want the Hereafter. We want the things that Allah wants for us.

Master Fard Muhammad has ordered us to start with the best that this world has to offer. He says that we have got to be a clean and productive people. He emphasized that our sisters must be clean. Their homes must be spotless. No Muslim sister should have a dirty home. Dishes all in the sink, garbage all in the kitchen, floors dirty and grimy, dust all over the place, dirty laundry stacked in the corners and beds unmade. No, no, not our sisters! We want the best and we must teach ourselves how to maintain the best.

There are some people with piggish and niggardly mentalities. If you put them in a Penthouse with the best of everything, in a week's time it will look like Prince Street and Broome Street used to look back in the 1950's, and that was bad! They will have it looking like most of Newark, New Jersey use to look before they tore it all down. We can't have that. Sisters, be clean! Brothers, that goes for you too!

You sit up in the house, and the sister won't clean it, and you see the dirt, well then, you are more at fault then she is. We are a clean people. Our children are in the hands of you sisters. Look around you today. We have people who were brought up in dirt as children, they were raised in dirt. Dirt is common place to them. They don't even know they are not supposed to be dirty and living in filth. They only know what they were brought up in.

Sisters, maintain cleanliness in all you do. Keep yourselves and your homes clean. Don't be afraid of water. Bathe all the time. Wash yourself from head to toe all the time and make your babies wash. Bathe them and make them stay clean and our people will be spotless.

Don't forget to pray!

May Allah bless you as I greet you in the New World's greeting of Peace in this World, and Peace in the Hereafter.

Peace! Peace!

Chapter Eleven
Our History

I thank Allah, my brothers and sisters, for blessing me to be able to stand up today, to speak to you today, to enlighten you, and to give to you Guidance and the Truth that was given to me from the Mouth of Almighty (God) Allah, in the Person of Fard Muhammad.

It is a miracle, my brothers and sisters, that I am among you today, teaching you these Divine words of Almighty (God) Allah. It is a miracle that you are able to receive these Divine words of Almighty (God) Allah.

Where did you get the courage, my brothers and sisters and the strength? Where did you get so much foresight? It is a miracle for you and I to get together today without fear. What is it that has erased the fear from your hearts? We are just a small few, surrounded by enemies. It is like being in the fiery furnace. The fire is raging all around us and we are right in the midst of it. We have no fear and we are not burning up. No, we are not hot, in fact, we are cool. Now ain't that right?

I want you to know, my brothers and sisters, that the truth you are receiving today is protected by Almighty (God) Allah. No harm can come to you or the truth without the permission of Almighty (God) Allah. He does not desire harm for me and you. He desires to establish you and I before the world, as an example of His Love and Mercy. Let us understand that we are receiving a Divine Truth today. The Truth stands for itself. You are a product of what you have heard of the Truth. That is proof in itself. Your very existence, having knowledge, wisdom, foresight, dedication, love, and unity, is the proof of this. Only Divine Truth could have brought this about and Divine Truth comes from Almighty (God) Allah.

Today, my brothers and sisters, we are going to tell you the truth about your history. We are going to tell you truth which no one has had a chance to hear. We are going to tell you our side of this story so you will know your roots, so you will see just how blessed you are.

The history of Master Fard Muhammad is the New Song that is prophesied. It is prophesied that in the last days they will sing a New Song. Our Father, the Honorable Mr. Elijah Muhammad, who made us Muslims, taught and raised us to understand that we make no distinction between Allah's Prophets or His Scriptures. We believe in and fulfill them all. This is Divine History, our history. Our history could not come until the end. The end of the workings of satan, the disbelievers and the hypocrites. When Wallace and all those like him, have had their say.

Surely Allah hurls the truth against falsehood so that it knocks its brains out. This is exactly what happens when we relate our history to you and the Black World. That is what we are dealing with today. Our History!

In the early 1950's, Islam, as taught by the Honorable Mr. Elijah Muhammad was just becoming well known. The general idea about the Nation of Islam was that it was a little hate group, united together by a mutual agreement that the white folks were the devils. Now most people, including white folks, felt that it was just something that niggers talked about on street corners, in alley ways and behind closed doors. Many Black people (players, gamblers, and slicksters) saw an opportunity to get on the gravy train, to use Our Father's teachings as a means of robbing the people. About this time Malcolm X came on the scene.

KNOWLEDGE OF THE GODS

When Malcolm came on the scene there was a different type of so-called Muslim in Chicago with Our Father. Wallace, Akbar, and other members of the family were caught up in the world around them.

Brother Fard went to Chicago to give Our Father a gift, and He was picked up at the train station by Elijah Jr., and the car he was driving was a "hot-rod." It had mud flaps, fox tails, and rock 'n' roll music blasting on the car radio. Master Fard Muhammad (Bro. Fard) was shocked! But this was the kind of mentality which existed among the people at that time. They felt Our Father was holding them back, that He was keeping them from enjoying the pleasures of this world, away from the partying and dancing. The generation coming up wanted to be hip and not old fashioned.

The sisters wanted to shorten the hem-line on the dresses and let half their hair come out from under their head pieces. This was the kind of mentality which existed when Malcolm X came on the scene.

Malcolm always did consider himself a "player" and he had a little "game" with him. But, the best thing that happened to Malcolm, was his meeting and coming together with Our Father. For a minute there Malcolm was acting like a believer. Because of this Our Father blessed him with a lot of wisdom and the man became a dynamic speaker and ultimately became the National Representative of the Nation.

Now let's look at the other side of Malcolm, the "player" side of Malcolm. The side of Malcolm, the side from the "Big Apple" (New York). Whenever he was in Chicago associating with Sharrief, Akbar, Wallace, Herbert, and the rest of the family of Our Father, he was the "hippest" thing going. He was a "dude" you could sneak off with and smoke a little reefer, drink a little wine, and party a little - just as long as nobody caught you.

A. M. Muhammad

This is what the people around Our Father at that particular time, especially Wallace, Herbert, Akbar, and Sharrief, these are the things they really wanted to get into. They had the means by this time. They had the financial means, to enjoy the things they wanted as teenagers. But these things could not be enjoyed under Our Father's dictate or what they called "Religious Dogma."

Malcolm represented a way for them to achieve this "fast life," the life they really wanted to live. But Malcolm wasn't quite ready to break with Our Father. He enjoyed his popularity and was acting like he was grateful.

Meanwhile, in the City of Newark, New Jersey, Allah blessed me to meet Brother Fard. Brother Fard came at a time when our Father called; when He made the first call for the soldiers of Allah to stand up and to defend the Nation of Islam. Brother Fard and myself were the first volunteers. We were the first soldiers and the first field decorated heroes. Brother Fard was made Field Minister because the Brother came up through the ranks like everybody else.

The only difference was that Brother Fard was just an exemplary soldier. At another time we will give you a beautiful history of how Brother Fard came up through the ranks. Brother Fard was Commissioned by Our Father. It wasn't because someone was doing Him a favor, or that He "lucked up," it was because the Brother qualified for the highest rank of any brother in the Nation. This honor was given to Brother Fard at the 1960 Saviour's Day Convention.

This was during the time when everyone in the Nation was more enthusiastic about hearing Minister Malcolm than hearing Our Father speak. Many times Brother Fard took note of this and called my attention to it. The people were blinded by Wallace and Malcolm. They were saying that Malcolm was the successor of Our Father, the next leader of the Nation of Islam.

KNOWLEDGE OF THE GODS

Malcolm had recruited the support of most of the Ministers and their congregations. So when Our Father conferred the rank of Field Minister (which is the highest ranking Minister in the Nation) upon Master Fard Muhammad, Malcolm took an attitude. He had a fit! They began to say, "That Brother is too young," instead of respecting the Wisdom of Our Father because of His choice. They rebelled because they saw their "good thing" crumbling to the ground.

They had intended to take the Nation, loosening the reign, and giving everyone the freedom to do as they pleased and party. But with the Field Minister given Supreme Authority over everyone, and knowing that He was a fanatic in following Our Father's teachings, they knew they would never get away with those things with Brother Fard at the leadership. So they opposed Him. They got together with their little secret council. When Brother Fard and myself went off to school (prison) they tried to take the Nation from Our Father. That's right! Tried to take it! This happened so the Scriptures could be fulfilled. Pay attention because you must know your roots.

The Kingdom of Heaven would be like someone having a garden and loaning it to someone else. And then, when they came to reclaim their garden, the people beat them in the head, threw them out and attempted to take the garden from them. The Kingdom of Heaven would be like someone trying to take the Nation from the rightful owner. You all know these things. The history had to be fulfilled.

This is the history of Joseph's brothers trying to destroy Joseph because they discovered Joseph had been given authority over them, that he would inherit the Nation. They figured that Joseph was too young, that he should not have been given the favor and that they were better qualified. This is our history. We want you to keep in mind that this is Divine.

It is a miracle that you are even able to receive this truth today.

A. M. Muhammad

Think about it. For thousands and thousands of years people have been talking about when this day would come, when this truth would come to the people and that God Himself would be walking among His people. For thousands of years everybody has been on guard waiting on this God and these people to come on the scene. Now that they are here and everyone knows they are here, there is no one who can do anything about it.

Don't you see? Don't you think that the devil has been waiting on this? Don't you know that they were given an extension of time until these people were raised? All praise is due to Allah, the Lord of All the worlds, the Mighty God and the Protector of We, His poor servants.

We have no other protection besides Allah. We want you to know your history brothers and sisters. We want you to understand that you can really see your history when you know where you came from, then you will not have a problem holding into focus where you are going. Being able to see the accomplishments of the past, this will keep you in touch with your abilities to perform the same feats of success in the future. It is your history which preserves the species.

This New Song makes you a New People. This new Song is what our Father meant when He said, "Turn the hearts of the children back to the Father," and that is what he did. So this makes our history our roots. It is our heredity. It is the thing that keeps us going. It is the thing that makes us The Family that we are, right here today! A small group. It is the development, along with the results of the history of Our Father coming on the scene looking for that one man. It was our Father knowing that He was the God and that He had the work of passing the Seed of God onto the future. This is what establishes our roots.

When Our Father met Master Fard Muhammad, Praise be to

KNOWLEDGE OF THE GODS

Allah, of 1930, that was not Master Fard Muhammad of today. Of course their histories in many places are similar. But to set the record straight, Master Fard Muhammad who came in 1930, Who met Our Father, and Who Our Father recognized immediately as Almighty (God) Allah in Person, and Who told Our Father that, "Yes, I am God. I am Allah, but don't you tell anyone Elijah." This is the Fard Who stayed 3 1/2 years and then left.

Our Father waited twelve years before He began to teach that Master Fard Muhammad was God in Person. This Fard was a Mighty Man. He was Almighty (God) Allah in Person, until He met Our Father. Master Fard Muhammad of 1930 was a specially prepared man.

My brothers and sisters, the Holy Qur'an has the written Revelations given to Prophet Muhammad of 1400 years ago. These Revelations are so important to us, the God Tribe. The Tribe whose head is Alpha and Omega. The Tribe possessing the keys of heaven and hell, and of life and death. The God Tribe, the Tribe of Shabazz. This is the Tribe of the Mighty God, Who all the prophets spoke of, Who would appear in the Last Days. The Greatest and the Mightiest God known.

Prophet Muhammad of 1400 years ago, did us such a great service in re-establishing the signs and setting up the keys, the Holy Qur'an and his faithful service to Almighty (God) Allah. The Honorable Elijah Muhammad said that Prophet Muhammad of 1400 years ago (PBUH) was a white man. Allah promised him in a dream that he would see heaven, and that he would see the Face of Almighty (God) Allah in Person. This is the greatest blessing that a prophet could ever aspire to, hope for, or pray for.

We put down in the history, that in the Last Days, from the seed of Prophet Muhammad (Peace and Mercy of Allah forever be upon him) that of his seed, his lineage, a child would be raised. That this child must be of two worlds, Caucasian and Asiatic. That he must be taught the keys, given Supreme Wisdom and sent in search of the Mighty God. No prophet could ask for or receive a greater blessing than meeting God face to face.

Master Fard Muhammad of 1930 was the manifestation of Prophet Muhammad. We thank Almighty (God) Allah for blessing Muhammad in this world and for blessing Muhammad in the Hereafter. So remember your roots. Remember that we are talking about your history, your heredity. That is the history of Master Fard Muhammad of 1930.

Our Father, the Most Honorable Mr. Elijah Muhammad, Almighty (God) Allah, was only looking for one man, and that was Master Fard Muhammad. When He found Him, a soldier, He began to teach Him, cultivate Him, and gave Him that which He needed to become independent. After Our Father had given Brother Fard the keys, Brother Fard ascended to the throne of Almighty (God) Allah. Because of this particular history, because of this heredity and because Master Fard Muhammad is the embodiment of Our Father, the only way that the teachings, that the Tribe can continue in existence, is that it must reproduce itself so it can be passed on. Yes, some of you guessed it. Here I am. Your poor Brother Muhammad.

My awakening passed the truth on to the general Family, or to the general Nation of Islam. I am like the gate, the Spokesman. And because I am the Spokesman, the soil for reproduction is made possible. I gather around me those few who hear and recognize the truth. Those who hear the Song and bear witness that We are the seeds of Our Father, those who bear witness that Our Father is God, and always has been. Those who bear witness that the Son of Man, the Great Mahdi is Master Fard Muhammad, as Our Father the Honorable Mr. Elijah Muhammad taught us. The few that wake up as a Family (We are a Family), are the first of our kind, our species,

KNOWLEDGE OF THE GODS

Shabazz! The only Shabazz that exist are you and I. We are the Family that must carry this wisdom, this way of life on into the world. We are talking about *your history*. We are talking about *your heredity*. We are talking about the preservation of our kind, our species.

This is an important subject. Because as you can see, we are a Family, just a small unit. We are our own brothers and sisters, our own mothers and fathers. In the history where Jesus was asked to leave the believers, he was teaching in a room. There came a knock on the door and someone approached Jesus and said, "Behold thy mother and thy brethren without seek for thee." And Jesus answered saying, "Who is my mother or my brethren?" And he looked at those sitting around him and said, "Behold my mother and my brethren! For whosoever shall do the Will of God, the same is my brother, and my sister, and my mother." (Mark 3: 32-35) Meaning that the believers were his family.

You are the prototype of what the New World will be. You are the first manifestation of the New World. You are like ripe seeds to be planted in the field, to produce thousands of our kind. This you cannot do without a knowledge of your history, your heritage and the step by step procedure of where you came from. I am talking about those of you who are knowledgeable about the Deportation, from 66 trillion years ago. Brothers and sisters should be able to trace their history, especially from the time we were brought here, to the hells of North America 400 years ago.

You understand that Our Father traced our history back to the rich fertile valley of Egypt. Our Father has given us the Supreme Wisdom that all people must respect and submit to. Being that we are that special people, that small little Family chosen to be the best who know the true history of where we came from, and that we are the God Tribe, then we waste no time taking advantage of everything in our environment to preserve the species, as well as to reproduce it. The Tribe of Shabazz must be preserved and the only way it can be preserved is to reproduce.

The habits that we force ourselves to keep now, are what we pass on to the next generation. This gives them the strength to preserve and establish higher aims and goals. But we cannot set our sights on being the God unless we can see the history that the Gods have made.

You look at the work of Our Father. His work was the work of a God. Look at the work of Master Fard Muhammad of 1930, it was the work of a God. If you go back further, to all the prophets, you will find that their works were the works of Gods. You come up to this day and time and look at Brother Fard's work, you can see it was the work of a God. If we can make ourselves understand this simple little truth that we are the God, then we can begin to preserve our species. This is our history. It is our life.

Let us take a look at nature. Go into the world of nature because it is important that you understand that we are Family. Nature casts out its seeds and offspring, and thereby reproduces itself. We are faced with the same kind of difficulties. Life is a struggle, always has been and always will be. Existence is a struggle.

Praise be to Allah, in the Person of Master Fard Muhammad. The struggle for existence is the only true heaven. Heaven is a place where you work and love to work. We know you just don't go to heaven and lay down. You must have shelter and clothing. You need industry and farms and this requires work. Heaven is a place where you must work! But in heaven you can be occupied with the work you love best. You have freedom, justice, and equality. When a man loves his work he never gets tired of it. All he wants to do is work because he loves doing what he is doing. That's what heaven is but it is a struggle.

KNOWLEDGE OF THE GODS

When we look at nature we see that the black ant is creative and constructive. It is not like the other ants. When it's time for it to expand and reproduce its species, the queen ant will go out on her own and re-establish a whole colony of ants.

In the plant world, a flower or weed scatters their seeds far and wide. The wind will blow them to distant places or animals and insects will take them away. This is what causes them to expand their territory and also increases their population. There are certain rules which governs their life-span. This is true for plant and animal life. In every world, plants, animals, humans, insects, all have specific rules they must live by. There are certain enemies to stay away from, particular diets that must be followed and a particular work order which helps care for their kind, also, reproduces and protects their kind. We must follow the rules of health, cleanliness, education and those things which are relevant for us to maintain our particular identity.

In order for us to maintain our heredity, we must become living examples of our history. We had God as an example in our midst, in the Honorable Mr. Elijah Muhammad, Who walked the earth forty years looking for one particular man. In all that time He knew He was the only one with Supreme Wisdom to fortify His Mind to such a degree that He would be able to search a country for forty years looking for that one man. We have this God's history. It was preserved because Our Father acted in a particular way. He made His followers eat a particular diet, spiritually and physically. Do you see what I am saying brothers and sisters? The rules that we have to live by are rules which preserve us as a people.

Now we are a Family. You are of My Tribe and by My Tribe I am talking about Master Fard Muhammad. We are the first twelve thousand of our Tribe of 144,000. That number only covers men, the Fruit of Islam. Also, there are women and children bringing the number to 600,000 in all. These are our people. We are not interested in no one else. Only those who see and understand that which we see and understand can be of us. Therefore, we must eat a particular diet, practice certain habits, and do all of the things which will keep our minds channeled on being who we are supposed to be. We must enforce these things or we will lose our purpose and aim in life and we will get carried off our course. We must occupy 24 hours a day with being Shabazzians, being the God Tribe. Then we truly inherit our reward from God.

If we want swift success, all we have to do is be more like Our Father and Brother Fard. That is, polish ourselves, practice Godly habits that have been given to us - fasting, praying, and studying. We must keep our minds on our purpose, our aims, and knowing our history (know who we are). When there is nothing left for us to do after we have become such a solid unit of people, then comes the *Bursting Asunder*! Praise be to Allah, in the Person of Master Fard Muhammad, Whom we forever thank for blessing us with the Supreme Wisdom. We thank Allah for blessing *us* to be able to give you this Supreme Wisdom and be able to tell you and teach you what Allah has taught me. It is a miracle that we can be in the fiery furnace, in the midst of hell, and give you instructions to build God's Kingdom right in the midst of the enemy.

Some of what I am saying might seem a little drawn out. But brothers and sisters, I know you understand by now, whenever I take the time to tell you something, it is important. When you study our words, you discover just how important they are. So let us get on with this subject; our history.

We thank Allah. The history of Brother Fard, and the history of you and I is a New Song. We have on the job training. We are learning as we go along, working hard, and doing all that we know how to do. This is good! Our efforts of training ourselves to follow

KNOWLEDGE OF THE GODS

the principles given to us by God have made us solid. We have become one body, small though we are. Because of the little bit of work that we have done, we are now the most courageous Black men and women on the face of the planet. We are the Original Family of the planet Earth. That is who we are! The odds which you and I face are tremendous. People are sitting back waiting to see if the devil will destroy us. We are not paying the devil or any of our enemies any mind. We know that Almighty (God) Allah is our Protector. Because of this attitude, people far and wide are watching us and bearing witness that we are some crazy, but loyal Muslims who really believe that some God is protecting us, because we aren't showing any fear.

I thank Allah because now that we have practiced some of the Supreme Wisdom and have become a small solid group, the First Family, we are now prepared. Because of our on the job training and development, we are now proud to stand up anywhere and represent ourselves as New World Muslims. Isn't that something? You didn't know you had that in you, did you?

Every one of you know enough about our traditions, customs and heritage because of practice, study, going to classes, listening to tapes and writing essays. This is our way of life, passed on to us from Our Father and Our God, Master Fard Muhammad.

This has made you a great people. Your past is so great that you can now go anywhere and be recognized as the wisest individuals in the country. Because of your on the job training, you have become ripe, you have become infectious. You are now ready to germinate wherever you go. Your history is the creation of the seed. You and I are that seed brothers and sisters. We are not to *Burst Asunder*, we are to stretch forth. We are to become planted in the Earth; in the West, in the North and in the South. You and I are obligated brothers and sisters, those of us who are qualified. Those of us who have been to enough classes, prayed, fasted, studied and supported the Nation. Those who know how the Muslim Girls Training and Fruit Of Islam are set up and know the teachings, and who have all the books and have read them - we are obligated!

Didn't I tell you that we were here to qualify you as the head of the New World of Islam? Well, my brothers and sisters, I am happy to tell you today, that you are now qualified! You can go anywhere in the United States and raise companies of brothers and sisters, just as you yourselves have been raised. You can teach them to follow the principles of Islam. You can wake them up to the Supreme Wisdom that Almighty (God) Allah, Our Saviour, Master Fard Muhammad is in our midst. You have been taught directly by the Spokesman. We are talking about Our History. It ends if we do not reproduce ourselves. It will be gone and we won't know who we are.

Nature opens the way for every new generation to find its own and to establish its own. Look at the Robin Redbreast. A common bird. You can see them popping up in the spring, one of the early arrivals. When their young get big enough to go for self they are pushed out of the nest. They have to fly or die! They are not wanted if they are not good for the preservation, or continuance (reproduction) of the species. Don't you understand?

The eagle nests way up in the mountain top. They build their nest out of thorns and they put the straw on top of the thorns and when the young bird is big enough to go for self, they pull the straw out of the nest so that there is nothing left but thorns and the bird has to get out of the thorns and leave the nest. Fly or die!

When any bird gets out on their own, they find new territory and they begin to reproduce their species. Man has the same history. As he branches out into new frontiers, he re-establishes his own and this is what we are faced with today. I'm trying to give you the importance of your history so that you will know who we are, and

KNOWLEDGE OF THE GODS

you know that we are qualified to go forward, like all things in nature. Allah is with us.

In the Holy Qur'an it says, and this is not a quote, I'm paraphrasing. That after the believers had been with Muhammad, peace and mercy of Allah be upon Muhammad forever. After they were around him for a certain period of time, and they became wise, and they knew the doctrine, Muhammad told them that they should go out into the land and help Muhammad, if they believed in Muhammad. That they should go back to their people exalting Allah and bearing witness to the great blessings that Allah had bestowed upon the true believers, carrying the truth far and wide and reproducing the species. We must go in and among our people in search of the lost sheep. You, my brothers and sisters are qualified to go forward.

In the Holy Qur'an, the *Bursting Asunder* represents a time when the believers were prepared to go forth and spread Islam throughout the whole country. This is what we are about to do today. The devil's time was to last until 1914, 6,000 years, but his time was extended until we were raised. You and I are now raised and are bursting. Our preservation of our species depends on you and I going forth like all things in nature must go forth, leave home, get away from the nest, and break right into a cruel world, to reproduce the species, to help resurrect the dead and find the lost sheep.

Remember the history of Our Father and the history of Fard of 1930. They started alone looking for just one of our kind to reproduce the species. Do you understand brothers and sisters, the importance of the history that I'm trying to teach you? For, when you know and understand this history as I do, then you will be out there with Poor Bro. Ali in some part of the country, city, town, district, community, somewhere, reproducing the species, teaching Islam and staying tight with the family.

A. M. Muhammad

We love each other brothers and sisters, because we're only a few people and we have to fight against the world. All the odds are against us. It makes us that much tighter. We are struggling. Nobody has to struggle as hard as we have to struggle. People are looking at us, brothers, and they are saying, "Ain't no people like the brothers. What they are doing out there is hard." And this is true. Only the God Tribe can do this. We love each other. We help one another. We protect one another. We fall out, argue, fight and sometimes we get mad with each other but we don't hold no grudge. And when we recognize that we're wrong, we are the first one to admit we're wrong. We ask for forgiveness, we repent and come back and everything is fine. No love lost. We don't hold no grudges. Allah is Most Merciful. That's how we feel about our brothers and sisters. I might be the one to mess up tomorrow. You might be. Who knows?

All we know is that Bro. Fard said that we don't have any limits on forgiving each other for our sins. We love one another and we look out for each other. We share our clothes with each other and we share our food with each other. How do you think I feel when people say, "Brother Ali, I got to give it to you and your people. There's not a whole lot of you but you are some together people." How do you think that makes me feel? I know we are some together people and we do love each other. We don't worry about nobody but ourselves. We mind our own business and we're struggling alone. Every success we have is our success. Nobody gives us nothing. We've gotten everything we have with our own hands and we are some proud people. We love each other. We don't care if our mother doesn't look out for us. We look out for us. The only mother we have is the believers. We are family. We're that way because Allah made us this way. We thank Allah in the Person of Master Fard Muhammad.

We thank our Father, the Most Hon. Mr. Elijah Muhammad, the

KNOWLEDGE OF THE GODS

Last God of the Old World and the First God of the New World. He got up, left His family, friends, property and everything else. To do what? To do His work! Of what? Reproducing the Tribe of Shabazz. That's our heritage, brothers and sisters, that's our history brothers and sisters! That's what we have to do. The time has come for us to break out, scatter far and wide, teach Islam, and raise the dead. This is the time.

Those of you who think you are qualified, volunteer! This is important work. Go out there somewhere, to the West, to the South, or to the North, but teach Islam and stay in touch.

We are trying to see if we can establish a meeting hall to start having regular Mosque services but we changed our mind. This is because at this time we are unable to open a hall elegant enough to represent Almighty (God) Allah, and Our Father the Most Honorable Mr. Elijah Muhammad. We just *cannot* worship God in a broken down place. No! Not you and I. We must have a place that we can be proud of. So until we have the funds to establish a place that we can be proud of, we are not going to have regular Mosque meetings. Therefore, the regular monthly meetings will continue. But, as we said, we want brothers and sisters to volunteer.

You have received your training. Some of you have been crying for months because Allah has blessed you. He has put in you the desire to want to go out. Some of you have been saying, "I feel like I am supposed to be in charge of something. I am just as wise as the others, and I have been in the Nation just as long as the others. I am tired of taking orders, I am ready to give some orders."

Some of them got put out. Some of them would argue with the officials. Well now brothers and sisters, those of you who feel qualified, you are obligated to pick your place in this country. Allah will bless you. Do you think He lit the flame of faith in your heart for nothing? To hide it? To place it under a basket? No Sir, Brother.

No Ma'am, Sister. It was so that you could carry that torch to our people who are living in a state of total darkness. We are obligated, just as Master Fard Muhammad of 1930 and Our Father were obligated.

We want you to know that this is our very life. We are not saying that it would be nice if brothers and sisters would go out and teach. We are telling you that this is our life! We MUST teach Islam in order to preserve the species. Our whole tribe is depending on you and I to wake them up. We are like the Action Centered Ants, the first ants to wake up after the winter sleep. We have the obligation of waking up everyone else. If we don't wake them up, then the whole tribe will die. Do you understand?

Brother Ali has taught you. Ain't it funny how you use to argue about going to classes, writing essays and making it to the meetings? Now the sisters have made their dresses and are ready to wear them and the brothers are well trained. You have completed your graduation fasts. Am I right? Well now you have got it! What else did you think you were going to get?

We told you that you were getting on the job training and now, you know as well as I, what the program is. So you have made it and are graduated and you are now ready to go and do your work, as I have done mine. You cannot come up with an excuse today brothers and sisters for not going out and teaching Islam. You have said that *your life and your death are all for Allah.* You have said *come what may, and that hard trials did not matter*, and obviously they don't.

Your families have turned against you and your friends have turned against you. Wives have left husbands and husbands have left wives. All this to establish this nucleus, the First Family of the Tribe of Shabazz. You are qualified! All of you know what is in this wicked world because you have been raised out of it. Like our Father said, "You are now ready to teach the students what you have

KNOWLEDGE OF THE GODS

received." You are the Angels that will be directing our people to a place of safety. You can go in and among them, without falling victim to this society because you have come out of it.

You know the science of moderation, how to adhere to God and how to stay away from the extreme. You know how to keep yourself away from evil things. You know how to go among those who want you among them and to stay away from those who don't like you. It is our time! It is the *Bursting Asunder*. The earth is now stretched with a severe stretching. It is now ready to tell its news. People all over the country are ready to see the First examples of True Muslims. They are waiting to see just what we are going to do. They already know who we are. They have grand stand seats.

There are many pioneer brothers and sisters who lived the history with Brother Fard and Myself. Some were even there when We were Commissioned. They are taking a back seat attitude, a wait and see attitude. But, my brothers and sisters, I say to you, they are getting ready to see that we are the people and bear witness and will soon be our good helpers. There is no doubt about that! We thank Almighty (God) Allah.

We haven't begged anyone for any help. And just because we know that there are people watching us, and that they will eventually identify with us, this does not mean that we will change our ideas or attitude one bit. We are not interested in pacifying anyone for their friendship. The truth is all that we are interested in and we accept truth from wherever it comes. But we don't want anyone to get the idea that as soon as we have a few dollars that they can tell us what we should and should not do. We are the Tribe of Shabazz, the God Tribe. We will not be dictated to by anyone as to what we should be about.

We want all of you who are qualified. This is your Islam. This is your Family as well as it is mine. Get out there and help me do this work! Allah will bless you. Don't be scared to go forth.

There are some people who have never been outside the city of Newark, New Jersey. They have the same mentality as the people had in the days of Columbus. Back then they thought the Earth was flat. Some folks think once you get to the perimeter of Newark that that is the end of the world, that there is no more and you will fall off. Don't be scared to go forth brothers and sisters. Go forth in the Name of Allah and He will bless you with everything you need. You will be able to return to the Family as one who preserved the species. I want you to understand that this is what I am talking about. I am talking about self-preservation. Without teachers in the land there will be no self-preservation. We are fulfilling the history of Allah scattering His Angels far and wide. We will be a mighty success, my brothers and sisters, if we just do what we are instructed to do.

Our main *national project* is establishing our newspaper, ALLAH IN MUHAMMAD SPEAKS. We are saving money and working on that right now. It looks like we are making progress, but it is still too early to tell. We may have about $1,500 to work with. We are trying to contact our brother Mutakabbir. Maybe Mutakabbir can edit our newspaper for us. If things go right we will have a newspaper shortly. We must have a voice. So that is our project.

The sisterhood and brotherhood have their own individual projects. The sisters in Trenton, New Jersey have their project of getting transportation and establishing nurseries, and the sisters in Newark have the same situation. Brothers, you have your tasks. Continue with your projects. Our main project is establishing ALLAH IN MUHAMMAD SPEAKS. As soon as we can do that, we can say that we have accomplished one milestone.

We thank Allah for blessing us to be His people. The First people of Almighty (God) Allah, in the Person of Master Fard Muhammad. We are a proud people and we are happy, humble, and close knit.

KNOWLEDGE OF THE GODS

Our word is our bond. We don't gossip and we uphold one another. We don't play with our religion!

We thank Allah, in the Person of Master Fard Muhammad, Who was to come and has come. We thank Our Father, the Most Honorable Mr. Elijah Muhammad, Who, like Abraham, raised us as the Seed and made us Muslims. We pray that Allah continue to bless us with the light of wisdom, knowledge and understanding. We continue to pray for the togetherness that love and unity brings, for much success and the continued protection of Allah.

I greet you, my beloved brothers and sisters, with the New World Nation of Islam's greetings of Peace to you in this world and Peace to you in the Hereafter.

My special greetings to our beautiful and beloved sisters. Brothers we have the most beautiful women in the whole world. We thank Allah for our sisters. All praise is due to Allah.

May Allah forever bless you!

Peace! Peace!

Chapter Twelve
The Event

We thank Almighty (God) Allah for blessing us to be on the scene today. We are happy, thankful and grateful to be living. We are happy to be alive.

We have eyes, ears, feet, hands, and we are blessed to be able to speak. Those of us who are completely healthy are so blessed. But there is much more than that. Not only are we blessed with good health physically, Allah has also blessed us with good health mentally. We have peace and are prepared now for the material heaven that Allah is bringing upon us.

Our subject today is THE EVENT. I would like to quote one section from the Holy Qur'an on THE EVENT. But before getting to that let me remind you that Our Father, the Honorable Mr. Elijah Muhammad Who we love and praise forever, raised from among us the Son of Man, the Great Mahdi, the Crusher of the wicked, the Christ, Our long awaited Saviour. Without Master Fard Muhammad you and I would be totally lost in the graves of mental death and ignorance. But due to our Beloved Saviour, Master Fard Muhammad, recognizing our Father as Alpha and Omega, you and I now have the greatest practical Islam - The Supreme Wisdom. This is what the whole world has been waiting, praying and preparing for. We are the first people to receive this Divine Wisdom of the identity of Allah, in the Person of Master Fard Muhammad. I want you to remember that you must study and continue to learn.

Study the chapter THE EVENT, and continue to learn to practice the Islam that you are being taught. THERE IS NO MORE TIME!

KNOWLEDGE OF THE GODS

Our Saviour said to me just the other day, "Well Ole Straggler, this is it! And what fascinates me is the round-about-way, the seemingly indirect route, that Allah used to bring Us to this particular point."

That is something to think about. The Course of Allah never changes. When He intends to elevate a people there is no way those people can stay on the bottom. Wisdom reigns Supreme. Superior Wisdom cannot be subjected to inferior wisdom. Therefore, the world is now being made aware of the fact that the Great Mahdi is now among us.

The Wisdom that we have is definitely Superior to all the practical Islam in the world. We are the first to inherit the promised heaven that is to be enjoyed right here on earth. No more doing without silks, satins, good homes, real jewelry, cars, airplanes, boats and the best that this world has to offer. This is only the beginning of the heaven that is promised to you and me. Not to come, but right now brothers and sisters. This is what the Holy Qur'an says about **The Event in Chapter 56 in Section 1**:

"In the Name of Allah, the Beneficent, the Merciful.

When the Event comes to pass

There is no belying its coming to pass

Abasing (some), exalting (others)

When the earth is shaken with a (severe) shaking,

And the mountains are crumbled to pieces,

So they are scattered dust,

And you are three sorts.

So those on the right hand, how (happy) are those on the right hand!

And those on the left, how (wretched) are those on the left!

And the foremost are the foremost

A. M. Muhammad

These are drawn nigh (to Allah).
In Gardens of bliss.
A multitude from among the first,
And a few from among those of later times,
On thrones inwrought,
Reclining on them, facing each other.
Round about them will go youths never altering in age,
With goblets and ewers, and a cup of pure drink
They are not affected with headache thereby, nor are they intoxicated,
And fruits that they choose,
And flesh of fowl that they desire,
And pure, beautiful ones,
Like unto hidden pearls.
A reward for what they did.
They hear therein no vain or sinful talk
But only the saying, Peace! Peace!
And those on the right hand; how (happy) are those on the right hand!
Amid thornless lote-trees,
And clustered banana-trees,
And extensive shade,
And water gushing,
And abundant fruit,
Neither intercepted, nor forbidden,
And exalted couches.
Surely We have created them a (new) creation,

KNOWLEDGE OF THE GODS

So We have made them virgins,
Loving, equals in age,
For those on the right hand.
A multitude from among the first,
And a multitude from among those of later times.

We thank Allah for blessing us to understand the Holy Qur'an in this day and time. You see, heaven is not in the sky. Heaven is your peace of mind, heaven is your peace and contentment right now. This is what Allah promised those of us who do good and keep the principles, even though we are in the midst of the fiery furnace of hell.

Even though we are surrounded by all manner of evil, we have shown the strength to not only accept truth and right guidance, but to put it into practice. Because of what we have done and the efforts we have made, Allah NOW blesses us with the promised heaven of food, clothing, good homes, money in the bank, and friends in all walks of life. This is so! Some of us have waited a long time for this day, and some came at later times.

The Foremost are those who are foremost in going forth; the first of those that practice Our Father's Islam. And those of later times are those who came and worked just as hard, if not harder, as those who struggled at first.

Because of these two groups of struggling, desiring, and yearning Muslims, Our Lord has now opened the gates of heaven for you and I. This means that the work we have done only qualifies us to do the great work that is now open to us, in a society that can only be defined as Heaven. Do good brothers and sisters, we are getting ready to be blessed with everything we need. Our society is going to be so sweet, that it can only be described as Heaven.

A. M. Muhammad

Every brother and sister who have kept the principles (practiced them) has been elevated above the masses, and they all have good homes and money in the bank. They have only themselves to associate with, and their society is respectful. Their rules and laws are rigidly kept! Anyone coming among them with evil, who is not in tune, who gossips, causes discontent, having sinful action, ways and manners, will not be allowed in the society. Heaven is for the Believers, those who work hard and strive, that is who heaven is prepared for.

Some people take their religion and actually sit on it. They take Our Father's books and put them in a closet and consequently, they accumulate dust. They never crack the pages to read a word. As the Believers begin to step through the gates of heaven because of the Guidance they receive, those who did not practice the Wisdom, will be unable to follow the Guidance which brings one through the gates of heaven. They will be left behind. We thank Allah and are most grateful, to be among the blessed few to enter the promised heaven.

We thank, thank Allah, in the Person of Master Fard Muhammad and we forever love and praise Our Father, the Most Honorable Mr. Elijah Muhammad, for Our Day, which is not to come. Our Day Is Here! All Holy Praises are due to Allah, the Lord of all the Worlds.

We have been blessed. Our Father, the Most Honorable Mr. Elijah Muhammad, has prepared the table for us in the presence of our enemies. He has established everything for us. At Our Father's Last Sermon, He had Islamic Scientist from the East on the rostrum with Him. He told us that we have many people (Muslims) all over the world, who are prepared to come to our aid the minute they see that we are good Muslims. He told us that the Sun was setting but a New Sun would rise.

All Muslims are taught from infancy to believe in the Qur'an. They are taught that the Mahdi will rise in the West in the time of

KNOWLEDGE OF THE GODS

the Last Days. All 700 million (close to 800 million) Muslims on the planet Earth are waiting for you and I, brothers and sisters, to start showing signs that we do practice Islam as taught by Our Father, the Honorable Mr. Elijah Muhammad. His Islam is the only accepted Supreme Wisdom known.

The Scientist of the East, the Old Orthodox World, confronted and questioned our Father in Mecca concerning the doctrine of Islam. They wanted to see if He was truly the Wisest Scientist of Islam on the Planet. They all bore witness at the conclusion of the meeting, that the Most Honorable Mr. Elijah Muhammad was none other than the True Messenger of Allah.

Brothers and sisters, all you have to do is think about this for a minute. Right here in this country there are millions of Muslims. Some are publicly known and others are in secret. They are looking for evidence, which they will see in our society's practices that we are Our Father's Children. When this happens, as it is reflected in the history of the birth of Jesus in the Bible, then you will see the fulfillment of that scripture. These are the wise men who accepted Islam, who were waiting for the birth of the Saviour, and who came immediately when they saw the signs in the sky.

This is the exact position we are in today. We have just become large enough to form that little Muslim Society - that small New World Community. The people are now turning their attention towards us and saying, "What about those New World Muslims over there? What are they about and what are they doing? I see some of their sisters wearing long dresses. I see some of their brothers wearing tams and combat boots. What are they up to?"

The people are now beginning to see who we are. They are beginning to see our Wisdom being practiced. This marks the time for the opening of heaven and the closing down of hell.

A. M. Muhammad

My brothers and sisters, we are the first recipients. Our God and Saviour, Master Fard Muhammad, told me to tell you to fight the devil's evil suggestions. Have no envy or jealousy among yourselves. As Allah begins to bless us with the heaven that is mentioned in the Event, and as you see Muhammad and the True Believers being blessed, do not become envious or angry, just because you think you should receive a certain blessing some other sister or brother received. You should be wise enough to know that Allah knows the difference in all Believers. He answers the prayers of every Believer. Therefore, you cannot get what someone else is praying for. You can only get what you pray for. There is no God besides Allah and He is Just!

We must understand and keep the attitude that WE WANT ONLY WHAT ALLAH WANTS FOR US. Our Society can be destroyed by petty thoughts like, "I don't like the

house that brother so-and-so just bought. If I had it I'd fix it this-way-and-that-way. He has fixed it like so-and-so and I don't like that." Brothers and sisters, we have left the old world, let us throw away its practices. Stay with the Truth!

When you see Allah blessing a Believer, be happy for that Believer. Say, "All Praises are due to Allah!" It is only evidence that Allah is blessing the Believers. Just as He is giving that Believer what he or she prayed for, it only proves that you will get what you have prayed for. Do not become jealous of each other. We are all some blessed people. Be content with what Allah has for you. Keep up prayer, practice the Islam that is given to you, and you will reap what you sow. Our Father said, "Give you nothing!" You have got to practice this Islam yourself.

If you see your brothers and sisters being blessed with heaven, and you are not, then the best thing for you to do is to practice the teachings. Follow the Guidance that has been given to you and pray

KNOWLEDGE OF THE GODS

for what you want. Remember, be careful, because when people start getting a little money, like we use to say, they act funny.

As Allah blesses us to grow, we want to make sure that no evil practices enter into our Society. I am referring to things which can destroy our unity, like gambling. There will be none of that. We have more important and constructive things to do. When brothers and sisters sit down at the gambling table it either ends up in arguments, fighting, hatred or envy. We don't want that! All Holy Praises are due to Allah in the Person of Master Fard Muhammad.

We must rid ourselves of pettiness. Let us be forgiving when a mistake is made. Forgive one another's transgressions. Do not be so quick to argue and fight with one another. Learn to safeguard each other's property. Learn! All Muslims are obligated to learn. We must always seek to advance our Society. Each of you is required and obligated, to continue to learn. If you do not continue to learn, you will be left behind. We can overcome most of the pettiness and evil which holds us down. These practices, which keep us from being a productive people, we can overcome if we hold onto the strongest principle of our faith, which is to hold fast to Allah in Muhammad, regardless to whom or what.

You can only receive what you work for. You are born into this world and you die according to a measure. No one comes on this planet, or leaves this planet, or does anything on this planet, except that it is written in a book. Therefore, you are not the judge of your brother or sister. Allah in Muhammad is the Only Judge. So why waste time getting angry with a brother or sister because they make a mistake or commit a sin? You should get the drink from that particular lesson, or that particular mistake, and pass it on to the rest of us so it will not be repeated. This is the way we must learn to live. Hold fast to Allah in Muhammad regardless to whom or what! Let nothing, person, place, thing, or evil suggestion come between you and Allah in Muhammad. This rises you above the pettiness and puts you on the Divine Plane of Understanding, which allows you to maintain your peace and contentment.

If you do not practice this then Allah will replace you with a new generation, and that is easy for Him to do. As a matter of fact, we can find this right in the Holy Qur'an in Chapter 35 verse 11:

"And Allah created you from dust, then from the life-germ, then He made pairs. And no female bears, nor brings forth, except with His knowledge.

And no one living long is granted a long life, nor is aught diminished of one's life, but it is all in a book. Surely that is easy to Allah."

We thank Allah - we are blessed. The Holy Qur'an as interpreted by Our Father for us to practice, is what the Orthodox Scientist of Islam in the East are trying to get the world of Islam, the old world of Islam, to accept. They are trying to get them to go back to the Qur'an.

We are now practicing the Qur'an. Not only in the light that they understand it, we are also practicing it in a greater light. This is what Brother Fard called GOLD ACTIVITY. He said this is when you have strived for a certain period of time to achieve an end and once you have achieved that end, your whole attitude changes. Your whole physical being changes because you successfully accomplished what you set out to do. All Holy Praise is due to Allah.

Because we have the Supreme Wisdom, people interested in being taught a higher form of Islam, they are all being directed to turn towards us. We thank Almighty (God) Allah for blessing us with this Divine Supreme Wisdom, which has made us the Head of the Universe after being the dust of the Earth.

The Holy Qur'an says in chapter 35 verses 15 to 22:

KNOWLEDGE OF THE GODS

"O men it is you that have need of Allah, and Allah is Self-Sufficient, The Praised One. If He please, He will remove you and bring a new creation.

And this is not hard to Allah.

And no burdened soul can bear another's burden. And if one weighed down by a burden calls another to carry his load, naught of it will be carried, even though he be near of kin. Thou warnest only those who fear their Lord in secret and keep up prayer. And whoever purifies himself, purifies himself only for his own good. And to Allah is the eventual coming. And the blind and the seeing are not alike,

Nor the darkness and the light,

Nor the shade and the heat.

Neither are the living and the dead alike. Surely Allah makes whom He please hear, and thou canst not make those hear who are in the graves."

Praises are due to Allah. So you see, it is not up to us, it is up to Allah. So hold on with the firmest grip because He is in control. Praise be to Allah!

Let us go now into the history so we can see what kind of Wisdom Our Father has given to us, and why all Muslims must submit to the teachings of Master Fard Muhammad, Almighty (God) Allah, in Person among us today.

Prophet Muhammad of 1400 years ago, may the Peace and Blessings of Allah forever be upon Him, discovered that Mecca had turned into a den of polytheistic people. They were worshipping all kinds of gods. The Angel Gabriel gave the revelation to Muhammad that He was to restore the Faith and re-establish the Signs of Allah.

The Christians and the Jews had took the Truth of the True Teachings of Islam, as brought by Jesus, Moses, and all the other

A. M. Muhammad

Prophets, and removed and hid some of it. They damaged the Scriptures so badly that they were no longer the same.

So, Prophet Muhammad of 1400 years ago, (PBUH), though He was a white man, re-established the signs of the Holy Qur'an, the people, the History of the Black Man, that there is no God besides Allah and Muhammad is His Prophet. He taught that we must believe in all the Prophets, and that we should serve the One True and Living God, Who would make Himself manifest to the entire world at Judgment. He would call Himself *The Great Mahdi* and He would rise in the West. Therefore, all Muslims, due to the great work of Prophet Muhammad of 1400 years ago (PBUH) would look to the West for the Mahdi's emergence.

He made babies recite the Qur'an. In turn, they taught their children and each generation up until the Last Days (The Judgment) to look to the West for the Mahdi. And when He appeared, to submit to Him because He would have a higher form of Islam. Can you see the position you are blessed to be in because of the work of Prophet Muhammad of 1400 years ago? Do you see how We repeat these messages, but is there any of you who will understand?

Because of His work, Allah blessed Muhammad. He showed Him in a dream that He would ride a horse with wings to the Seven Heavens, meeting along the way all the Wise Men, all of the Prophets and Apostles of God, until He came Face to Face with God Himself.

This was done by keeping the seed of Prophet Muhammad alive in the Holy City of Mecca. In the year of 1877 a specific child was born and given specific instructions. This child was the manifestation of the promise to Muhammad. He is Muhammad of 1400 years ago (PBUH). We are talking about Master Fard Muhammad who came in 1930. He was half and half, having one parent black and the other white, who came to the shores of North

KNOWLEDGE OF THE GODS

America with the Keys and the Crown to meet Alpha and Omega. He who was dead, but is alive forever more. The First Man to recognize God in Person Face to Face.

Master Fard Muhammad who came in 1930 was the Personification of the promise to Muhammad of 1400 years ago - and because of His great work, that He would see God Face to Face, and that was fulfilled when Master Fard Muhammad met God, in the Person of the Honorable Mr. Elijah Muhammad, in 1930.

The course of Allah never changes and we are the most blessed people on the planet. You have a great heritage. You have the greatest. It is up to you to practice those rules, laws, and principles that Our Father gave us. We will then be seen as the good Muslims following the Mahdi and serving no God other than Allah in Muhammad. Do you understand? Well this is it! You can see why the more we practice Our Father's Teachings, the more obvious we become to the help that has already been prepared for us. We can be very happy because we are now being seen as Good Muslims. Praise be to Allah!

Before closing, here is a word to our sisters. We thank Allah for our sisters. We have the best women in the world. We are all learning how to do right, to shun evil, rid ourselves of laziness, and all other negative things which keep us from being what we are supposed to be - Righteous Muslims! Our sisters must practice cleanliness. Our sisters should realize that our children are our future, they are what we are living for. It is through them that we, as a people, continue to exist. Our existence is threatened when we do not prepare our children for the future.

Sisters, be dedicated to your children! Do not be lackadaisical in studying and learning child care (how to handle infants), and how to take care of your children. Our children are the Family Jewels. Never leave our babies alone, make sure they are always protected.

This shows that we are a wise people. Do not use baby talk with our children, talk to them as individuals. Treat them with justice, never lie to them and make them keep the principles that we must keep. Most important, you must learn how to handle our babies!

I remember Brother Fard teaching us how to study nature, how to learn how to get the drinks from the trees (the plants) the insects, fish and from the beasts of the fields. Brother Fard taught us how to get drinks from everything in nature. He taught us about bears. He said the bear is one of the most dedicated mothers on the planet. He said that one of the reasons for this is because of the male bear. If he catches the bear cubs alone and unprotected away from the mother, he will kill them on the spot. Because of this action on the male's part, the female bear will not let her cubs get out of her sight, nor will she allow anyone to come near her cubs.

You, my brothers and sisters, represent the Human Family of the Planet Earth. How much more should we protect our children? How much more should we go all out for the best treatment and education for our children?

Sisters, you are the Mothers of Civilization, be dedicated to your children. Do not allow our babies to run wild with no guidance, with no education and with no upbringing. They don't know how to wash their faces and their hands, they can't put on their clothes, and they don't know how to tie their shoes. We cannot have this. These are the practices of the old world. We, Muslims of the New World take care of our children. They are always first priority! Sisters, I know that you are going to be on the job. Get into those books, go to the library. Learn about taking care of children and learn about weaning babies. Learn all of these things. Learn the symptoms to look for when babies are sick. Learn to care for them sisters!

We thank Almighty (God) Allah for this day. I am down with a little cold, but this is the happiest cold I have ever had in my life. I

KNOWLEDGE OF THE GODS

thank Allah for you. I thank Allah for Me because our striving is now being rewarded. We can be happy. We can rejoice.

Our Father once told us that when our day came we can sit back and laugh at them, because we would be safe in heaven and they would be burning in hell. The old world is gone out and the beautiful rays of sunlight, of the New World of Islam, are now obvious to the entire Universe. It is our time to act! Brothers and sisters, please, let us act right. In the manner that will keep our Saviour proud and happy with us and in the manner that we know will make Our Father proud.

So, without any further delay, I greet you, My Beloved Brothers and Sisters, with the New World's greetings of Peace as I encourage you to continue to strive. I congratulate you for being the First to come forward, and the First to receive the Divine Blessings promised to us by Almighty (God) Allah.

May Allah forever bless us as I greet you in the Name of Allah, the Beneficent, the Most Merciful, in the Person of Master Fard Muhammad. And in the Name of Our Father, the Honorable Mr. Elijah Muhammad, to whom we forever Love and Praise. I greet you my beloved Brothers and Sisters with the New World's greetings of Peace in this world and Peace in the Hereafter.

Peace! Peace!

Chapter Thirteen
Saviour's Day

Saviour's Day. Our first Saviour's Day. Saviour's Day, February 26th, 1979. The First Saviour's Day celebrated by the New World Nation of Islam. Our Father, the Most Honorable Mr. Elijah Muhammad, fixed our Ramadan observance at 30 days during the month of December. We have changed our mind about celebrating the falsehood of Christianity, and the keeping of our minds on Islam for the month, while all the people in the wilderness of North America, this hell, were celebrating falsehood.

We take these forty days to commemorate all the Prophets of Almighty (God) Allah. We make no distinction between the Prophets and we believe in them all. Also, to show that we will be the best Muslims on the Planet Earth, we fast ten days longer than all other Muslims - We observe a strict fast from sun up until the sun goes down for an extra ten days. We want you to understand that it was Our Father, the Honorable Mr. Elijah Muhammad, Who, in His last instructions, declared that the world was watching to see if we would be good Muslims. He also said that the Sun would set and a New Sun would rise.

We thank Almighty (God) Allah for blessing us with the desire to be good Muslims in this day and time. The 26th of February is a happy day for the New World Nation of Islam's Muslims. Not only is our Ramadan Fast for 40 days, we also adhere to strict sacrifice; and at its conclusion, February 26th, we recognize that a New Sun has come, that the Dawn of our day has appeared and Our Saviour

KNOWLEDGE OF THE GODS

Has Arrived. We are happy, and give thanks, that we have our peace to celebrate the ending of the fast, and the starting of a new year.

We declare on the 26th of February our New Covenant with Almighty (God) Allah, in the Person of Master Fard Muhammad. We declare our faith and declare that we will do better in the year to come. We collect all of the good that we have done in the past year. We cleanse ourselves with fasting and praying, to get away from all the bad things we might have done in the past year. Now, on this day (the 26th) we reaffirm to Almighty (God) Allah, in the Person of Master Fard Muhammad, that we will throw away the bad things and not repeat them in the year to come. We set these goals and we follow them.

My Family has decided that meat will no longer be eaten in our household. Everyone who was on the 40 day Ramadan Fast are feeling so good from just eating vegetables, fish, and fowl every now and then. We no longer have a desire to eat meat. Every year we must, as a duty, strive to do better, take on greater obligations, and greater duties in the year to come. This is the way that we celebrate our Ramadan and our Saviour's Day.

We are very happy and thankful to Almighty (God) Allah, for all who were able to make the 40 day fast. We are very happy and We thank Almighty (God) Allah, for those of you who tried and did not complete the fast. Allah is Most Merciful and He does not intend hardship for any of us. Those of us who did not make it, Praise be to Allah for what we did get in. We will fast a like number of other days at another time, which is convenient for those who desire.

Today, our subject is Saviour's Day. We thank Allah. We cannot thank Allah enough, and We forever praise and love Our Father, the Most Honorable Mr. Elijah Muhammad. For if it were not for Him we would still be a dead people. We would be deaf, dumb, and blind. We thank Muhammad ibn Abdullah (PBUH) for all of His life's work, his dedication in re-establishing the signs of Allah and giving to us the Holy Qur'an. O' my brothers and sisters, the Wisdom and the Guidance of the Great Prophet was aimed directly at you and I. This is our Saviour's Day and we thank Allah so much.

Our Father said, and I would like to quote this from chapter 19 entitled, **The Black Man** from *Our Saviour Has Arrived*: *"According to the teachings to me of man's histories by Allah (God) in the Person of Master Fard Muhammad, praise is due to Him forever, The Great Mahdi and the Messiah that the world has been expecting to come for the last two thousand years, has come and is going about His work as has been predicted that He would do."*

This quote is very significant. He does not say the Saviour will come, He says that He is here, and that He is going about His work. That was in 1974! I want you to pay attention here, my beloved brothers and sisters. I want you to understand that Our Father did not waste His time. Our Father stayed up nights reading over the scriptures, fasting and praying, to put these things in Black and White for you and I as Guidance. He was not wasting His time or fooling around. He was giving us the Keys of Life.

Allah is among us doing His work. The Great Mahdi, the Messiah is in and among His people, doing His work. He was present and doing His work in 1974. This is according to Our Father, the Most Honorable Mr. Elijah Muhammad, Who never lied and never dies. The Holy Qur'an says, "Speak not of Him as dead, for He is not dead." The foolish people know not, nor do they understand. As long as there is a breath of life in any member of the New World Nation of Islam Our Father lives!

Our Father told us that Master Fard Muhammad was present, and doing His work in and among His people, as of 1974. The title of the book is *Our Saviour Has Arrived*, not that He is coming. For years, before the publication of this Great Book, Our Father was

KNOWLEDGE OF THE GODS

teaching us that He was only preparing us for the coming of the Saviour, Master Fard Muhammad. Then he tells us Our Saviour Has Arrived and that He is among us doing His work! He sent word to the Mosque (Newark, N.J. Temple #25) - "Be careful of how you talk to strangers, for you might be talking to the Mahdi" and that, "Master Fard Muhammad was in the city, look out for Him."

Beloved brothers and sisters, if Master Fard Muhammad was on the scene in 1974, and He was, because Our Father said He was. And if he was going about His work of raising, gathering and separating His people (the sheep from the goats); and He was because Our Father said He was, then *someone* should have met Him! Some brother or sister somewhere should have met Him. If He was among our People in 1974 somebody should have known Him. Now I ask you, who of you believers, following the Honorable Mr. Elijah Muhammad, recognized the Saviour in 1974? Where is he or she? Which brother minister recognized the Saviour? You do know Our Father had many ministers. Not one of them met the Saviour? You mean Brother Fard was among all of us, and no one could see Him? Nobody met Him? Then how could He have been doing His work of gathering His people?

My brothers and sisters, the teachings of the Honorable Elijah Muhammad have been a mystery to the people. They have not understood the finer science of His teachings. To arrive at this understanding, the Saviour had to study and fast. It took Him less than a year and a half of studying and following Our Father's teachings before He began to recognize the higher science. It took Him two years before He was absolutely certain that Our Father, the Honorable Mr. Elijah Muhammad, was God in Person - the Last God of the Old World and the First God of the New World.

Our Father recognized the Saviour on the right path of understanding in 1958. Our Father recognized Him and declared it to the world. He said, "I see the Saviour, Master Fard Muhammad. I see Him. He is sitting in the audience right there. Don't you see Him?" Then He said, "No, I don't guess you can. It ain't time yet." Don't you understand? Our Father in His infinite wisdom gave us complete guidance, perfect guidance. His science was so high only the Saviour could recognize it, and then turn around and teach it to us. All Holy praise is due to Allah, in the Person of Master Fard Muhammad.

How come no one recognized the Saviour? What is He? Some kind of spook? All those hundreds of thousands of people who said they believed in the teachings of the Honorable Mr. Elijah Muhammad, never rejected the fact that Our Father was teaching the presence of Master Fard Muhammad in our midst. They accepted it at that time. They gave their word that they believed in it. They would sit and scream at the top of their lungs, "Teach them Holy Apostle, that's right!" The Man could hardly get a word out of His mouth without hearing, "Teach 'em, wake 'em up, that's right!"

Where are those who met the Saviour? Who can stand up and say, "Yes brother, the Honorable Mr. Elijah Muhammad was telling the truth, I met the Saviour. He is in the land doing His work." The only individual who can point out Master Fard Muhammad to you, is your Poor Brother Muhammad. And I am teaching the truth! Not from myself, but directly from the mouth of the Honorable Mr. Elijah Muhammad. Why? Because the first thing that the Saviour taught me, upon recognizing Him, was all Praise is due to Our Father, the Most Honorable Mr. Elijah Muhammad, the Last God of the Old World and the First God of the New World. His word is scripture and we must live by it. We cannot change one period of His teachings. Where are all the Ministers? Where are all the Captains and Lieutenants? Nobody knew the Saviour? Our Father said He was here.

KNOWLEDGE OF THE GODS

Let me share another quote from Our Father. We thank Allah so much for having it all in black and white. No one can deny these teachings. Our Father made the world accept them and bear witness to them. You and I, my brothers and sisters, the children of the Most Honorable Mr. Elijah Muhammad, His seed who will carry out His work, word for word and step for step. We are proud and we are blessed. This is what He said, "Jesus Christ? And who is Christ? What Jesus Christ? Jesus wasn't even a Christ back then, 2,000 years ago. According to the meaning of Christ, that name means one coming in the Last Day or Crusher. He crushes the wicked. Christ, the Crusher. Jesus didn't do that. That is the Mahdi Who will do that today. The one whom we are representing to you, the Great Mahdi, the Restorer of the Kingdom of Peace on Earth. All Holy Praise is due to Allah."

All Holy Praise is due to Allah in the Person of Master Fard Muhammad, just as Our Father taught us. Be not deceived. The coming of God, the Christ, the Messiah, the Son of Man, or the second coming of Jesus. In Islam it is referred to as the coming of the Great Mahdi, the coming of Allah to the birth of Muhammad.

Brothers and sisters, we are sharing all of this with you because we want you to understand that this is not My doctrine. I did not create this. This came to Me, this understanding of Our Father's teachings, from the mouth of Master Fard Muhammad; and I will forever praise, serve and look to Him for guidance.

Is it so strange that I met the Saviour? I was down-trodden, ignorant, dumb, and could barely read or write. Aren't the Saviour's people supposed to be the down-trodden? Many of you brothers and sisters who follow the Honorable Mr. Elijah Muhammad think you are lost because you are in the wilderness, in the mud, are dirty and have fallen in the slime. Well you are blessed because this is the exact place and condition Master Fard Muhammad is collecting His people from. He comes to the man in the mud.

You should be wise enough to know, when you hear Him teaching you the same thing the Honorable Mr. Elijah Muhammad gave to you, that you should stand up because this is our day - Our Saviour Has Arrived! You will not hear me saying that, "Yes, I believe in *some* of the teachings of the Honorable Mr. Elijah Muhammad. I am saying that I believe in ALL of the teachings of the Honorable Mr. Elijah Muhammad. I will not change one word!"

Our Saviour is here and He is doing His work! Why can't you see Him? Is it the same reason why the people before did not see Him? They did not pay close enough attention to the teachings of Our Father. You cannot accept Master Fard Muhammad unless you first accept Our Father, the Most Honorable Mr. Elijah Muhammad. This is the truth. I bear witness with my life. I know Him like I know myself. When I first met Him He was upset over a problem in Islam which He could not solve. He was sorrowing over it when I met Him. As We talked the problem was solved and He was so happy. He took Me out shopping and we celebrated. We bought a whole lot of food. He said, "Brother, all praise is due to Allah." He said, "I am so glad I met You. Now I know what I must do in life. I am a soldier for Allah."

It was sometime later that I realized that I was a soldier too, because it seemed to be the only life that I could really identify with and help the Messenger. So we began to do the work of a soldier, and as you know a soldier's life is not an easy one. Sometimes you are up and sometimes you are down. It also gets pretty dangerous. But the greatest reward that a Muslim can receive is Jihad (fighting in the way of Allah).

In the old days, coming up as young men, we loved Our Father. We did everything we could and all that we knew how to do to serve Him. He recognized this. He began to watch this brother, along with

KNOWLEDGE OF THE GODS

a few other brothers who responded to everything He said. When He finally came to Newark, New Jersey, He said, "I see Allah in the audience, don't you?"

Don't you understand? He sent for us in 1960 to make sure we'd be at the Saviour's Day Convention. And just to show you the wisdom of Our Father, this was during the time that the hypocrites, Malcolm X and Wallace, were trying to take the Nation. They even had the devil behind them saying Malcolm was going to be the next leader of the Nation of Islam. The Ministers and the followers were even in on this thing with Malcolm and Wallace.

At the 1960 Saviour's Day Convention Our Father made this announcement, "I have been made equal in knowledge with Allah. I control the winds and the seas. I have power over the Sun, Moon, and Stars." He also announced to the Nation and all of the Ministers, that He was appointing Brother Fard as a Field Minister for the Nation of Islam, the highest ranking Minister in the Nation and that He would be in charge of all Muslims wherever He went.

Malcolm and his crew of hypocrites were upset. They said, "We ain't recognizing the young brother! He can't tell us nothing! The young brother is a jailbird!" But Our Father had already put it in black and white.

Consequently, Malcolm and his devilish crew tried to take the nation from Our Father and failed. Evil is always destined to fail when confronted with truth. So, the rank which Our Father gave to Brother Fard is irrevocable. Then He declared that no one had the power to appoint a Field Minister and that no one had the power to bust a Field Minister that He places in authority. This means that the same rank He received in 1960, on Saviour's Day, is the same rank that He maintains today.

Saviour means one who saves. Our Father said, "Accept My

teachings and live, reject it and die!" The Saviour must come on the scene with Our Father's teachings in order to save us, the so-called American Negroes. He cannot come on the scene with a teaching saying this is what He thinks. He cannot come on the scene saying Elijah was short-sighted, and that we should not pay attention to Elijah's teachings anymore. He comes on the scene saying, "All Praise is due to Our Father, the Most Honorable Mr. Elijah Muhammad." He gives us insight into the wisdom of Our Father. He guides us into the foot-steps of Our Father in the creation of a New World of Islam, as Our Father directed us. We want you to understand these points brothers and sisters, because it is very important to your life. What I say to you is proof that you are receiving the truth. All Holy Praise is due to Allah.

My work, thanks to Allah, and My words demonstrate that I am with Him and that I know Him. You bear witness that before My meeting Master Fard Muhammad and recognizing Him, I had no keys to help uplift you. This comes with understanding. I bear witness that I did not understand Our Father's teachings, until the Saviour taught me the truth of Our Father's identity. He, the Saviour, Master Fard Muhammad, the Great Mahdi, is among us today and He is doing His work. He didn't just start.

Almost twenty years ago the Saviour went into the prisons and set up the First Academy of Islam. He sent for Me a year later and We started the First Graduation Class. We taught and We trained every day for five years and three months. We graduated many Ministers. Then we returned to Our Mosque, Mosque #25 in the city of Newark, New Jersey, only to be rejected and persecuted because of our belief. We fulfilled the scriptures, my brothers and sisters. We paid the price.

Today our accusers are gone. They call themselves Bilalians and they hate Elijah. Their tree has withered in three days (years). You

KNOWLEDGE OF THE GODS

can hardly find a Bilalian, and if you do they are ashamed to admit it. Our day has come and Our Saviour has arrived. There is so much we can say about the history of Our Saviour and what qualified Him to be who He is. But let us look into what is happening today.

Saviour's Day finds us in a time of being on the brink of World War III. Nations are rising against Nations, depression has set in and America is falling. Our people are hungry, naked and out of doors. This is the time that our people must have a Saviour or be destroyed. We must be a strong people in this day and time. Our Father's number is 25. The Saviour's number is 26, and I, your poor Brother, was commissioned the 27th. We will say more on this subject at a later time.

We want to thank Allah for our beautiful sisters. We are creating a new people, and you cannot create a new people without the sisters. The sisters are getting stronger and more beautiful every day. You will have to respect our sisters. Not because we say you must respect them, and not because we threaten you with serious repercussions if you don't respect them. Their strength of character is becoming so strong that eventually the whole world will marvel at, and respect the women of the New World Nation of Islam, here in the wilderness of North America. Praises are due to Allah.

Brothers, our sisters don't want weak husbands. If you are too weak to get rid of the cigarette, too weak to stop lying, too weak to stop drinking, too weak to stop using drugs and too weak to stop eating the hog, our sisters will have nothing to do with you. If you cannot keep your duty to Allah in Muhammad by keeping up prayer and fasting, our sisters will not have anything to do with you. Our sisters have been raised to the level to throw out of their houses the drinking, smoking, using drugs and the eating of the swine. They will not let you brothers, who are weak, take them back into the grave.

So what does this mean for the future of the New World Nation of Islam? It means that our strong sisters will be raising some strong children. It means that our civilization will be built on strength. You look over in the East and you find Muslims fighting Muslims. In Iran and other Muslim Nations they are struggling to get the brothers and the sisters to go back to the tenants of the Qur'an. It is a hard struggle because the devil has contaminated the planet with his devilishment and wickedness. Their people want to be like Europeans. They want to be like the white man. They want cities like New York. They do not want to live a pious life. They do not want to live the righteous life of the Qur'an. They want to smoke, drink, lie, cheat, steal, and murder each other, as the devil has taught them to do. So the great Imans of the East, who are trying to fight with their brothers and sisters, attempting to get them back into the Qur'an, are having a hard way to go. But not you and I. All Praise is due to Allah.

I just heard recently on the news that the women of Iran were demonstrating and fighting because they did not want to put on the long dresses and wear veils anymore. They don't want to come out of the make-up and the displaying of their beauty in the public. But look at our beautiful sisters, they want to cover themselves, they can't wait to put on the veil. We thank Allah so very much for our sisters. Praise be to Allah.

We must learn to fight the devil, not only physically but mentally as well. When negative thoughts come up in your mind concerning the promises of Allah in Muhammad to you, you should not entertain those thoughts. Any thoughts of opposition, distrust, or ungratefulness to Almighty (God) Allah in Muhammad, you should run those thoughts from your mind - chase them away. When the negative thought comes up like, "Allah promised that we would have heaven overnight, and I haven't received any heaven yet!"

KNOWLEDGE OF THE GODS

Don't entertain thoughts like that. The minute you recognize the negativity of those thoughts say, "I seek refuge in Allah against the accursed satan. Get away from me devil, I am going to think about my prayers and my lessons."

Learn to fight the devil. When people come and suggest negative things about your brothers and sisters, do not join them in gossiping or making fun of your people. Change the subject. Tell them, "I'll see you later. I don't talk about my brothers and my sisters." We are a strong people and we are going to get stronger. As we learn to fight the evil suggestions our peace and contentment becomes more permanent, more enduring. It is only when we allow the devil to make those suggestions that we entertain, that we lose our peace, become restless, and dissatisfied. Fight the devil brothers and sisters!

We thank Almighty (God) Allah, in the Person of Master Fard Muhammad. He is here to create a New World. Newark, New Jersey is the Holy City, designated the Model City by Our Father. It is a Divine dictate that no one can change. Mecca means the place where the knowledge and wisdom of the Original man first started when the planet was found. Master Fard Muhammad said that we will set up, in the city of Newark, an advanced Muslim Society that the entire Muslim world will recognize, respect, and pay homage to. That's right! He intends to do that with you and I, brothers and sisters, and we are well on the way.

You must know that after darkness comes light, and you know it has been spiritually dark since the passing of Our Father. We thank Allah for Our first Saviour's Day. He will teach us love, peace and happiness. Not the kind of love you have learned of in the devil's civilization. No, no, my brothers and sisters! It is the kind of love Brother Fard taught me to have for Him - unlimited love! I don't have to see Him or be around Him. I just do what He tells me and continue to love Him for blessing me to have this life.

I remember in our early soldiering days, when there was no money. We had to make do with what we had. In those days we were lucky to just keep up our appearance. Brother Fard felt that we should wear a suit, white shirt, and a tie every day. And that is what we did. Even when we were broke. The people thought we always had money but we didn't. During those hard times, Brother Fard would wear my clothes and I would wear his. I use to have a little thing about my clothes. I wouldn't allow anyone to put on my clothes. I wouldn't wear anyone's clothes and I didn't allow anyone to wear mine. The Brother taught me what real love was, and that real love transcends clothes, cars, houses, money and time. Real love goes on, and on, and on - it is above everything. Real love will not allow you to accept negative criticism about that which you love.

No one can tell me anything bad about Brother Fard. If that was the case I would have turned against Him like the rest of the Nation, when they turned against Him because of His appointment. No! You can't tell me anything against Brother Fard. And as many times as people have run to him about me, it is obvious that you can't tell Him anything bad about Me. That is love! It is true love. It is unlimited love. It is love which transcends all the foolishness we have to face in our daily lives.

He is to teach us happiness. I just got through telling you how to fight the devil, how to keep him out of your mind so you can have peace. Brother Fard taught me true happiness. The happiness we must teach our people in the New World Nation of Islam. Happiness is in the work! There is pride in the work. Heaven is not a place. Our Father said, "It is not a place where you go and sit down. "It is a place where you go to work." The work is your heaven. It is your happiness.

Brother Fard teaches a brother and sister how *they* can help Allah

KNOWLEDGE OF THE GODS

in Muhammad, not how somebody else can, but how they can help. So when a brother sees the little work he is doing in helping the Nation, this makes him happy. So Allah gives him a life of happiness and He gives him more life. The more work you do the happier you become. And the happier you are, the more work you want to do. The happiness is in the work. These successes, one after the other, makes us a proud and accomplished people. We can't help but be happy.

Brother Fard teaches that when you get on the prayer rug to pray, kick the devil out of your mind, communicate with your Lord and thank Him. You are showing Him that you are truly grateful for all the happiness, progress, and love. Brother, when you get off that prayer rug you will have some peace. Your peace will be so strong that anyone coming in contact with you will say, "That is a peaceful brother there." Your day will go so smooth. That is heaven! Brother Fard said our civilization will promote this kind of thing 24 hours a day. Our customs and traditions will be in accordance with those particular basics of civilization. All Holy Praises is due to Allah.

This is a great day. Our Saviour is among us and He is doing His work. You are the proof of that. I, your poor Brother, am proof of that. Our Father did not lie. He did not leave us without guidance. A good Father provides for his children. Our Father told us David was not around to see the completion of his Temple, but he did get the material for the making of that Temple. Solomon, his son completed the Temple of his Father's (David's) desire. Our Father said, "So I say to you like David, even though I may not be around to see the completion of the Temple, nevertheless, I will get the material for you."

Don't you understand? He has prepared a table before us in the presence of our enemies. All of this is given to us by Our Father. All we have to do is really believe in the teachings of the Honorable Mr.

A. M. Muhammad

Elijah Muhammad and we would recognize the Saviour today, just like that! Every individual who will believe in the Honorable Mr. Elijah Muhammad will see and recognize the Saviour. He is not a mystery god. We do not believe in spooks and spirits. Our Father said, "Spookism is the number one thing that keeps us from being a productive people." We do not sit at home and wait for spooks and spirits to bring us food, clothing, and shelter. No, no, we get up and go and find what we need, and we thank Almighty (God) Allah for every blessing that we receive. I thank Allah, in the Person of Master Fard Muhammad, and we forever give praise to Our Father the Most Honorable Mr. Elijah Muhammad.

Don't forget Muhammad ibn Abdullah of 1400 years ago, brothers and sisters. There is a whole lot of science in that Great Prophet's life which we will teach you shortly; that which Brother Fard taught us to give to you. Read the Holy Qur'an! Get up at night and pray! You will discover that Almighty (God) Allah promises you, and He never fails in His promises. You are already a mighty Nation. We thank Almighty (God) Allah.

We want to give a word to our brothers, fellow Muslims in the East, and all over the world, before we bring this to an end. If we, of the New World Nation of Islam, seem a little fanatical or antagonistic, it is not because we do not love and respect all our brothers who say, "We bear witness to Allah and Muhammad is His Messenger." We do love and respect you and we will never fight with an enemy of yours against you. We are brothers and sisters under the same God.

We are in a different situation here in the wilderness of North America. We are a people who have been lost from home and made slaves for well over 400 years. We, your poor Black brothers and sisters here in the wilderness of North America, must strive hard to achieve perfection.

KNOWLEDGE OF THE GODS

Our Father, the Most Honorable Mr. Elijah Muhammad, whom we forever praise and love, said to us as a last instruction, "The world is watching you to see if you will be good Muslims." That is what Our Father said. So we owe it to Our Father, the Most Honorable Mr. Elijah Muhammad, to raise our people, the so-called American Negroes, who were once lost but are now found. They are the Holy Tribe of Shabazz! We must raise our people to be recognized as the best Muslims on the planet earth, and we have a very short time to do this. So, our beloved brother and sister Muslims all over the world, be patient with us. Watch us, for Allah is with us. You will soon see that our guidance is your guidance too. This is a happy day. We are taking our first steps towards becoming the greatest Nation the world has ever known. We can be happy and we must rejoice. Our Father said we can even laugh at the enemies in this day and time if we want to.

In bringing this Saviour's Day message to a close, I would like to extend to you the special greetings of peace and love from Our Saviour, Master Fard Muhammad, Almighty (God) Allah in Person. Not a spook, not a spirit, but a Man! He said that He is very pleased. We can be very happy. This year, 1979, is to be a big year for the New World Nation of Islam. Some of you have already sneaked a peak of what is happening to us. So without any further delay . . .

In the Most Holy name of Allah, in the Person of Master Fard Muhammad, the Great Mahdi, the Crusher of the wicked, Our Saviour and Deliverer. And in the name of Our Father, the Most Honorable Mr. Elijah Muhammad, to Whom We will forever praise and love, and in the name of Muhammad ibn Abdullah, and all the beloved Prophets of Almighty (God) Allah, and We make no distinction between them. I end this Saviour's Day message with Our New World's greetings of Peace in this world, and Peace in the Hereafter.

A. M. Muhammad

Peace! Peace!

Chapter Fourteen
You Can't Accept One Without Accepting The Other And The Difference In Fard Of Today From Fard Of 1930

I am your Poor Brother Ali, Spokesman for Allah in the Person. Not one to come but the one who is here and has been here for more than 20 years, doing His work of gathering His people. He is my Saviour and He is your Saviour. The only difference between you and I is that I met Him first. And now I am pointing Him out to you.

Heaven, as we have been taught by Our Father the Most Honorable Mr. Elijah Muhammad, is the place where we will have no more Messengers, Apostles, and Prophets because everyone will be with God, Face to Face. They will know Him as they know each other. Master Fard Muhammad, Almighty (God) Allah, is now ready to take you, my brothers and sisters, into a heaven which is called the Promised Land.

I am so happy to celebrate this day with you, July 4, 1979, our Independence. We are a blessed people. We are the poor Righteous Muslims who know who the True and Living God is. We are poor people. We are the people who held onto our Father's teachings. We are a tried and tested people. No wonder there is just a few of us. You see, when the going gets rough, and the trials are hard, you won't find too many people hanging around. The few that are present today are the most blessed people in the universe. We are a happy people. Yes, we are a poor people but we are a happy people. We are a peaceful people. We are a wise people. And more than anything else, we are Our Father's children.

Today we can be happy we are celebrating our Independence. Few though we may be, we are happy because the Sun, Moon, and Star is our National. That's right! It is a National that is respected everywhere in the Universe. It is our Flag. It is our National Flag that hangs over our Nation, infant though we may be. It is our National Flag. It is our National Heritage. We are proud of our Nation, our Flag and our Independence which we will forever fight for. So let us be happy, let us enjoy, and let us discuss the seriousness of the times.

My subject today is, "YOU CAN'T ACCEPT ONE WITHOUT ACCEPTING THE OTHER, AND THE DIFFERENCE IN FARD OF 1930 AND FARD OF TODAY." We thank Allah much. But before I begin I would like to extend to you the peace and love from our God and Saviour, in the Person of Master Fard Muhammad. His words to you are, "Now that you see the help of Allah coming to you, you should run fast to Allah through prayer, fasting, studying your lessons and also, reading the Qur'an and Our Father's Books." He said, "Tell them a word to the wise is sufficient." I know all of you know what that means. So all praises due to Allah. You really don't know how blessed we are. God walks amongst us brothers and sisters. He talks, He goes to the store, He drives an automobile and He flies in planes. He is not a spook. He is not a spirit. No wonder there are only a few of us.

Supreme Wisdom is very scarce. It is very rare. It is a very rare commodity. We are blessed to have a well that has no end to its flow of Divine Supreme Wisdom, right from the Mouth of Almighty (God) Allah in the Person of Master Fard Muhammad. You, my beautiful Black brothers and sisters, are now ready to become the head instead of the tail. We thank Allah in the Person of Master Fard Muhammad and we forever give praise and love to Our Father, the Most Honorable Mr. Elijah Muhammad.

Some people may ask, "Why does Master Fard Muhammad, our God and Saviour, need a Spokesman?" And we say to you as Our Father often said to us, "Ask your questions and learn all about yourself." That is a good question. Why a Spokesman? Let us take for example the Scriptures concerning the Seed of Abraham. We would be lost in a strange land not our own and we would be referred to as the so-called American negroes. And in the Last Days, in which we would be found, we would be slaves of one of the most powerful nations on the planet Earth and it would take God Himself, to restore this Holy Nation to its rightful place. This history is talking about us today. It is also an illustration of all other prophecies that are to be fulfilled by God, who has promised that He would come in the Last Days Himself to save you and I, the Holy Vessels, the Lost Tribe.

In fulfillment of all the histories, as promised, the history of Moses could not be fulfilled without his brother Aaron. The history of Jesus could not be fulfilled without His brother Simon Peter. The history of Abraham's two sons, Isaac and Ishmael, could not be fulfilled if it were not for Brother Fard having a Spokesman. So the Spokesman is a sign of the Saviour being in our midst.

In the Last Days we will be raised with Wisdom and Understanding to the status of Gods. But, if we are to fulfill all of the Scriptures then we must have two Gods in the Last Day and Time. One would be called God and one would be called the Holy One. These two would be inseparable and Commissioned by a God, whom they both respected as a Father, being above them both. You see, we can have no imposter in the Person of Master Fard Muhammad. All of the prophets laid out a scripture in which He would have to fulfill and only one Man in the Universe can fulfill all of these scriptures with His life.

In every pattern they coupled the two Gods in the Last Day and Time. So I am here before you as proof that the Saviour is here. I have met Him and lived with Him day and night for more than five years. I was with Him when He was Commissioned by Our Father and when the public record was made that the Saviour was now here and He had arrived. I am the first witness. I am your proof. You must bear witness to this Truth you hear coming from the mouth of Poor Brother Ali. You must also bear witness that this Great Truth does not start, nor will it stop, with Poor Brother Ali. Its Origin can be traced directly to Our Father. And what is more, you must bear witness that Brother Ali understands Our Father's teachings better than you. Superior Wisdom cannot be subjected to inferior Wisdom. Unless I had been taught Superior Wisdom, I would not have these arguments to make you bear witness that you cannot accept one without accepting the other and that every knee must bend to Allah, in the Person of Master Fard Muhammad, just as Our Father, the Most Honorable Mr. Elijah Muhammad taught Us.

If you do not believe that Master Fard Muhammad was long Commissioned before Our Father passed and that Our Saviour was among us when Our Father was teaching that He was, then you cannot say that you are a follower of the Honorable Elijah Muhammad. In the letter you wrote to Chicago, asking to be accepted in the Nation of Islam and be given a Holy name; then receiving a reply, which was referred to as an X, acknowledging receipt of your letter by the Laborer's Board, and advising you that it was not up to them in the final analysis as to whether or not you would be accepted in the New World, or accepted by Allah in the Person of Master Fard Muhammad. It was made clear to you that your letter had been accepted by the Laborer's Board and that they hoped that it would be accepted by Allah.

KNOWLEDGE OF THE GODS

Every Muslim who received an X and who does not believe that their entering Heaven depended upon their acceptance by Master Fard Muhammad in Person, cannot say that they are a follower of the Honorable Mr. Elijah Muhammad. You cannot accept the Most Honorable Mr. Elijah Muhammad and not accept Master Fard Muhammad, our God and Saviour in the Person. These things you must understand. You must believe in the Honorable Mr. Elijah Muhammad's teachings 100%. Taking nothing from it, and adding nothing to it!

Our Saviour taught me that when Our Father said the Day Sun would set and a New Sun would rise, this was referring to the Spiritual Night of Islam predicted to take place. During this Spiritual Darkness, when the Day Sun had set, the night of confusion and falling away would take place. He taught me that during this time of darkness a few of us would remain up all night praying and fasting and that we would be ridiculed and persecuted because of our strange actions. Everyone else would be doing what everyone does when it gets dark and that is, going to bed and falling asleep. But when it was *time*, and that word is important, for the Sun of the New World, the New Day, to come up, then all of the sleepers would begin to stir. Muslims would begin to wake up and start to pray, to prepare themselves, by making amendments and cleansing themselves through ablutions, in preparation to meet their Lord (making prayer). Brother Fard said this Spiritual Darkness would last 3 1/2 years, and any time after that, our people lost in the House of Israel would begin to stir and wake up. It would almost be like they never went anywhere and passed the night in sleep. The continuous consciousness of Our Father's teachings would flow so rapidly it will be like someone rang a bell, blew a horn, or yelled and everyone will stand up at once.

You, my beautiful brothers and sisters, who are now with me

suffering. Suffering even though the help has come, and you can now see this help and the work that comes with it, are blessed. I am so happy to have you here with me, to help me do this work. My job is to prepare you for Master Fard Muhammad. WE are a blessed people to be on the scene today.

You cannot accept One without accepting the Other. You must accept the Honorable Mr. Elijah Muhammad's teachings 100%. You must submit to Master Fard Muhammad 100%. You must do all that the lessons say you must do. The Rules and Laws must be kept. We are the Elect! We are the First! The example of Our Father's teachings will be seen through us. Therefore, don't take lightly the warning of Master Fard Muhammad to us today. Don't take it lightly. Get into your lessons brothers and sisters, because when you see people coming into the Faith in companies, students wanting what the teacher has, you will be able to teach them, not what you think, but what you know are the teachings of the Honorable Mr. Elijah Muhammad. Fill your head with our Father's Books. Practice your lessons, make your prayers.

"O Allah make us steadfast in prayer, and also our children." We *must* pray brothers and sisters. We have come this far and have gone through a lot of trials in order to be the greatest people in our Nation. We will be the best examples of true and righteous leadership for our people, as directed by the Honorable Mr. Elijah Muhammad. Now that the Help is coming are we going to just sit down and enjoy? No, no! Our Father said, "Heaven is not a place where we go and sit down and rest, that's where the work just starts. That is where we start at!"

You must get into your lessons now. You must understand that there is no difference between the two. You cannot make a separation. You must accept them both! There is no contradiction in the teachings of the Honorable Mr. Elijah Muhammad. You cannot

KNOWLEDGE OF THE GODS

accept Master Fard Muhammad and not believe in Muhammad. You cannot say you believe in Muhammad but you do not believe in Master Fard Muhammad. You cannot accept One without accepting the Other. All Holy Praise is due to Allah.

Study, fast, and pray because that is what time it is brothers and sisters. Those of you who follow these instructions, when the companies come, you will be the only teachers prepared to set an example. Those of you who do not, you will receive the reward of those who were just on the scene, and the young brothers and sisters will turn to you and say, "Those brothers and sisters did nothing with their blessings but sit on them, so they are not examples for us to follow. Those who followed the instructions of studying, praying, and fasting are the perfect examples of the Honorable Mr. Elijah Muhammad's teachings. Let us strive to be like them. They took their blessings and increased them by practicing the teachings." It is up to you. All Holy Praise is due to Allah.

Now is the time to be as strong as you can in your Islam. Drink from these fountains! Don't do what the Old World did. They took their lessons and put them in a closet and stashed Our Father's Books somewhere in a drawer. Drink, drink, drink the Wisdom! You may not think that you are learning, but every time you read the Divine words of Our Father it goes into your heart.

Master Fard Muhammad made us write essays on all our lessons until we understood them perfectly. Is it any small wonder that Brother Ali can answer all of your questions concerning Our Father's teachings? And can answer questions of Muslims who have not yet come? Our Supreme Wisdom is the highest Islam on the planet today. We are proud and are a blessed people. So follow the advice of studying, praying and fasting. We thank Almighty (God) Allah for blessing us with Supreme Wisdom.

In the year of 1930 Master Fard Muhammad came to the shores

A. M. Muhammad

of North America with a crown and some keys searching for Elijah. Elijah recognized Him as soon as He saw Him. He had been waiting for the Saviour. After 3 1/2 years Master Fard Muhammad of 1930 had fulfilled His mission, which is what He was born for. Coming to find God, Alpha and Omega (the First and the Last) He Who was dead but is alive, forevermore. He (Fard) gave the keys and crown to God, Face to Face. That is Who Master Fard of 1930 was and is. He was a specially prepared Man, Half and Half. He was given all the keys of the 23 Scientists. Taught by them all until He was wiser than them all. So they had to increase the number of Scientists and add the number 24.

Master Fard Muhammad was never mentally dead. From the time of His birth until the time He took on His mission, He lived a pure life. Free from hog, alcohol, drugs, wickedness, evil, lies and deceit. He was protected from murder, robbery and hell. When Fard, Praise be to Allah, of 1930 (Peace and blessing of Allah be upon Him) came to the shores of North America, He came in fulfillment of Muhammad of 1400 years ago (Peace and blessings of Allah forever by upon Him) That was His fulfillment. "Lightening coming out of the East and shining even unto the West." That is Who Master Fard Muhammad was and is. The first prophet to meet God in the End, Face to Face.

Our Father, the Most Honorable Mr. Elijah Muhammad taught us that the Son of Man, the Messiah, the Christ, is the bringer in of Judgment; and in the Last Days He will rise up among His people, save them and destroy their enemies. Master Fard Muhammad of 1930 did not have this job to do. For this job was referring to a future Man, who would be raised up and given a Commission that would be made public record by the Honorable Mr. Elijah Muhammad.

The Honorable Mr. Elijah Muhammad is the First Man that we, the so-called American Negroes can claim as our own. He was the

KNOWLEDGE OF THE GODS

only one to stand up in our midst and claim us as His people and force the world to bear witness. He rose up and proclaimed that He was above all men and was the Messenger of Allah, and the world bore witness to Him. He was from among us. He raised Our Saviour. Our God placed the title of Fard Saviour on His head in fulfillment of the name Fard living for 1,000 years, as it is prophesied.

This Son of Man is raised from you and I. This is the Master Fard of today. The One Who Our Father said was doing His work of gathering His people in our midst. He said, "Fard is not interested in everybody. Our Saviour (Master Fard Muhammad of today) is only interested in His people. That is, those who have accepted the Honorable Mr. Elijah Muhammad 100%." You are accepted by God according to your acceptance of the Honorable Mr. Elijah Muhammad. That is the truth. How else could it be? There can be no imposters. Brother Ali could not understand the teachings of the Honorable Elijah Muhammad and He could not understand the science of Elijah Muhammad's teachings unless He was taught by somebody wiser than He.

Our Father said, "You aren't the people unless you fulfill all the histories." He said, "And we would be fools to take the history of Jesus as referring to a man of the past." He said, "This History is talking about a man of today."

Well alright! Let's check it out. John the Baptist was teaching that he was preparing the way for the Saviour (the Messiah) and when Jesus came to John the Baptist to be baptized, John the Baptist told everyone, " . . . Behold the Lamb of God, which taketh away the sin of the world." And, "This is he of whom I said, after me cometh a man which is preferred before me." (John 1: 29, 30)

Even before Jesus appeared they were questioning John the Baptist as to who he was. The Jews sent priests and Levites from Jerusalem to ask him Who art thou? And he confessed, and denied not; but confessed, "I am not the Christ." (John 1:19, 20)

And they asked him, "What then? Art thou Elias?"

And he saith, "I am not."

"Art thou that prophet?"

And he answered, "No."

Then said they unto him, "Who art thou? That we may give an answer to them that sent us. What sayest thou of thyself?"

He said, "I am the voice of one crying in the wilderness, Make straight the way of the Lord, as said the prophet Isaiah. I baptize with water; but there standeth One among you, whom ye know not." (John 1:21-26)

According to the scriptures, it says that John the Baptist and Jesus were of the same tribe and that they would represent in the Last Day and Time the coming of Elijah, Who would prepare the way for the Lord, for the Lord's Great and Dreadful Day.

Elijah's job was only to make record; that is, to turn the children's attention to the right direction, to give them the right teachings. This was so they would accept Him (the Lord) when He appeared. When Jesus came on the scene the first thing that John the Baptist said was, "This is the One I have been telling you was coming."

History shows that John the Baptist and Jesus were cousins, meaning they were from the same tribe. We are not to accept that as referring to past history, it is referring to today. This means that God, and I say God because according to recorded history, when Jesus came on the scene, John the Baptist praised Jesus as being the One He was talking about, Who was preferred before Him and was greater than He was.

However, Jesus taught, "Verily I say unto you, among them that are born of women there has not risen One greater than John the Baptist . . . " And that, "All things are delivered unto Me of My

KNOWLEDGE OF THE GODS

Father; and no man knoweth the Son, but the Father; neither knoweth any man the Father, save the Son, and he whomsoever the Son will reveal Him." (Matt. 12:11, 12:27)

This is what Master Fard Muhammad is supposed to be saying today, if the Honorable Mr. Elijah Muhammad told the truth. And you know He told us the truth. It is real. That's right!

As the history points out, a record was made when the Saviour appeared. We have the history and we have the tapes wherein the Honorable Mr. Elijah Muhammad said in the Rickery Auditorium in 1959 that, "I am so happy for this day. I waited 379 years for this day." He said, "I see the Saviour sitting in the audience." He said, "I see Him. Don't you?" He then said, "No, I don't guess it's time yet."

Do you understand what I am saying? Well, this is the scripture and We must fulfill all of the scriptures. The Saviour must come up among His people. He is the Son of Man because *you judge the tree by the fruit it bears.* If He is His Father's Seed, then He will produce the same Fruit that His Father produced. He wouldn't change anything. All He would do is advance the Seed. No one following Master Fard Muhammad will be able to say that He does not love and praise the Honorable Mr. Elijah Muhammad with all His heart and soul, because this is His Father! He is Elijah's Seed! No one knew the Father but the Son. No one knew the Son but the Father.

As soon as Jesus, or as soon as Fard Saviour, recognized Who Our Father was, Who the Honorable Mr. Elijah Muhammad really was - that He wasn't just a Messenger, that he was the Last God of the Old World and the First God of the New World; He began to teach. Do you understand? Read Jesus' history in the scriptures of how He was among His people all His life. Everyone knew Him, His mother, His father, and His brothers and sisters. He had come up in the Temple. Everyone knew He was a smart man. As a child He was smart. As a youngster in the Mosque He was smart.

A. M. Muhammad

Everyone agrees on the fact that Jesus was known and considered very smart, right up until He got Commissioned (baptized by John the Baptist) by Elijah.

Then what happened? They put Him out of His own Mosque. He was no newcomer to Jerusalem, He was no newcomer to the Mosque. But what happened? They ran Him, His Disciples and everybody who sympathized with Him out. What was the difference of opinion? Why were they upset with Jesus? They said Jesus had a new teaching. That he was teaching that no one was greater than John the Baptist in the Heavens or the Earth. Why were they mad with that?

They wanted to accept Him as a prophet. They were willing to accept and had accepted, John the Baptist as a prophet and their Leader and Teacher. Why did they get mad at Jesus? Because He wanted to give Him all the praise? Why did they want to limit the praise for John the Baptist? Why did they put Jesus out? Do you understand? This is the Fard of Today. We would be fools to try to apply this history to a Saviour 2,000 years ago. This history applies to the Jesus of today, who was double-crossed by His own people whom He grew up with in the Nation. This is the Fard of Today, Who fulfills all the scriptures. Our Saviour!

You cannot misquote Our Father's teaching around Him. You cannot say anything and say that Our Father, the Most Honorable Mr. Elijah Muhammad, said it and Our Father did not say it. You can't do this and be in the presence of Master Fard Muhammad. Because He knows and can recite Our Father's Books and all of the lessons. You see, that is Our Saviour. Because of His belief in Almighty (God) Allah, He was persecuted from city to city, and those who believed in Him were persecuted from city to city.

The night of Spiritual Darkness will continue until the man of sin has had a chance to show whose son he is, whose seed he is.

KNOWLEDGE OF THE GODS

Whatever is in your heart that is what your hands will manifest. Wallace loves the President and being a so-called Negro and a patriot of this country. This is what he is about and advises others to do.

Master Fard Muhammad says this is Judgment and we must prepare ourselves to fight for independence. The arch-enemy (the devil) has no plans of love for our people. If God did not come when he did, in the Person of Master Fard Muhammad, Allah would have destroyed the Earth. You can be thankful that Master Fard Muhammad studied His lessons, fasted, and prayed until He received Divine Revelation to the True identity of the Honorable Mr. Elijah Muhammad; thus, qualifying Himself to be the Wisest Scientist on Earth and succeed Our Father as God. Not as a prophet, but as God, as Our Father's God. This is the difference in the histories of the two Fards. All Holy praise is due to Allah in the person of Master Fard Muhammad.

All Holy Praise is due to Allah. We forever thank Our Father for raising from among us our Leader and Saviour, and God in the Person of Master Fard Muhammad. Our Father, the Most Honorable Mr. Elijah Muhammad did not leave us Leaderless. Nor did He appoint a staff or an elective board to choose leaders for you. He said, "There is no successor, after Me comes God." That is what Our Father said and We know that the God He was referring to was none other than Master Fard Muhammad. There is no doubt about that!

Our Father taught us that Allah, in the Person of Master Fard Muhammad, would build the New World of Islam with the true believers of the Nation of Islam. The ones He (Elijah) Our Father, had raised. Our Father taught us that He was just preparing the way for the Great Mahdi, Allah in Person, Master Fard Muhammad. You know that your acceptance by Allah, in the Person of Master Fard Muhammad, would depend on your acceptance of Our Father, the

A. M. Muhammad

Honorable Mr. Elijah Muhammad. There had to be a falling away first. We know that Allah doesn't bless us while the hypocrites are still among us. Allah separates us by our Faith, and that is the job of Master Fard Muhammad to separate the faithful sheep from the goats.

We thank Allah and say, "O Allah, the Lord of everything, we have no help besides Thee. We love Thee, and Praise Thee, and we teach our children to submit to Thee. O our Most Gracious Lord and Saviour, we want only what you want for us, and we thank Thee for blessing us to be Your people, whom you will make the Head instead of the tail. We bear witness that Truth has come and falsehood must now be vanquished. And if You do not come to the True Believers aid at this time, the only Believers that You have will be destroyed by the enemy. Surely Allah answers him who Praises Him. Our Lord, Thine is the Praised."

I bid you to enjoy and celebrate your Independence Day. Remember who you are and start being yourself. A perfect example of an Elijah Muslim, Leaders of Our Black New World Nation of Islam.

In closing I say, In the Name of Allah, in the Person of Master Fard Muhammad, the Beneficent, the Most Merciful. Master of the Day of Judgment in which we are now living. And in the Name of Our Father, the Most Honorable Mr. Elijah Muhammad, the Last God of the Old World, and the First God of the New World, to Whom We forever Praise and Love. I greet you My beautiful Black Brothers and Sisters in the New World's Nation of Islam greetings of Peace in this world and Peace in the Hereafter.

Peace! Peace!

Chapter Fifteen
Ramadan

January 17, 1980. The first day of Ramadan. I am your Poor Brother Muhammad Ali, Spokesman for Almighty (God) Allah in the Person of Master Fard Muhammad and the Official Representative of the New World Nation of Islam, here in the wilderness of North America.

We are some blessed people. We are a mighty people. We are the Chosen of God. We are the Family of God. We have so much to be thankful for in this day and time. You and I, in this day, will be fashioned and guided into the Head Spot, not the bottom spot, but the Head Spot of all the Muslim Nations on the planet Earth. It is a promise that is binding by the Prophets. We know that We are rejected. We know that this world does not think We should be the people, or that We don't look or act like what they think the people are supposed to look and act like. But Praise be to Allah! Allah is the God in the Heavens and the Earth. He elevates whom He pleases, and He brings low whom He pleases. They do not have to like our God, Master Fard Muhammad, My God, your Saviour. But regardless to whether they like Allah in the Person of Master Fard Muhammad matters not, because every knee will eventually bend to Him.

He is the Great God. Not a spook. He is the Almighty God. Not some spook sitting up on a cloud somewhere, but a real live man, just as all the Prophets. Our Father was a Man Who taught Us to believe in God being a Man and not a spirit. I am the first witness of Almighty (God) Allah, in the Person of Master Fard Muhammad, being in our midst today, doing Our work. Muhammad and His followers may not look like the people to you, but where Muhammad is, Islam is, and you must come to Muhammad to get this Islam. There is no other way. Allah is the City and Ali is the Gate. You must come through Muhammad.

We thank Allah, even for the rejection. Because the prophecy says that We are the Lost Seed, that We would be rejected and that We would be in a strange land that was not our own. That We would be the reject of the nations. We are proud to be the rejected. All Master Masons know the story of the Master Builder and the Black Stone that was rejected. The Master Builder's name was Hiram Abiff.

Hiram Abiff was the Master Builder and he had three sons. The King had employed Hiram Abiff and his three sons to build for him a beautiful Temple. The three sons of Hiram Abiff, the Master Builder, were wicked and evil sons. As the Temple neared its completion, the wicked sons, Jubela, Jubelo, and Jubelum, began to see how beautiful the Temple was going to be. Because they wanted to steal the credit for themselves, they hit the Master Builder, Hiram Abiff, over the head with a carpenter's mallet. They dragged his body into a rubbish heap and buried him in a wooden box in the Northwest corner. After hiding the body they came back to complete the Temple and get the credit for themselves.

The Temple was complete except for the Cornerstone. Jubela, Jubelo, and Jubelum set to work, trying to find a Cornerstone for the Temple so it could be completed. They looked all through the rock quarry. They saw a big Black and odd shaped Stone but they rejected that. They felt there was no way in the world that could be the Stone. They didn't even try it, because they just knew that wasn't it. It looked too funny to be the Cornerstone. So they tried to make a Cornerstone. Nothing they fixed up or cut would fit right. The schedule for the completion of the Temple came and went, and the

KNOWLEDGE OF THE GODS

Temple still wasn't completed.

The King becoming suspicious, came to the Temple to find out what was the hold-up. When he questioned the wicked sons, Jubela, Jubelo, and Jubelum, he could easily see that they were hiding something, that they were lying. He asked them where was the Master Builder. He couldn't get right answers, so he decided he would investigate for himself. The King walked around until he finally came to the Northwest gate. There he saw a box. It was hidden under a rubbish heap, in a shroud of evergreen. He opened the box and there was Hiram Abiff, the Master Builder laying in this coffin-like box. Praise be to Allah.

The King reached down with the Master's Grip, which is the handshake that all Muslims recognize all over the world, and he said, "Come forth Hiram Abiff." If I remember correctly, he said it three times. Incidentally, the Master's Grip is also called the Lion's Paw. By using the Master's Grip, Hiram Abiff woke up. After he came out of the box (the shallow grave in which he had been buried) he explained to the King what Jubela, Jubelo, and Jubelum had done to him. They returned to the Temple site and the Master Builder went straight to the Black Stone, and they put it in place.

When they put the Black Stone in place, the whole Temple shook and rocked. When the Temple settled on the Black Stone it seemed to take on a new appearance. It became so beautiful, cut so perfect, that instead of the people coming to see the marvels and beauties of the Temple, they were coming to see the Black Stone.

That is the story of the Stone. The Black Stone that the builders rejected. It is a sign of you and I, in this Day and Time. We are rejected because the people don't think that we are the folks. We thank Allah, in the Person of Master Fard Muhammad, to be the rejected in this day and time. Praise be to Allah. We thank Allah much. Al-Hum-du-illah.

A. M. Muhammad

Our subject here is Ramadan; the Holy Month of Ramadan. **Holy Qur'an Chapter 2, Section 23 Fasting**, Verses 185-186. Praise be to Allah.

> *The month of Ramadan is that in which the Qur'an was revealed,*
> *a guidance and the Criterion. So whoever of you is present in the month,*
> *he shall fast therein, and whoever is sick or on a journey, (he shall fast) a (like) number of other days. Allah desires ease for you, and He desires not hardship for you,*
> *and (He desires) that you should complete the number*
> *and that you should exalt the greatness of Allah for having guided*
> *you and that you may give thanks.*
> *And when My servants ask thee concerning Me, surely I am nigh. I answer the prayer of the suppliant when he calls on Me, so they should hear My call and believe in Me that they may walk in the right way.*

All Praise is due to Allah. The Holy Month of Ramadan is the month in which the Holy Qur'an was revealed to Muhammad ibn Abdullah of 1400 years ago, (May the Peace and Blessings of Allah forever be upon Him). It is because of this that we commemorate the Revelations of Gabriel that was to be the final Revelations before the Judgment. We bear witness that these Revelations in the Qur'an were the clearest Light, until the coming of Our Father, the Honorable Mr. Elijah Muhammad. He revealed the identity of this wicked devil, in this wicked civilization, and the Judgment of the Earth.

KNOWLEDGE OF THE GODS

One is on the scene today greater than Yakub, with the Supreme Wisdom, in the Person of Master Fard Muhammad.

Ramadan for all Muslims is 30 days, but for us, the New World Nation of Islam, Ramadan is 40 days. It is 40 days because we not only commemorate Prophet Muhammad ibn Abdullah of 1400 years ago, we bear witness to all the Prophets. We make no distinction between any of the prophets, and because we are New World Muslims, we must do more. We must suffer to be the best Muslims on the planet earth, the perfect Tribe of Allah, the Godhead Tribe. During this time of suffering the most, we must get knowledge and do good to others. This means that for these 40 days we are supposed to keep our minds on Allah and Muhammad. We are supposed to read the Qur'an, read Our Father's Books, and get knowledge to benefit self and kind.

Knowledge is the key. We must get knowledge. We must also practice in the doing of good towards each other. We must start the fast off with a resolve. We should on the night of the 17th, the beginning of the Ramadan fast, resolve to be better in the year to come. More than we have ever been. We should keep in mind that this is supposed to be the most peaceful time of the year for us. Make an extra effort to be good, not only for our own sake, but towards our brothers and sisters. We thank Allah for blessing us to be His people. We want to do all that we can to be close to Allah and Muhammad. To show the world of Muslims that we do more to serve Allah than all others. We thank Allah!

During this month we eat only after the Sunset Prayer. We eat fruit, whole wheat bread and pure dairy products. Incidentally, the devil's civilization is corrupting everything. You have to be careful with the dairy products that you buy from these people. We know that cheese, the commercial brands that you're use to finding on the shelves in the stores, are full of pig. Full of hog! Just a few years back Philadelphia Cream Cheese was a good cheese and we ate Philadelphia Cream Cheese. But today, even the Philadelphia Cheese has hog in it. So, you have to be careful. Our Father said we can eat cheese but don't try to eat too much. I say to you that those of you who want cheese should go to the health food stores and try to get pure dairy products. During this fast we must eat whole wheat bread, fruit, milk, butter, and like I said, cheese if you desire, when you can get it pure.

Now, sure this is hard. Sure it's suffering but that's who we are. We suffer the most because we're given the most Allah has promised to make us the head and not the tail. Because of that we must do more. When we speak about suffering for Allah, it brings to mind how Allah raises us from one stage to the next. Each stage representing a certain amount of difficulty. Each difficulty that we overcome brings us closer to Allah. Until eventually, we understand that the trials are not for Allah, the trials are for us, that we may turn loose this wicked world and place nothing between us and Allah and Muhammad, and be perfect examples of leadership.

All of the suffering we do for Allah is only to get us in a perfect state or condition. We should be happy to suffer for Allah. All of our suffering proves that we are qualified. Because if we can hang on to Allah and Muhammad when things are bad, and things are hard, and we're going without new clothes, when we're suffering without proper shelter, when food is scarce, when there's no money. If we hold on to Allah during these trying times, Allah blesses us to achieve a high degree of peace in the midst of all this fire. Like Shadrach, Meshach, and Abednego, when they were thrown in the fiery furnace and had to suffer because of their belief in Allah. They went into the fire saying, "Praise be to Allah." So Allah said, "Fire be cool to Shadrach, Meshach, and Abednego." And the fire was cool.

KNOWLEDGE OF THE GODS

What we have to learn here is that the suffering that you and I are going through is only purifying us and making us learn to maintain our peace regardless to whom or what. Once we learn to maintain our peace then we are in heaven, forevermore. If you can maintain your peace during the time of adversity, how much more peace will you have when everything is going the way you think it should go? Suffering for Allah is the greatest gift.

Brothers and Sisters who have difficulty in maintaining this fast of whole wheat bread, milk, and fruit, you do the best you can. Brothers in prison (Brothers in school) you do the best that you can. Allah is God and He does not intend hardship for us. He intends that He elevate us and bring us closer to Him. Our Spirit, our outlook towards this fast should be as only another step towards getting closer to Allah. This diet, according to Master Fard Muhammad, is the diet that the Nation will eventually be on. All of our foods will be bread, fruit and milk. That's a fact! Brother Fard taught me that our bodies do not need anything else. That all of the elements, all of the nourishment and chemistry that our body needs is in whole wheat bread. He says milk is a near perfect food. The only thing that it is lacking is the solid matter. Whole wheat bread has all of the solid matter, all of the protein, all of the vitamins, everything that we need, is there, plus more, in the whole wheat bread. He says, that in the near future, when the Nation is eating every other day, which we are progressing to, we'll take on a new growth. Our bodies being clean, our system mentally and physically being given the right foods will automatically take on a new growth. And He says that it is not too far off that the Scientists will be eating one meal a week.

Every Ramadan we want to try to do a little bit better. Every year we want to resolve to do a little bit better. We thank Almighty God Allah, in the Person of Master Fard Muhammad, and we forever love Our Father. If it were not for Our Father we would be lost. We would be dead! If it were not for Master Fard Muhammad waking up to the true identity of our Father, the earth would have been smitten with a severe chastisement. You and I are the most blessed people in the world. We must now begin to take our seat at the Head of the Muslim World. We are thankful for the opportunity to do better.

In passing, let me make mention about junk food. Allah provides us with pure foods, good foods. He tells us, eat pure whole wheat bread, eat pure butter, eat fresh fruit, and fresh milk. These are the best foods for us. These are the things that prepare our minds for our job. For the heaven we are now laying the foundation for. This is the best food for us. It's the best food that we can acquire on this planet. He puts this before us in abundance. Because we have been brought up in the devil's civilization and taught to accept the weak, the lesser, we turn to the junk foods. I have seen it happen over and over again, that a believer will walk into a store or a market and he will step all over the fruit all over the lawful things and buy candy and cookies and junk food. We must get out of that habit, Brothers and Sisters. Nothing looks worse than a Muslim officer eating junk food. Praise be to Allah for His Guidance. Praise be to Allah for our willingness to hear and obey.

My instructions are for the Tribe of Shabazz, Our Family. We don't want everybody with us. We want only our people who are the strong, who are going to be the examples for the Nation. There is no other way for us to enter Heaven except through this process of learning to be better, of cleanliness. We must clean ourselves up! We must be strong. This is the only way we can establish our leadership. When we relax the laws of Our Father and Master Fard Muhammad, we relax the quality of officers in our midst. We should never try to weaken a law or go around a law because some brother or some sister feels like the law is too hard to uphold. The law is hard because the work we have to do is hard and we only want the

KNOWLEDGE OF THE GODS

strong. If we take away the hard work then we can't find the strong people. Never relax the rules of Our Father and Master Fard Muhammad. Uphold those rules all the time. Envy and jealousy destroys. Get rid of envy and learn to love each other. We are to be the best Muslims on the planet, that's what we are about. That is our job.

We want the officers to remember; and this is important brothers and sisters. It is unlawful to speak evil of your fellow Muslims, to curse them or to gossip about one another. Do not use profanity or slang. You are an officer. You must be humble. You must be amiable towards the believers. You are not to chastise the believers. Your job is that of a director. Always be a humble officer. Never allow anyone to speak to you of evil about your brothers or sisters. Just as you have to fight against suggestions about your Lord and Muhammad, you must also fight the evil suggestions that come up concerning your brothers and sisters. We must uphold one another. If we are wrong, we will come together and do what we have to do to make ourselves right. If we are dirty, we will get together and clean ourselves up. We are one family and we must fight to stay strong! We must help each other to be strong and not help each other to be weak. We thank Allah much.

This world's life is a passing thing. It is like a grave yard with dead bodies lying on the ground rotting away. Those who desire this world are like birds of prey, scavenger dogs! Do not, officers of the New World Nation of Islam, uphold this world, and the joys and pleasure of this world at any time. This world must be destroyed. It is on the way out. We do not love it, we hate it.

We must do good acts of charity. Even if it is just a good word to the believers, that is a good deed. It is a good act and Allah will bless you for it. When a bad officer is in charge, there is constant trouble and the people mourn. We are all leaders of the highest order. We are with Allah to stay. We are not going anywhere.

You, officers are responsible for the believers just as the shepherd is responsible for the general well-being, the maintenance and unity of his flock. You are all shepherds. Uphold the law officers! You must always Praise Allah, in the Person of Master Fard Muhammad, the Beneficent, and our Most Merciful Saviour. You must always honor and Praise Our Father, the Most Honorable Mr. Elijah Muhammad. This should be your regular routine in the presence of the believers. You should constantly be giving Our Father and Master Fard Muhammad the Praise that is their due. You may also honor Me, if you want to.

We thank Allah. Collect all of Our Father's columns that you can. Keep your notebooks. As Brother Fard told us, our notebooks are the True Gold. The wisdom that is in our notebooks, is the wisdom that will be the foundation for the civilization which we are now beginning to form. At first Allah brings together a small group, a clot of people. Then He begins to put in the bone structure. Classes are started and then a graduation program. As the structure comes, so comes the growth. This little clot of people is the Nation.

We are being fashioned right now into the most proficient staff, governmental staff that the world has ever seen. They need all of our knowledge. You would be surprised at some of the knowledge We have lost. We have lost essays written by the hand of Master Fard Muhammad. There are still a lot of them around in the notebooks of some of the old angels. Go to each other. Check out one another's notebooks and get the things you don't have. Search for knowledge. It is the knowledge that makes us great.

Praise be to Allah. We want to make this Ramadan the best Ramadan we have ever experienced. Help each other to do that. Let's tighten up our unity.

KNOWLEDGE OF THE GODS

Before closing I have just a few more things to say. As you know, the world is in a grip of war. A third World War can break out any day now. This Third World War is supposed to be the last and final war. It is to usher in Armageddon, or the Judgment. We must learn self-defense. Watch the news on television. Look at the war torn countries struggling to survive. See what it is to have bombed out cities, refugees on the road, no food and no water. Understand that we must try to prepare ourselves so that when war comes, we will have first aid, water, food and be able to defend ourselves. This is important. Praise be to Allah.

Every Muslim household should have a survival kit. This is necessary brothers and sisters. If an atomic bomb blew up in Canada, the radiation fall-out could possibly damage the food, water and the very atmosphere that we breathe. We have to start thinking along these lines and realize this is a very serious situation that we are living in, and if we do not take the proper steps we can make some grave mistakes. We must realize that we are all that we have and we must do all that we can to survive. Praise be to Allah. It reminds Me of a little history about the Old Man in the Mountain.

We know that we don't look like the people and we are happy that we don't look like this world, or anything in it. To our sisters, keep yourselves close to one another for protection in this world. Do not allow yourselves to be degraded by this dead civilization. Sisters, don't be in the streets befriending the enemy of Islam, stay close to your family. Brothers, get ready to defend your sisters. We will not allow any man to degrade our sisters. Our women must be respected and the time is coming when a brother will have to be prepared to take a head about the degradation of our sisters.

Our sisters are the most precious jewels that we have. We must respect them and they must respect themselves. The relief, blessings and the joy to our eyes is now in sight. Let us qualify ourselves to receive it and be good examples for Allah in the Person of Master Fard Muhammad. Let us act in a way that Our Father will be proud that we are His children. We are doing this and we are happy. We can see the Divine Hand in the work. Hang on in there. Some things may seem strange but Allah will prove to you that His Hand is above our hand. All Holy Praise is due to Allah.

So in closing, I encourage you and exhort you, to continue to do good, especially among each other. Let this be the best Ramadan we have ever made and let us look forward to many more.

The conclusion of this Ramadan fast is the 26th of February. This Saviour's Day, in which we commemorate Master Fard Muhammad of 1930, Who came and gave the crown to Our Father, the Most Honorable Mr. Elijah Muhammad. He came in July of 1930 and He left in 1934. He was the Personification of Muhammad ibn Abdullah of 1400 years ago, Who was promised by Almighty (God) Allah that He would be the first one Resurrected when God Himself would stand up. He Who had been dead and is alive forevermore.

We will remember all of the Prophets on this day. And we make our sacrifices and we do it with a happy and cheerful heart, because Allah has made us the Head and not the tail. We do more than all other Muslims in our service to Allah, because we are the Head and not the tail. It is out of the Mouth of Almighty (God) Allah, in His promise and covenant to the Prophets, that He, Himself would rise up and make us the lost, mentally dead and disrespected ones, the Head instead of the tail.

Let us complete this Ramadan with high spirits. Let us help ourselves by looking out for our brothers and sisters. Sisters, maintain your unity and love one another. Don't be so quick to condemn each other. We all make mistakes. When a brother or sister makes a mistake, or has made a mistake, learn how to forgive your brother. Learn how to forgive your sister. Don't be so quick to

KNOWLEDGE OF THE GODS

condemn each other. We don't claim to be holier than thou. You know that we are all we have. When a brother makes a mistake or when his spirits are low, that is when he really needs a brother, that is when a sister really needs a sister. Let us practice these things of love and unity.

In closing: In the Name of Allah in the Person of Master Fard Muhammad, the Beneficent and the Most Merciful Saviour. The Master of this Day of Judgment in which we are now living. It Is to Allah alone that we forever submit to and seek for help. And in the Name of Our Beloved Father, the Most Honorable Mr. Elijah Muhammad, to Whom We forever Praise and can't Praise enough. Lord knows, if it don't be for Our Father there would not be anything. I greet you My Beloved Brothers and Sisters, in the New World Nation of Islam's greeting of Peace in this World and Peace in the Hereafter.

Peace! Peace! May Allah bless you and I love you.

Chapter Sixteen
A Brief Talk

All Holy Praise is due to Allah, the Lord of all the Worlds. The Beneficent and the Most Merciful Saviour. He is in the Person of Master Fard Muhammad. That's right! He is the Master of this Day of Judgment that you and I are now living in.

We can't find no refuge anywhere else. He is the only One that will help us that I know. When you get through running around searching for something else, and taking twenty years to discover that there is nothing else, you then realize that nothing will help us, you and Me, but Allah in the Person of Master Fard Muhammad. I don't submit to nobody else. Forget it! I don't want to see it! I don't even want to hear it. I don't want to talk about it and I don't want to see it! I want no part of anything other than Almighty (God) Allah in the Person of Master Fard Muhammad. I think we all can understand that. He is our only hope and help, if you understand.

The Blackman has no beginning. He is older than the Sun. He is older than the Moon. He is older than the Stars. The Blackman has no beginning, nor does He have an ending. I begin in the Name of Our Father, the Most Honorable Mr. Elijah Muhammad. We have no choice but to bear witness that We have no other origin, that We have no other awakening, and that We have no other life. Elijah was the First Man to stand up among the so-called American Negroes and tell the truth, at a time when they (the devil) were killing niggers for smiling at white folks. Our Father stood up and declared that the entire white race was a race of devils and that they must be destroyed off the face of the planet Earth. I don't even have to tell you the description He gave to you and I, the identity that he gave to you

KNOWLEDGE OF THE GODS

and I, and of the roots the Most Honorable Mr. Elijah Muhammad gave to you and I, brothers and sisters. We have no other Father and there can be no end to Our Praise for the Most Honorable Mr. Elijah Muhammad. He was the Last God of the Old World and the First God of the New World. We thank Almighty (God) Allah in the Person of Master Fard Muhammad.

No! We have no beginning. We know that it was in six (6) cycles that all was completed. That is why we call the Seventh Day the Lord's Day (the Perfect Day). This is the Day when everything is supposed to be in tune with Righteousness, the Judgment Day. During this time there would be a change in the atmosphere, in the solar system. For as it is above, so shall it be on earth. When thy Kingdom come, thy Will be done, on Earth as it is in Heaven. There is no God besides Allah. So We know that the Creation, though We can find no beginning, has been a point of reference for civilizations for as long as man has been known to be in existence. Islam.

During this time everything in nature would have experienced so much discord and evil, that the entire planet would be ready for some Righteous people. I mean, some folks that are really right. Not a people who are hypocritical and who lie, but real people. People with no shame in so far as trying to do right.

Not those who would say, "Well we had better do this thing over here because we don't want them to know over there; and being that this is a shameful thing we are doing, let's hide this action from the other brothers and sisters who are Righteous."

So, from the reference, We know without a doubt that the Lord Created Himself, from whatever and from wherever. And then from Himself, He created all else. The positive and negative forces of the universe were created at the same time. The one being an authority over the other. Thus a regeneration of establishing populations, societies and civilizations came about.

A. M. Muhammad

The first men and women formed a society in their living together, breeding together and in their struggling for survival together. They grew as a distinct people that is, the way they survive, the foods they eat, the clothes they wear, the music they listen to and the customs they practice. In all things there is that chief element; the God that they worship. It is through the God that they worship that we can trace their origin.

Islam is the only religion known that has no birth record. We can date all others because We were here when they came into being and We will be here when they leave. In fact, thanks to Allah, We usher them in and We are the ones that will usher them out. Thank Allah, because Our Father turned the Heart of the children to the Father, and the Heart of the Father to the children. We have no Father other than the Most Honorable Mr. Elijah Muhammad.

As the society (the clot) is established and because of its awkwardness and newness in a world that it is not fully accustomed to, it must now set up an order. It must have an area in which to function; that is, establish certain tendencies, characteristics and aptitudes of learning. Then it is realized, "Look, we have been getting together here, now we should start having classes. Every Sunday we meet and just sit around talking, listening to a little music (Jazz) and that's nice. But now we should do something constructive because we are Muslims. So why don't we start having classes here for the sisters and classes for the brothers?" Thus We establish structure. The clot takes on bones.

This is the same process and pattern of growth in the human body, the civilization for man. We can see the parallel. It is the same. With that view, we all have no difficulty in seeing how our past is from the Gods. We have built every civilization the planet has ever known anything about. We know them all.

The encyclopedia of human existence is in the very protoplasm

KNOWLEDGE OF THE GODS

of the black germ. It is our record, it is in all of us. Brother Fard taught us that this protoplasm exists in all things and it is done that way so there would be no doubt of the Judgment. He went on to explain that it is like a person not having a particular reference book or encyclopedia in a library. And then, someone comes along and puts that missing encyclopedia in that library; that missing part will make all the difference in the world, in the way of enlightenment.

He said Allah, being the All Wise God put the protoplasm in the very core, which the white world has just discovered at this late date. This is a kindergarten lesson Master Fard Muhammad taught us when We were in school. He called this element Deoxyribonucleic Acid (DNA). He (the devil) is trying to break it down so that he can read the encyclopedia of history that is in the Blackman.

However, because this particular history is microcosmic and being in the substance of all living things, there is no way that its maturity will be known to the devils by the time the Lord of all the Worlds has completed His experimentation concerning the type of civilization He wants to build.

The animal kingdom is ready for heaven; they have survived. That is why We say, "Respect the animal kingdom." Look at them! They have survived brothers and sisters. Don't you understand this? Don't you know what a hell it is to survive out there? We catch hell just trying to survive. If we are given a chance look at all the tools we'd have at our disposal.

Examine the animal kingdom. Look how overwhelmed they have been by the devil himself, but you still see them surviving. They have survived. And because they have survived, they are a lesson for you and I. We must respect everything in nature, for it has the right to exist just as we have the right to exist. As long as the harmony is there, no one has any trouble. That is Peace. That is the nature of the Universe. That is Islam. That is Our identity. It is natural.

The society that We are forming now is laying the identity. It is writing the encyclopedia for the future. We are to take all of the knowledge that we can get. We want what the Scientists know. We want to spend our money on developing modern techniques towards getting the proper education, because we must be the best that ever did it.

The civilization that We are getting ready to establish under the guidance of Master Fard Muhammad, will be respected by the whole planet, immediately! Right away! Because the Muslim World is spiritual, they are going to recognize that We have the highest spiritual doctrine on the planet. Supreme Wisdom! The next thing they will recognize is Our material advancement. Our type of government and society, in the civilization which you and I are now establishing. By looking around at this universe, being a species alone, a family, we can see there are only a few of us. But the one thing we are going to do is survive because we have God on our side.

We must acquire all the modern wisdom; we must put ourselves in a position to get all that and more. Set up establishments that will be continuously on top of all new knowledge developed anywhere on the planet. We have got to be the most advanced in knowledge. Every little bit we can get, anywhere, we have to get. I cannot express this enough. Knowledge! Knowledge! Knowledge! Knowledge!

You must establish an order of worship towards your God that will take in all of the good of the old and push it into the future, so everyone can see the association. The connection will be there and will stand out, and they will be able to see the association. The connection will be there, and will stand out and they will be able to see God's people. The people will see that all they needed were the

KNOWLEDGE OF THE GODS

brothers and sisters with the right ideas. All they needed were the Technicians, who are spiritually called the Shabazzians. We are the Master Builders. We will build a civilization quick!

White folks weren't dumb when they sent the good ship Jesus to Africa. He did not bring back dummies. He came back with people who knew how to build civilizations. The proof of that is the civilization We have built. Now if someone wants to say that is a lie, well, if it wasn't before, it is now! What arguments do you want to make about that? We did it, and because We did it, it was always in Us. Being that it was in Us, it had to come from somewhere. We always did that - build civilizations. That's right. We are the best. We are the Master Builders.

When We were taken from our homeland, it rocked, settled and went to sleep. The devils invaded every Holy place. Every statue that gave any indication of Black dominance from the past was disfigured. Even if they (the devils) wanted to hold them for their beauty, they would still bruise the noses, or any other features that were distinctly Black. In the museums, when they showed the King Tut Exhibition, and other exhibitions pertaining to Egypt and its Pharaohs, they would portray them as Europeans. White folks have always tried to steal Our identity; like the Jews trying to claim that they are the seed of Abraham, which is a lie of the highest order.

We thank Almighty (God) Allah for blessing Us to be His People. We were on the bottom. We were the least, that one who knew nothing. The only thing We had was that sense in the back of our head, which use to always say, "Now man, you know that's the Truth." That is what made Us different. And because of that ability alone, Allah has made Us the Head. We are the First Scientist and the Last Scientist. The history is so beautiful. It is so beautiful and We thank Allah so much.

It seems just like yesterday. I can see it so clearly. They (the

A. M. Muhammad

devils) had turned your Poor Brother loose from the military. I had come home and began to roam the streets, trying to find the fellows I use to hang out with. But the world goes on and you can never go back. Me being an illiterate, there wasn't much I could do in looking for a job; so, I just hung around and decided I would try to be a part of a singing group. Back then, in those big city ghettos, everyone belonged to a du-wop group. I was no different. So I du-wopped for a while, getting a meal here and a couch to sleep on there. Never nothing real. We would go to a house party and sing our hearts out. You couldn't tell us we weren't the top rated singing group in the country the way we performed at those drunken parties. Anytime something real came our way, we would automatically shy away from it. On those occasions group members wouldn't show up. You and I, we come from the same place.

One day I was sitting around listening to Horace Silver. As I remember, the album was *Seven Pieces of Silver*. This brother came by named Saul and started talking to my partner, Brother Rudy. What I had not known was that Rudy had been talking with this brother all the time, had been visiting the man's house and they were both Muslims. Elijah Muslims. I knew nothing about Muslims. I was totally dumb. If you had asked me what a Muslim was, I would have thought you were talking about some kind of bread you eat or a muffin. I didn't know anything about Muslims.

As this fellow was talking to Rudy, I stopped listening to the records, and started listening to what he was saying. He said, "Yeah, the Black man is God." And, "Praise be to Allah. Civilizations that we built many thousands of years ago before the Pyramids, were like living out in futuristic space. It was so peaceful and beautiful. The Palaces were unimaginable. This was how the civilizations we use to live in back home, in the East, thousands of years ago, use to be. And you know something else? Flying carpets ain't no joke!"

KNOWLEDGE OF THE GODS

When he said that, something like a telephone ringing went off inside my head. I could feel pins and needles running through my body, like electricity or something. I was excited and said, "Wait a minute brothers! Wait a minute man! What did you just say?"

The brother was stunned. I could see him thinking, *looks like I have got myself into something here*. Then he repeated it, "I said flying carpets ain't no joke."

I said, "Yeah, that's what I thought you said. Where did you learn that at?"

He said, "At the Temple."

I said, "Well how much does it cost to get in?"

He said, "You don't have to pay nothing to get in." Then he turned to Rudy and said, "Rudy look, why don't you bring the brother around sometime? This brother wants to hear this, why don't you bring him on around?"

Rudy said, "Alright."

That's when I said, "You mean just come around? Where is it at?"

Saul said, "Rudy will bring you. Rudy, bring him around."

Rudy says, "Yeah." You could see Saul wanted to get out of there, so he left.

Then I turned to Rudy and said, "Look Rudy, what's this man? What's going on?"

He said, "Those are the brothers."

I said, "Brothers? What is brothers?"

He said, "Muslim brothers."

I asked him, "Do they teach that stuff? Can anybody get in?"

He said, "Oh yeah. I'm going to take you around there."

I immediately asked him, "Well when are you going to take me around there?" He told me he would take me around there that night, and I said, "Okay, but you don't have to pay anything to get in do you?"

"No, you don't have to pay," Rudy said.

I said, "Well alright."

The place turned out to be at 13 Court Street. Solomon and Pat had just got married and they had heard Islam from another brother. Some brother had come over from New York. The few of us use to meet at 13 Court Street. There was Brother Jimmy Gross, Yusef, Everett, Randy, Solomon, myself, another brother named Solomon and Earl. I could go on and on, but this is where the few of us met. When Rudy took me around there for the first time, I met these brothers and I sat there listening to this Islam. To me it was right and it was the Truth.

All the way home on the bus I was thinking, "This is just too good to be true. Something has got to be wrong." I was nervous and I couldn't wait to get home. When I got home I went to my room and started pacing up and down. I was trying to figure this out. I was really thinking about this. This was something I was not use to, because like I said, I was ignorant.

My mind was moving. It was really cranked up. I was really cranked up. I was trying to figure this thing out. I was thinking to myself, "I have heard the truth. I cannot deny that I have heard the truth. But what is going on? What is this? I just got to know. I must know that this is the truth. I need a sign or something." Then it hit me. I did not know that I knew Allah was God, and I did not know I knew how to prostrate; but both of these things happened to me, as a consequence of what I am trying to tell you.

I got on my knees because that is how my mother taught me to pray. To stand by the bed, get on your knees and put your little hands

KNOWLEDGE OF THE GODS

up in front of you. So I did this and said, "Lord I need a sign. Just show me a sign. I know this ain't nothing to play with. I want to know. I just got to know this is right. Just give me a sign." Then I just started crying right there. I prostrated and said, "Oh Allah, please show me a sign that this is the truth. The way that You want me to go and I will serve You forever." Then I just cried for a few minutes. However, when I stood up, I felt different. I just felt different. My mind seemed to be clear. I wasn't worried and I just seemed to be calm.

The thought came to me to get the Bible and open it up. So I got the Bible and opened it up. Remember now, I told you I was ignorant and could not read. I had about a second or third grade education. The first thing my eyes turned to was *Job Chapter 1 verses 6-7*:

"And the servants of the Lord came to present themselves and satan came also.

And the Lord asked satan from whence cometh thou?

Satan said from walking to and fro on the earth and up and down in it."

And that was the sign of the cross and that the white folks were the devils.

I just got so excited, I started crying again. I grabbed the book I was holding, the Bible, and I walked up and down in the room. I then left my room and went and knocked on my mother's bedroom door. This was about two or three o'clock in the morning. She got up and came to the door. I excitedly said, "Ma, listen! I know the Truth! I know the Truth! Look! Its right here in the Bible!" I opened it up and showed it to her.

She was looking at me like she thought I was high off drugs or something and said, "Yeah, okay." At first she was saying, "What?

What?" Like she was irritated because I had awakened her. The woman was a working lady and here it was early in the morning.

When she opened the door and saw I was really serious, she listened at what I was saying. She probably thought I was high off something and decided to humor me.

She said, "Well yeah, now listen. Now man, man do you hear me?"

I said, "Yeah, I hear you. But do you see what I am saying?"

She said, "Look, okay. You just go to bed. We'll talk about this tomorrow. Go to your room and we'll talk about it tomorrow."

Seeing this I said, "Yeah okay, alright. Yeah, alright Ma. I'll talk to you tomorrow." I went to bed. That was my experience in coming into Islam.

From then on I started to go among the brothers as often as I could, hear as much as I could and learn as much as I could. Things began to turn and became a little different for me. All I wanted was to be like the Honorable Mr. Elijah Muhammad wanted me to be. But I began to notice that certain brothers were involved with drugs. Certain brothers were involved with prostitutes and certain brothers were involved with other things. I knew that was not what Elijah wanted. So I figured the best thing for me to do was clean myself up, get all the lessons, get a job, get married, and try to be the kind of Muslim Muhammad wanted. So that is what I did.

Meanwhile, the brothers were still growing. They were teaching and still meeting. I was trying to work. I stayed in touch but not as often as I use to. One day the brothers came to my house and said, "Look brother, you are staying up here in the mountains. Why don't you come on down and meet some of the new brothers we have?" I said, "Yeah, well alright. I'll be down." So I went down to the meeting at 13 Court Street. There was a bunch of new brothers. They

KNOWLEDGE OF THE GODS

were all upstairs talking and sciencing up (discussing Islam). I was introduced to these new brothers. Praise be to Allah.

I went upstairs and they introduced me to all the brothers. As I was being introduced to the brothers someone said, "Brother Al, this is Brother Belton X." I said, "Salaam Alaikum brother." I looked at the brother and he looked at me; then I smiled and he smiled. So I said, "Brother I know I know you. I have got to know you from somewhere."

He said, "I was thinking the same thing."

Then I said, "Well, where did you come up?"

And he answered, "I came up around 15th Avenue."

I said, "Oh yeah? Do you know Brady?"

He said, "I came up with Him and Mason Anthony."

Then I said, "Well I hung out with them guys. I used to be with them all the time." And he said, "Oh yeah?" Then we got to talking and I went home.

I was working like a slave. One day a knock came at my door. As I opened the door and saw Brother Belton I said, "As Salaam Alaikum."

He said, "Wa Alaikum Salaam."

I said Peace Brother Belton, how are you?"

He said, "I'm alright Brother. Can I talk to you for a minute?"

I said, "Yes Sir, come on in."

He then told Me how He had been over to Brother Wesley's place and talked with a few of the Brothers. They had told him I was a member of the Council and that he should come over and talk with Me. I said, "Yeah, well alright Brother, what is it?"

The Council was the only Brothers in Newark. There were 13 of us. This came about through our coming together and deciding that we should start having something. That was, having dinners, meetings or something because we were getting too big. People were coming and standing all out in the street because there was not enough room in the houses. The sisters would stay up day and night cooking, making bean pies and fixing coffee. And before any of us could get any rest, there would be more Bothers just wanting to hear some Islam. We would be dog tired. We had to set up some kind of structure. We called all the Brothers together. All 13 of us to solve the problem.

I was the 13th registered Brother in Newark. When anything would go on, most of the Brothers would refer younger Brothers to one of the Brothers in the Council. So that is what happened in this case. They had referred Brother Belton to Me after he had spoken to other Brothers on the Council.

This is what Brother Fard had to say: "Brother." He said. "I waged war on the devil, and I went to bless Our Father. When I came back the other brothers said I was wrong and that I shouldn't do that because Muslims don't do that. They said I was making things hot. They told me that Muslims don't carry pen knives and that Muslims aren't aggressive. I got upset because I didn't know what was going on. Am I wrong?" He asked.

So I said, "Well Brother. First of all, a Muslim can't do anything wrong to the devil."

He said, "All Praises due to Allah! Brother I feel so good! That's all I needed to hear! I feel alright now! Praise be to Allah! Brother Wesley was right when he told me to come over here and talk with you. I'm so glad I came over. Brother I am hungry," He said. "I feel like my appetite is back."

I said, "Well Brother, I have a little something. You are welcome to whatever is here. I am kind of poor you know."

KNOWLEDGE OF THE GODS

He went and looked in the pantry and the pantry was bare. Then He looked in the ice box and it was bare. So He said, "Brother look, Praise be to Allah. Allah is going to bless You. Come with me."

I said, "Where are We going?"

He said, "We are going to get some groceries."

I said, "Yeah?"

He said, "Yeah."

I said, "Well alright."

I got my coat and we left. We got into His old raggedy car. It was an old 1951 Fleetwood Cadillac. Then off we went to the supermarket. He said, "Come on Brother, get a shopping cart." I got a cart and He told me whatever I saw that I wanted, to just put it in the cart. I am standing there thinking, *this Brother must have a whole lot of money*. So I started putting stuff in the shopping cart. Now we got two baskets full of food. I mean they were full. Again, I'm thinking, *this Brother must have a whole lot of money*, and *why is He buying all this food?* You know how it is coming up in the city. You expect a sucker to be doing something wrong. The thought hit me that it was on Him and I wasn't going to worry about it.

When We got to the cashier He said, "Okay, you check everything in. I've got to go cash a check." As the cashier was counting up the groceries, I was bagging them up. When she was almost finished, I looked to see where Brother Fard was. He was in front of the Customer Service window. I saw him shrug his shoulders and hold his hand out. Then it looked like the cashier was shaking his finger in the Brother's face. But then it looked like the Brother was shaking His finger in the man's face. At that point the man just reached down and gave the Brother some money. He then came over and paid the lady. As We were leaving We looked at each other and He said, "I told You Allah was going to bless Us." And that is how We got together.

From that point on the brothers who remained with the original Council were down the hill. Brother Fard would go out night and day looking for young brothers and sisters. He sometimes would trick them up to my apartment just so I could teach. I quit my job and my wife threatened to leave me. We put her out!

I remember and I still tease Him about that today, about how He ran my wife off. And that tickles Him too, because He never did like her. I told Him the sister was talking about leaving because she said, "You have too much company."

He said, "What?"

I said, "Yeah, every night when there are folks up here and I am teaching, she starts fussing. Saying things like, *She is not going to be staying up all night*, that, *She ain't got no family life, and that, all I do is entertain my guests*. Then I told Him how she said, *Somebody has got to go. Either these folks and all the noise go, or she would.*"

So He said, "Good! Send her on away from here."

At that point I told Him, "You can't be telling folks to send their wives away." At that time I was in charge. I was the one who issued the lessons to the Brothers, and the one teaching the Islam. So I said to Him, "You can't tell a man what to do with his wife. Where is your mercy?" But after I thought about it, I knew the Brother was right. So I told the sister to pack on up and go, because this was no place for her. We put her out and then it was teaching wall to wall. Many nights We would stay up with no sleep at all; and would not get sleepy. Yes, many nights. And there were a lot of nights We were exhausted. Praise be to Allah.

Another group of brothers started to form with Myself and Brother Fard. It's like I said, He would keep on bringing folks. He would tell them, "Look, I've got a friend named Brother Al. He's got

KNOWLEDGE OF THE GODS

a beautiful apartment and I just want you to see it." He'd get them there like that. He'd tell them I had lots of jazz records. Knowing they liked that jazz, He'd get them to come see My collection. Once they got there, "Po' Boy" would have to teach. As We began to teach, brothers and sisters began to come around and stand up. So here again, We had to start establishing some kind of structure. We started teaching, We began training, and We were even marching in the City Streets. They really thought We were crazy then. It was about this time that Minister James came to the City.

I don't want to leave out any valuable history here. We were just getting together and decided that We needed a bigger place. We decided that the teachings were too important to be worrying about personal grievances or problems that might have taken place between Captain Yusuf, who was a Captain in the New York Mosque, and brother Hasan. They had had some trouble in New York with Malcolm. We figured Islam was more important. So We got in touch with them in order to get an official Minister to come over and officiate our meetings.

We had opened up a store front at 142 South Orange Avenue. The place wasn't big enough to hold 20 chairs. You know how those little small store front churches are. If you could squeeze in 20 chairs it was good. Brother Assistant Minister Chris from New York would come over to teach for us. Malcolm wanted Newark to be an annex of Mosque #7 and we didn't want that, so confusion started. Malcolm demanded our poor-rate; he wanted to know where the money was. The brothers formed their Council and let it be known that we were doing our own thing and that we just wanted their help with a Minister. Our attitude was, this is ours and we keep our money.

Malcolm, wearing his shoulder holster with a little .45 snub nose, came over with a couple of car loads of Fruit (brothers). We met at

A. M. Muhammad

13 Court Street. Malcolm started making demands and telling us that if we didn't straighten up, and do things like he wanted, some heads were going to roll and all that other kind of funny stuff. The brothers responded with, "Yeah, well that works two ways." This was the first time I stood up and said something in Council. I said, "Hold on! Listen! We all follow the Honorable Mr. Elijah Muhammad. Is there anybody here who does not follow the Honorable Mr. Elijah Muhammad? Since we have a Leader and Teacher, and we have a telephone here, then whatever the dispute is, being that it is serious, somebody get on the phone. Whoever is in charge get on the phone to Our Father. Tell Him what the problem is and let Him solve it. Because we are acting like we don't have a Leader."

"Yes sir, brother. Yes sir. That's right Brother Al!" came the responses. So Solomon Thomas goes upstairs and makes the phone call. Our Father tells him to tell Malcolm to go back to New York, He was sending us an agent and that Minister James Shabazz was coming there as an agent to help us establish a Mosque, until one of the brothers among us qualified to be the Minister. And that was it. When the brother gave us the message, Malcolm storms out and we started cheering.

We now had our own. The Honorable Mr. Elijah Muhammad said He was sending us an agent and that one of us should stand up and be the Minister but everybody got quiet. Who was going to stand up and be the Minister? Nobody wanted to be the Minister. Everybody present had an excuse, even Me. My excuse was that I was dumb and could not read or write. They needed someone who could at least read and write. But everybody had an excuse.

Minister James came and told us what his instructions were. That he was just an agent sent to set up the Mosque and that a Brother from among us would have to qualify to be the Minister of the Mosque. Nobody stood up. Minister James went about his work of

KNOWLEDGE OF THE GODS

establishing a Mosque. We all gave him our support. We became the fastest growing Mosque there was.

Finally, Brother Fard (Brother Belton at that time) had completed all of His lessons. Me and the Brothers who were with us, became the most dedicated brothers in the Mosque. Every time the doors opened we were right there. We were seen as the soldier Brothers and the other Brothers, they were the Scientist. We were the soldiers. We were doing all the work. Now the other Brothers would show up at the Mosque or they might not, but if they did, everybody would crowd around them. They would get all the attention. The people would say, "Guess who's at the Mosque?"

"Who?"

"Brother Hasan."

"Oh yeah, he's there? Let's go see Brother Hasan."

But Brother Fard and I were there as soon as the doors opened. We were right there dusting off the seats and standing post. As a matter of fact, We would take the post just like We took post for them devils when We were in the army. It became such a thing that everyone wanted to stand in front of the rostrum so they could shine.

We were the soldiers of the Mosque. The history of how we were the First Soldiers for Our Father is very clear; also, how Minister James had only to say what was needed, and We'd be out there in the land fighting. We would always be successful. We became known as The Soldiers of Allah. Being soldiers, We spent all of our time working for Allah and studying our lessons. We knew our lessons backwards and forward. We could recite our lessons like We made them. Because that is all We did, all the time.

Brother Belton and Myself got entangled with the beast and they put Us in the Newark Street Jail. While We were in Newark Street Jail I got bailed out. When I got out, Our Father was making a sneak stopover in New York because He was on His way East, to Mecca. He made a stop at Mosque #7. Me, Isaiah and Brother Ike, went over there to hear what Our Father said at that meeting.

These are some of the things that He said:

"I can give you to Allah now because you are ready." He said, "Look at all My, good helpers up on the rostrum." He had Malcolm, Farrakhan, Minister James, and some more of His Ministers up there on the podium with Him. He said, "These are My good helpers. Many people say that they are ex-convicts and come from bad walks of life, but when I look out here and see your smiling faces - seeing that you have come to see your Leader and Teacher on a Friday night, when most people are out there doing what they call having a good time. I thank Allah for these good helpers." He continued with, "I think it's time for Elijah to go back to prison and get some more of these good helpers." I don't know why I was so excited, but Me and Ike wrote that down. Then He said, "Don't worry about a job. Too long have you been worrying about a job. If you are going to work for anybody work for Allah!" Me and Isaiah wrote that down too. There were many more things He said.

The very next day they turned Brother Belton loose from the jail house. Meanwhile, Minister James kept asking the Fruit for someone to stand up and be the Minister, because no one had yet stood up. He kept reminding them that he was just an agent for the Mosque, to get the Mosque established and that they had to have a Minister from among themselves like Our Father ordered. Yet, no one stood up. Nobody wanted to be the Minister.

As I said, the very next morning, after we saw Our Father getting ready to go to Mecca, Brother Fard gets out of jail. As soon as He got home He called Me. "Brother Al, guess what? I finally found out what I want to be."

KNOWLEDGE OF THE GODS

I said, "What's that?"

"I'm going to be a Minister," He answered.

I said, "Yeah?"

He said, "Yeah, and I'm going to take a name. My name is Aziz. But I don't want to be a regular Minister," He went on. "I want to be a Minister going in the prison to teach. I was thinking while I was in jail walking up and down in that cell, I was thinking about Brady, Mason and all the fellas. All of them are in the prison and if I could get down there we'd have the soldiers we needed in a minute. We'd be able to bring the beast's civilization down over night."

I said, "I hear you. I hear you. Now let Me tell You something. We went over last night to hear Our Father and He said, "He thought it was time for Elijah to go back to prison and get some more good Ministers.""

Brother Belton fell out. He said, "What!"

I said, "Yes Sir."

He said, "Praise be to Allah! I'm going to go see Minister James now." So He went to see Minister James.

When He told Minister James He wanted to go into the prisons to teach, Minister James jumped about two feet off the floor. He said, "What did you say brother?" Brother Fard got scared. Minister James said, "Just tell me what you said. Just repeat that."

"I want to be the Minister, but I want to go into the prisons to teach," answered Brother Fard.

The Minister said, "Brother let me tell you something. The Honorable Mr. Elijah Muhammad told me that a brother would come to me to ask for permission to go into the prisons and preach. He told me when that happens to come straight out to Chicago and let Him know. So brother, I have to go right now! You be at the Fruit meeting Monday night. I'll be back by then and I'll tell you what Mr.

A. M. Muhammad

Muhammad says." And he left.

The Brother came back all excited. He said, "I don't know what's going on. Minister James told me to meet him on Fruit night." When Monday came around We were at the Fruit meeting. We were standing tall and clean waiting for Minister James but Minister James didn't come. The next day We were out doing Our regular - selling MUHAMMAD SPEAKS. We didn't sell papers like the hypocrites sold papers. Whenever a Brother or Sister didn't have the money We gave it to them. We just made them promise to read the paper and not throw it away.

That Wednesday We were out in the streets teaching Islam and selling the paper. As Brother Fard passed the Shabazz Bakery on South Orange Avenue across from the Mosque, He saw Minister James there with an apron on helping the baker. Brother Fard I think had brother Samad with Him I'm not sure because I wasn't there. Minister James tapped on the window for Brother Belton to come in. Minister James told Him that from then on He was the Official Representative of Mosque #25. The Brother called and told Me He was the Official Representative of Mosque #25 and asked Me what did it mean. I told Him I didn't know but I guessed it meant He was the Official Representative.

During this time My folks had Me under house arrest. They didn't want Me to go nowhere because they had got Me out on bail by putting their house up. I kept telling them that the charges had been dropped. Brother Fard told me that they had dropped the charges and let Him out of jail. I tried to tell them I could go anywhere, even out of state, but they wanted Me to stay in the house. I was under house arrest. They thought if I left the house and got into some trouble they would lose their home. So they kept Me under house arrest.

Brother Fard got instructions from Minister James to go to

KNOWLEDGE OF THE GODS

Rahway State Prison and ask the Warden if He could come in and teach Islam because He was a Minister and the Official Representative of Mosque #25 in Newark, New Jersey. Brother Belton and a couple of the brothers came to My house to get Me to go with them. "We just got instructions from Minister James. He said We can go down to the prison and We are going down now. Come on, get your stuff."

"Wait a minute now Brother Belton," I said, "You know My folks are acting crazy." (See how you can miss history. I just want to point that out to you. I'm saying no because My people don't want Me to leave. Here's history in the making and I'm saying they don't want Me to leave).

He said, "You're not coming?"

I said, "Well Brother, you know I have to live here."

"Well alright," He said, "But let Me wear Your Janawl cap." I went upstairs to get it for Him and then they left.

When they got to the prison the warden wouldn't let them in. When He came back He was mad. Minister James tells Him, "Look Brother, don't worry about it. Mr. Muhammad said they probably wouldn't let You in. He said that when You came back disappointed to tell you not to worry about it because Allah has a way to get You into the jail house." We said, "Praise be to Allah!" From that time on this is how things happened:

There was Us on one side and the Old Council on the other. We are soldiers and they aren't. We are getting the glory and they're not. We are moving up in the ranks and they're not. We are the keepers of the Mosque and they're not. They had become the opposition of the Mosque because they had brothers and sisters out there selling dope and that meant We had become their enemies.

When it came time for the Brother to go to jail, which We call school, He got a sentence of six to nine years out of Somerville, New Jersey and He goes off to school. Just about everyone at school was expecting Him.

Just before He left I was getting everything together. I got the car, I got the clothes (We wore the same size) and I got the address book. I teasingly told Him, "You'll be alright, I'll be down to see You. Just get on away from here and give Me that shirt. No, no, give Me the shirt. You can't take it to jail." That is how We were. By the time He left I wasn't even thinking about going to jail! Who Me? I ain't going to no jail.

When Minister James would call Us for instructions he made sure We both were there. Minister James would see Me or he'd come to the restaurant and I'd be there. "How you doing there Brother Lt. Albert X?" "Fine sir," I'd answer. "I want to talk with You and Brother Belton. Where is Brother Belton? You go get Him. I'll wait here for you because I have to talk to you." I'd go get the Brother and bring Him back and he'd start talking about jail. I'd say, "Jail? You don't need Me do you?" Minister James would say, "Sit down there Brother, just stay there. I want You to hear this." They would make Me stay even though I'd be trying to get out of it.

If I was not there they would send somebody to get Me. If he found Brother Belton first, he wouldn't start talking until someone had got Me. They would bring Me in there, sit Me down and then he'd start to talk. He'd tell the Brother what His instructions were for when He got into the prison. That is all they would be talking about. I had to sit right there, bored to death, while he's telling the Brother what to do when He goes to jail. I'd be wanting to chase after some of the sisters or something.

When it became time for Brother Belton to go off to school, He went and I was out and happy. The Brother wasn't in jail a good week when I was on My way to jail right behind Him. He went to

KNOWLEDGE OF THE GODS

jail the last week of April of 1960 and thirteen days later, on a Friday the 13th of May, I too went to jail. He got six to nine years from Somerville, New Jersey and I got six to nine years out of Union County, New Jersey. When We got to the jail house we started working. I knew what His instructions were better than He did because I was a Witness. I was right there! It was My job to help Him because when He was Commissioned and at the time He was Commissioned, He Commissioned Me the Field Supreme Captain. So that made Me the Head of the Staff. By the time We arrived at school, I had been functioning in My role as a Captain for as long as He had been the Official Representative. I left out a lot of that history. We'll have to cover that subject all by itself.

So when I came to school it's straight to work. We followed the instructions that We had been given. We raised Scientists in school. When it was time to come home, in the summer of 1965, the Brother came home first. I came out in the Fall. When We got out the people didn't want to let Us in the Mosque. The Brother had to get a letter from the Honorable Mr. Elijah Muhammad before they would let Him in the Mosque. I also had to get a letter. Praise be to Allah. The history had to be fulfilled.

When We did get back in the Mosque they were scared. They had heard so much about Our coming home and taking over the Mosque. Minister James was making statements like, "He wasn't going to let no petty thief come from no prison and take his throne." There was a lot of corruption in the Mosque. Everyone was aware of that. The Mosque had got so corrupt until someone had stole the brass mold of the Crescent and Star from the top of the Mosque. And to make matters worse, rumor was that Minister James had done it. We heard he had pawned it. But that's the way the history went.

When Brother Mutakabbir and Myself got arrested, the Mosque was on the brink of putting Us out. We were too influential among the believers. Even though they would give Us the worse jobs and the worst duties to perform, We would always do it with a cheerful heart, and We would be examples in whatever We was told to do. Regardless to where they put Us We were an example. We had trained for years to be an example. We couldn't be anything but an example. My job was the garbage detail. As soon as We would arrive at the Mosque, it was My assignment to take the garbage out from the Mosque and from the restaurant across the street. It was really a job. Praise be to Allah! We did it with a cheerful heart. Not that Brother Fard didn't have to smack My jaws a couple of times, because I was really mad at them hypocrites. But after a couple of smackings My jaws were like they were supposed to be and We did it with a cheerful heart. They were on the brink of putting Us out anyway.

When the beast arrested Brother Mutakabbir and Myself it gave the Mosque an opportunity to blame everything on Us. They said that We were gangsters. That We were not Ministers or rather that We weren't Brothers in that Mosque. They were saying that they didn't recognize Us, and this was before We even got to the police headquarters. By the time We did get to the headquarters, Minister James was talking about how We wasn't this and We wasn't that.

The devil attacked the Mosque. They said We had told the police that We had hid the money in the Mosque. They burned some of the files in the Mosque and that was a big thing. Our Father wrote an article, **Whose Christmas**, in which He mentioned the case. He said, "The devils lied so bad you could smell it." The devil lied on us. They lied about all the things We said. He didn't say Minister James lied, He said the devils lied so bad you could smell it. It was a lie they told. The devils said We gave them justification to run into the Mosque and grab the files because We told them that the money was hidden in the Mosque. Our Father said they were a bare face lie!

KNOWLEDGE OF THE GODS

Lying on them Brothers like that.

That concluded the separation. In 1966 they had Brother Fard saying that He was teaching He was the Saviour and giving folks names. Our Father wrote a letter to the Mosque telling them to apologize to the Brother and said, "If they want to know Who gave Him the name Fard Saviour, I gave him the name Fard Saviour. All of us are Saviours!"

Now what do you have to say about that! Then He told them they would have to accept the Brother in the Mosque and give the Brother His administration. But Minister James wouldn't do it. They began to persecute the Brother. A few followers who had turned against Him, who were with us when the Brother was in school, were now doing so because it seemed like all the numbers were with James and his crew. When they condemned the Brother and said that the Brother was a liar, some of the people that were with us turned on the Brother and called Him a liar. My wife, Sister Freda, they told her I was the enemy and to leave Me and marry the brother of their choice and she did. The same thing happened with two other sisters who were on the scene, Sister Rosalyn and sister Azizma. Praise be to Allah!

While I'm in jail *The Trial of Jesus* is going on in the Mosque. I asked Allah for a sign because I was confused and uptight, plus Brother Fard had sent Me a letter apologizing if He had led Me astray. All the people and the brothers who were supposed to have been with Us were saying He was a false Prophet. I imagined He wanted to get My side of this thing. That was, whether I was with the rest of them in their belief. But Me being who I am and being what I've always been, immediately went to Our Father. I took the letter that Brother Fard had sent Me and what I had to say about the whole thing. And thanks to Allah, the record has always shown that whenever I reported to Him I reported everything. If Brother Fard was ever wrong, He got told on! I would tell everything to Our Father whenever I wrote. When I wrote this time, right after I got the letter from Brother Fard, I was upset because He was talking the way He was.

Our Father wrote Me back and everything lit up. I began to see Jesus' history being fulfilled and the Second Reign of going back to the jail house. The history of Paul and Silas going in to teach and raise the Second Reign and Our history of who We were. We thank Allah!

In the First School We were told all that We had to do. But We didn't know at that time that there had to be another period of time of graduating a Staff. We didn't know that the First Heaven would pass and then a New Heaven would come. We thought that in the First Heaven We would be able to establish everything. But that did not come about, it wasn't to be. It was the passing away of the First Heaven, that which We had from the beginning, which had to pass. Even the AL-FARD had to be updated. These things had to pass with the passing of Our Father, the passing of the time and the passing of the Old World. All those things had to pass.

Our Father, The Most Honorable Mr. Elijah Muhammad, We speak not of Him as dead because He is not dead. The fools think He is dead but We know better. My going back to school and raising another Staff was the fulfillment of Operation Second Reign. At the conclusion of the creation of the New Staff, the men and the women, We are then able to do all the things We were taught to do in the First Reign. From Our Father's teachings We were able to do all of this today, after the Second Reign, after the raising of the Second Staff. Now We are able to see Our place in the history. We are able to see Our roots and We are able to see where We come from.

We are able to see where We are right now and the formation of the Staff. The women are just about complete and the men have been

KNOWLEDGE OF THE GODS

waiting. The women are just about established. When the Staff is paired up, when there are as many believing women as there are men, then the Staff is complete. That is when the bounties of heaven will be poured out into our system. That is the blood, the life flow. The establishing of restaurants, homes, schools and the establishing of the community. That blood flow is ready to take place at the conclusion of the graduating of the women and the completion of the Ramadan Fast. The future is as bright as We can imagine. Our problem is to do things right and exact. We have all the time in the world.

When this life blood begins to flow through Us, when the finances come to Us, we must do right. Before you know it we will be a people existing forever, respected by all. Thank Allah for this *Brief Talk*.

In the Most Holy Name of Allah, the Beneficent, and the Most Merciful. In the Person of Master Fard Muhammad, Our Saviour. He is the Master of this Day of Judgment. And in the Name of Our Father, the Most Honorable Mr. Elijah Muhammad, I greet you My beloved brothers and sisters in the New World Nation's greetings of Peace in this World and Peace in the Hereafter.

Peace! Peace!

Chapter Seventeen
Brief Talk II

I am your Poor Brother Ali and I would like to continue our Brief Talk. There are so many things that I have to tell you. Things that Brother Fard taught us in the Old School. The Old School is the First Academy of Islam. A lot of the things He told me to tell you, your ears are not ready for at this time but they are there for you. Brother Fard taught me things fifteen years ago that you are now just being prepared to hear. We have so much to tell you.

There is no God besides Allah, in the Person of Master Fard Muhammad and Muhammad is His Slave. We forever thank Allah for Muhammad Ibn Abdullah of 1400 years ago (PBUH). The Seal of all the Prophets. We thank Allah for Him because this Brother came at a time when the devils were getting ready to divide and destruct the Divine Scripture in such a way that the true identity of the Lost Tribe would be totally lost, except for a few, to all on this planet. Prophet Muhammad of 1400 years ago (PBUH) stopped that process, gathered all of the signs and compiled them in such a way that they could not be disrupted again. He made sure with His life's work that those signs, those teachings of Islam, would be carried right on up until the last day, when God Himself would rise up to reveal the mystery of Almighty God Allah and the devil in person. Meaning that he is the Last and the First.

Prophet Muhammad of 1400 years ago (PBUH) taught that the Mahdi or God Himself would appear in the last day and usher in the resurrection and the Holy War. Allah revealed to Prophet Muhammad in a dream in which He saw himself on a flying horse, a winged horse, that took him from Medina to Jerusalem and from

KNOWLEDGE OF THE GODS

Jerusalem to the Seven Heavens in which He met all the Prophets until eventually he came face to face with God Himself. This dream is the prediction of Muhammad being the first to be resurrected in the last day and time. Where Muhammad is, Islam is. Where Islam is, Muhammad is. You cannot separate them. This was the gift given by Allah to Prophet Muhammad of 1400 years ago. That he would allow Him as proof of the resurrection, to be the first One resurrected in the Day of Judgment. We bear witness that Master Fard Muhammad (call it reincarnation if you like) was the manifestation of Muhammad's whole soul and body when He came to the shores of North America in the year 1930, July 4th. That was the personification of Muhammad. Nobody on the planet who contained the thought of Islam and all of the Divine signs and teachings of all the Prophets and the science of Muhammad but Master Fard Muhammad who came in 1930. There was no man on the planet who was familiar, who was knowledgeable, who was scientific in the thoughts of Prophet Muhammad of 1400 years ago (PBUH) than Master Fard Muhammad, Who was raised by the 23 Scientists in Mecca and who was sent here to the wilderness of North America to meet Face to Face with God. It was the manifestation of Muhammad ibn Abdullah. Let me give you an illustration.

In all living things you have genes, you have protoplasm. The protoplasm carries the heredity of the living thing. Meaning that if you go into the forest and see a squirrel, that squirrel is the exact replica of the squirrel before him. They all look alike, they all sound alike, they all do the exact same thing that their fathers have done as long as they've been on the planet. The hereditary traits are passed on through the genes.

Now let's take some material things like computers. Let's take the program which is like the genes or the work that that particular machine must produce. When we put the program into the computer, the computer does the work outlined by the program. In people, it is the thoughts which are the program and the body is the machine, it is the computer. If the program is Muhammad's thoughts then the body performs the same way Muhammad performed.

Meaning that if Muhammad learned the benefit of prayer when He programmed himself to pray, his body responded in a certain way. So if your body is programmed to pray like Muhammad prayed, then your body will respond the same way Muhammad's body responded 1400 years ago. You will act the same way; you will talk the same way; you will see things the same way; you will eat the same food you will have the same system reaction because it is the same program. Master Fard Muhammad of 1930 is the manifestation and the fulfillment of the promise to Muhammad of 1400 years ago. He would be the first resurrected because of the great work that he performed in re-establishing our signs, which point out our true identity so that the work in this day and time is lessened by 100 fold. Can you imagine how bad it would be if we didn't have Muhammad of 1400 years ago and his great work? If we didn't have the Qur'an letting us know about this blue eyed devil and of the resurrection and of the true identity of the Lost Tribe? We'd really be in trouble.

Yes! Thanks, thanks to Thee O'Allah for raising Prophet Muhammad of 1400 years ago. May the peace and blessings of Allah forever be upon Him and we must not forget that because we know these things makes us the Head of the Muslim World instead of the tail. Being the Head of the Muslim World instead of the tail puts upon us an enormous responsibility to be the best Muslims that there are, so we must train ourselves. We must be strong. We must help ourselves to be strong. We must discipline ourselves so that we can be strong. One of our biggest evils is our desire for this world and anything which is besides Allah. When we start loving material

KNOWLEDGE OF THE GODS

things, loving the things of this world, we become fixated. You see, there's a New World coming in. The New World is coming in and you can see it. In a minute the truth will be heard. It's only a matter of time. The Prophets knew. Every one of them when they came on the scene, knew, that what they were saying was a new doctrine to the people and it would be a matter of time before the people caught-up to those thoughts.

So it is the same thing today, we are moving into a New World. Soon everybody will catch up to the thoughts but the movement is real. If you have a love of this world, if you have some desire, something in this world that you are attached to, then that attachment will hold you there while the movement for complete separation progresses forward. You will move forward in another direction, in other things, but as long as you hold on to that particular attachment of this world, this world's life, that part of you that you devote to that, will burn in hellfire. If I were you, I'd make sure that all my parts are with Allah and Muhammad, bringing in this New World of Islam. Check it out. Look around you. Find out what disturbs you and what you want to do. Do a little self-analysis and every time you come to a point of dissatisfaction, nine times out of ten, it is because you are attached to something in this world. When we're with Allah and Muhammad everything is alright. How could anything be wrong when you're with God? Get away from the things of this world. The desire for the things of this world is our biggest evil.

We must demonstrate leadership qualities. You can't be talking about each other. You can't be gossiping and talking about each other in a hurtful way. You can't do that and build character. If you can't build character and add on to the reputation of somebody then don't say nothing at all. If so and so says, "Well what do you think about Brother so and so?" You think he's a good Brother but your only experience with the Brother might have been one in which the

Brother was making mistakes. There's no need for you to bad mouth the Brother. There's no need for you to say, "Yeah, well, Brother so and so, he's always making mistakes. I can't stand that guy. You know, I don't like him." There's no need for you to say that, being that you know that you are not the judge of anybody. The best thing for you to say is, "Well, I don't know." This is discipline. This is strength. It is hurtful to sit around and discuss the bad points of your Brothers and Sisters in a derogatory manner. "Oh, these are the no goodest folks I ever seen in my life. So and so, he's lying, and so and so be cheating. So and so is dumb and so and so." You don't do that and you don't participate in that. That's backbiting and that's cursed by Allah.

Anytime you utter hurtful talk about a brother or a sister, Allah does not forgive you for that until that Brother or Sister forgives you for that. Any Brother or Sister who witnesses a Brother or Sister backbiting another Brother or Sister, that Brother or Sister should come to the aid of the Brother who is being harmed by the hurtful talk, or Sister who is being harmed by hurtful talk. The Brother or Sister who comes to the aid is saved, according to Allah. His words to me, "If Brothers and Sisters defend each other against being defamed, against hurtful talk and against backbiting, that Brother or Sister is saved." If you want to be saved, don't participate in no backbiting and don't allow nobody around you to be talking bad about your Brothers and Sisters.

Stand up! Allah will bless you and Allah stands up with you. "Oh, hold on now! If you're not going to say something good about my Brother, just don't say anything. We are striving to be right. We try. We know we make mistakes. But We ask for Allah's forgiveness on all our poor Brothers and Sisters and we want to do right. I know you can find something good to say about the brother. The brother is always at class on time. Well now, there's something, Brother So

KNOWLEDGE OF THE GODS

and So is always on time."

If you stand up for your Brother, or stand up for your Sister, Allah will stand up for you. You are saved. That is important. You will see the love and unity that develops because of that attitude in us. We must realize that we are not an open society. We don't want everybody.

Brother Fard used to tell us in the Old School; the crits are always talking about, "This ain't no unity!" Because we would always separate ourselves from the hypocrites. And they are the ones who were saying that they believed in the Hon. Mr. Elijah Muhammad, calling him the Messenger and the Apostle, yet, doing everything against His teachings. The crits used to always come to Brother Fard talking about, "Brother, this ain't no unity. We supposed to be together." And Brother Fard would smile and say, "Well brother, the believers are together." And He would tell us, He would say, "What they propose is like a person cleaning up, doing spring cleaning in his house. And he cleans out all the garbage and all the excess and puts it out in the disposal. But before the garbage disposal or the sanitation company comes around to pick up the garbage, in comes the next door neighbors trying to bring the garbage back in the house, saying this ain't no unity. Believers unite with believers, they don't unite with no hypocrites. You don't unite the sheep with the goats."

We are now establishing the process by which we will try and test every believer that comes among us, to make sure that his trials and tribulations prove that he is a Shabazzian. That he is of the strong. We will have that in effect in a very short period of time and we will not have disbelievers, hypocrites, stool pigeons and backbiters, weak people, among us, the Tribe of Shabazz.

We are a closed society. We are a secret society. We don't discuss our business with everybody. We don't want everybody around us, we only want our own. We love our own, we protect our own, our own comes first in this world. We must have food first. We must have clothing first. We must have shelter first. We must take care of our own. We will build our tradition on the love and unity of taking care of our own self. This family takes care of its own and we do not allow just anybody in our family. No! No! We will not have weak people. We will make the rules hard just so that we can only have the strong. We thank Almighty God Allah in the Person of Master Fard Muhammad for coming or We would be dead. He is the first begotten of the dead, there's no doubt about it. Thank Almighty God Allah!

He's told me that He will save us regardless to what He has to go through. He said He doesn't care what He has to do. He said even if it means that He has to eat rattle snakes, He will gladly do it because He was born and raised to save you and I. You can't even imagine the love that the Saviour has for you. We thank Almighty God Allah in the Person of Master Fard Muhammad.

You have to kill all the pride you find in yourself. You can't have no pride. We have to stamp out pride. The pride is like a weight around your neck in the water and Lord knows you don't need nothing like that. If you want to be proud, be proud of the accomplishments of your Brothers and Sisters. And if you have set an example in that regard among your Brothers and Sisters, then thank Allah and know that it was him who made you great; not yourselves. Get rid of pride. Officers are humble and meek. They're modest and they're friendly to the Believers. They're kind and they're always helpful. That's the mark of a true believer and a true officer. You don't walk around with your chest stuck all out in the air, as if to say, "I'm better than you." Your job is to serve the Believers. Serve God's people. Never be big with pride. Humble yourselves before the people. Worry about what Allah thinks of you,

KNOWLEDGE OF THE GODS

not what the people thinks of you, which is the origin of pride. All Holy Praise is due to Allah. There is so much that we must learn.

There are many things that are hateful to Allah. The Lord hates adultery. He hates the old adulterer. He hates the King who lies. He hates the proud officer of the Faithful. He says that all of these are cursed. We must get knowledge. We can't get enough knowledge. We have to always stay ahead of the people in knowing. God is God because he knows more than everybody. We must get all the knowledge we can. Supreme Wisdom is not for everybody, it is only for a few people. When you realize that you know the truth of Almighty God Allah in the Person of Master Fard Muhammad, then you are obligated to dig up this Supreme Knowledge wherever you can find it. You're obligated to do this.

Many years ago, in the Old School, Brother Fard did not allow this truth to be taught outright. We could only suggest, make hints or ask questions. Brothers had to dig into their lessons and discover that truth for themselves. Brother Fard, myself, and Our Father, were the only ones who knew the truth for almost four years. During that period of time, or the earlier part of that particular period of time, I thought I was going to go crazy because I couldn't understand why the truth had to be kept secret when God Himself was supposed to be among us. I wanted to tell it. Brother Fard would always tell me, "Brother, it ain't time." And I would say, "Well, we are the only ones that know." and He would say, "It ain't time for anybody else to know yet."

I had become so confused. I went back to my room and opened up my Qur'an for guidance because I had to have some guidance. The weight of that knowledge was just too much for me. So when I opened up the Qur'an, the first thing I read was, submit to those in authority. I closed the book up and I've been straight ever since. What I'm trying to tell you is, Supreme Wisdom is scarce and only those who are most blessed by Allah can get this Wisdom and Knowledge at this time. You are blessed. Don't waste time. Get all that you can get, all of the time.

You should be sciencing all the time. You should be trying to find a clearer understanding of Our Father's books. You should be digging into these things. You should be into your lessons. You should be studying those lessons. You should know what those words mean. I remember in the Old School, when Brother Fard was teaching me, just before I woke up. He would ask me questions. He had asked me, "Who was the original man?" I was trying to explain that it was 4 billion 400 million all over the planet earth. And He said, "Well, no Brother. We got to take the lessons . . . you know you always taught me that Our Father says what he means and He means what he says. The lesson says, "Who is the Original Man? Not who is the Original Men . . . plural. It says, the Original Man. So why don't you go back and get in your dictionary and discover that 'the' means a particular person, place or thing. You understand? That's the benefit of study Brother." He said.

Brother Fard made us write books on the lessons. We didn't waste time in the field. We were either fighting, studying or praying. You should be happy to have another Muslim somewhere close to you so you can get together and study Islam. Get into the science. This is the Supreme Wisdom, brothers and sisters. You want to be on the top part of the Nation? You have to study. You have to know more about this than anybody else. Don't waste time. Fast, pray, study and make yourself be strong. Discipline yourself. Set up a study hour during the day, and make yourself carry it through. You have to learn to fight the devil on all levels. Our Father said any Muslim who is scared to fight ain't no Muslim at all. Check that out on a personal basis, look at that on a personal basis. Think of how many times you say, "Well, I'm going to take an hour today just to study Our Father's Book, *How to Eat to Live*." And then when it's time for you to take that hour, the devil says, "Aw man! You can start tomorrow. You don't have to do it right now." Or "You know Brother so and so said he's coming over. You might as well wait for him to come over to start because he'll probably get here while you're reading. No sense in starting and having to stop." The devil says, "Yeah, well you were going to go down the street. Its nice out and everything. Why don't you put that off and go out today and read your book tomorrow?" And you listen to that and carry it out. Leave Our Father's Book over to the side and go do something different. You got to learn to fight.

When you say, "I'm going to take this hour. I'm going to take from two to three to read Our Father's Book." And when the time comes you say, "Where's the Book? Nothing is going to stop me from serving Allah. Praise be to Allah! Allahu Akbar! You make yourself do it. When the suggestion says, "Man, you don't have to do that right now. You know you got time. Why don't you wait for another five to six minutes? Why don't you go listen to some music first? You know, relax or something. You don't have to do that right now."

You are supposed to say, "Be gone Satan! Get out of my face devil! You know that's weak! I found a way to serve Allah and you are going to show me how not to serve Him? Get behind me Satan! Allahu Akbar! I'm going to read this book this hour. I'm serving Allah this hour!"

Fight! Because that's what a Muslim is about. And be strong. You make yourself strong through discipline. That's the truth. That's who we are. Strong Muslims. Muslims who make themselves do the right things because they know what is right to do. None of us can say that we don't know what we're supposed to be doing.

Our Father prepared the table. He got all the material, everything.

A. M. Muhammad

The whole program is set now. Nobody can say they don't know what to do. All we have to do is make ourselves the strongest Brothers and Sisters in the world! That's all we have to do. We are doing that and I thank Almighty God Allah. Al hum-du-illah. We thank Allah much. If it weren't for our Saviour, the identity of God would still be a mystery and we would be dead. There is no God besides Allah.

The greatest teaching of Our Father was God, is in the Person of Master Fard Muhammad. He is a Man. He is not a spirit, not a spook, not unseen. But He is seen and heard the world over. That's what Our Father teaches. He taught the true identity of God. Once we could see the true identity of God, that God is man and not a spirit, then we Muslims wake up to that fact along with the fact that the white folks are the devil, just as real as God is the Black man. That's real. If it weren't for the Saviour, we wouldn't have this knowledge. It would be lost. Just like what happened to Our Father's books and lessons at the hands of the hypocrites and the devil. If it weren't for Brother Fard we would be lost. No doubt about it. We'd be dead thinking that the white folks are the angels and the Black folks are the devil. Praise be to Allah the Lord of all the worlds.

In a sense, we can sympathize with our people who have lived in the worst kinds of conditions all their lives. They can't really have the knowledge of what Heaven is all about. So you can see them misunderstanding Heaven. They believe that when they die, they will go to Heaven in the sky because they have no real knowledge of what Heaven is. But on the other hand, those very same people (so-called American Negroes) if they are going to believe that Heaven is a spiritual thing that you go to and see only after you die, then they have to believe that the devil and hell can only happen after they die.

Now you know the black man of America (so-called American

KNOWLEDGE OF THE GODS

Negroes) can accept that they are going to catch hell after they die. Then they are saying that the hell that they are catching day in and day out; that the hell that we have caught for more than 400 years with trying to live with these devils, with the hurt and with the pain. If they believe that this is non-existent, that this ain't hell then they may have a legitimate beef. But I know that every black man, woman and child knows that they are living in hell right now. They know that this is a devilish situation, all this hell we see around us. Murder, robbery, rape and killing of each other for hardly nothing. Cussing and gnashing of the teeth, all this hell. Real devils on the scene, wicked people, evil people, murderous people, robbing people, conniving people, peevish people, deceitful people, lying people.

There's no way in the world there could be another hell after you die. You're getting this now. So if we can bear witness that the devil is real; that this is a hellified situation that we are living in, then we can bear witness that Allah is God. And the only way we are going to get Heaven is to submit to Him against evil. We thank Almighty God Allah for blessing us with Supreme Wisdom, to know that God is real, that He is a man and there's nothing after death. Nothing! A live dog is better than a dead King. Nobody wants to die. The devils who advocate that foolishness, you don't see them trying to die. If somebody was going to go somewhere, if they were going to go to heaven after they died, then they would have to have special security police to keep the Popes on this here planet as long as they supposed to be here. Otherwise they would be trying to sneak off into Heaven, with all this hell on this planet. But what happens every time one of those folks get sick? They send for the physicians of the highest order to cure him, to let him stay on this planet, just to keep him alive a few more days because he don't want to go.

Don't you know if there was a Heaven after you die, white folks would be in control of it? As you've been taught, if Heaven was so good, then white folks would get there first. They would get their little passports and visas to Heaven first. You would have to pay to die.

What kind of society are you going to have where you (the Black man of America) has accepted that the white man is God? Now what kind of existence can he expect in Heaven if there was such a thing after he died?

Oh, we are so blessed. This is the most advanced country on the planet. We are of a very high caliber. We are of the Holy Tribe of Shabazz, the God Tribe. No superstitions, truth of reality, living proof of God being in our midst today, which could not have come about unless the Son recognized the Father and the Father recognized the Son. The Son of Man comes on the scene praising His Father and He says if you don't accept the Honorable Mr. Elijah Muhammad, then you can forget about accepting Master Fard Muhammad. You see how blessed we are? We thank Almighty (God) Allah in the Person of Master Fard Muhammad. We are blessed to be His people.

Study, Brothers and Sisters and prove all things. Just like they told Paul, "Prove all things and that which you find true you hold on to it." You hold on to it! If you bear witness that Brother Muhammad Ali is telling you the truth, then you better hold on to Him. You don't worry about Brother so and so and what he is doing or what Sister so and so thinks.

Brother, don't worry about whether your wife believes, you better worry about whether you believe. Sister, don't be worried about whether your husband is gone, you be with Muhammad. You'd better check out yourself. Are *you* with Muhammad? Think about it. Make sure you're with Muhammad. You study! Get your roots and find out why all this is so. Don't just take nobody's word. A leader

KNOWLEDGE OF THE GODS

is one who knows. Brother Fard told me in the Old School: He said, "When you make a man dig for this knowledge for himself, he establishes his roots. He establishes his own proofs. Then when it's time for him to defend his truth he can defend it with all that he has because he has discovered these truths himself. If a person just accepts what someone else has told them, then when it's time for the proof; it's time for them to prove what they're saying, they can't do it, because they've just accepted something someone said." We thank Allah much.

In the Old School, everybody knows the wisdom of the Angels studying under Fard. They know our accomplishments, they know that we can recite the lessons backwards and forwards and that we wrote essays on the lessons every week. We wrote essays on our Father's books every week. Every day we had to train. The only way we didn't train is when they did not let anyone out in the recreation yard. Brother Fard Saviour built giants. When Allah makes you great you are truly great. Poor Brother Ali was the Captain of the Old School and *earned* the reputation, *The Dean of Captains and Professor of Ministers*. Now only Allah knows that such history in the future will depict Poor Brother Ali as highest in His class in the First Academy of Islam; respected and honored with Supreme Authority over all those in His class. Only Allah could have brought that about. Master Fard Muhammad bore witness that poor Brother Ali was like Simon Peter, the Stone upon which He would build His church. When Allah makes you great, you sure enough are great indeed.

Here's a little history. In 1956, when I accepted Islam and came among the believers (the few believers that there were at that time) I found a lot of unrighteous practices among us. It disturbed me because at the time, Our Father was teaching us to be clean, stand up, and a Muslim should marry. A Muslim should raise his children and take care of them and live a clean life and this is what I had intended to do. So I rounded up my lessons and I went off into the wilderness for righteousness sake. I wanted to do right. I wanted to be like Our Father wanted us to be. Now, because I'm alone, I have nothing but my own direction in regards to the opinions that are formed of Our Father's teachings, our lessons, and a Muslim's conduct, so that my only instructor in my absence of the influence of the group that I came up in was that of Our Father. Having no personal contact with Him, I could only go and be what I read of what He was saying, or what I heard or saw with my own eyes at a convention in which He appeared. So what we're saying is, I was being raised without hands or without an instructor because it was during the time that we were waiting for an agent to come to help us establish a Mosque. Eventually, Minister James was sent to help us. What I'm saying, is in the absence of anyone's influence I had nothing but what I could understand of Our Father's teachings to go by.

So when Brother Fard came on the scene to begin to receive lessons from me, I had already formed opinions about Islam of my own from what I had received from Our Father. Therefore, my faith in the Honorable Mr. Elijah Muhammad, was brought about through Him, without His actually being there. The stone was hewn out of the mountain without hands. It was my faith in the Honorable Mr. Elijah Muhammad which caused Master Fard Muhammad to appoint me as His Chief of Staff and to declare even in the old school, years before any of the Angels knew who was going to leave and who wasn't. They were asleep on the scripture of everybody leaving except John or Simon Peter, the *Rock*.

The Angels in the Old School use to say, "Yeah well, we don't care." Or, "I don't care how many followers He's got. I know He's got one. I'm not going nowhere. My life and death is all for Allah.

KNOWLEDGE OF THE GODS

I'm with Brother Fard."

All the Angels were taught this and this was their attitude so nobody felt that they were going to leave, that they would ever turn their backs on Brother Fard. None of them! But as you remember, it was during this period of time, of early teachings, that everybody did not understand. So when brothers began to wake up, they woke up to Our Father's identity and they woke up to Master Fard's identity but they did not wake up to Brother Ali's identity until later. It is because of Brother Ali's identity that many of them turned around. The fact remains that the stone that was hewn out without hands under Our Father, was the same stone that Jesus (Master Fard Muhammad) declared to be the stone upon which He would build His church and consequently, like a miracle, everybody left but Poor Brother Ali. Proving with his life that He is the only true Spokesman and First Begotten of Brother Fard, Allah in Person in the midst of the Tribe of Shabazz.

When Allah makes you great, you are great indeed. And we thank Allah so much for being His people. Things look rough and sometimes it looks like we're not making progress, but that is because we are now in the nebulous region of a New World. Everything we get we will establish ourselves. Now, when you think about it, you will have to bear witness that we are doing all that we know how to do and all that we can handle at this particular time.

We can be happy. We must develop slowly at a right good pace, like Our Father says. He teaches us the sense to handle a particular job. He does not put a burden on us too heavy for us to bear. The Old Man in the Mountain, Ali Hasan, Praise be to Allah, took His people up into a high-mountain and this is where he taught them to live a life of bliss. They were taught to live every day as blissful and as peaceful as they could. This is heaven. All you've got to do is make it so. There are signs in this for us today, taking our small family up into a high mountain, the Nation that we are now establishing.

The executives of this particular Nation will live good. There is no luxury in this world that could even begin to compare with the Heaven that Allah has prepared for us. The few of you who believe as Muhammad believes will shortly be put on a level of existence all of your own in which you will receive unlimited funds to save your people. You will enjoy bliss. You will be as Ali Hasan's people were, soldiers, fighting the devil on all levels, all the time to preserve Islam. But enjoying all the Heaven that we could enjoy every minute of every hour of every day that we live. A strong, beautiful people, a healthy people. A people who do not mix and mingle their blood with others. They keep themselves pure and righteous and safe from wicked outsiders and strange people. As Soldiers for Allah, we cannot endure weakness. Study your lessons, the principles are there.

Yakub was successful because his people obeyed his laws and those who failed to obey his laws, they were killed. Officials, the time is near when you will not be able to disobey a law or an order and live. Very serious time coming up. Very serious time.

We're getting ready to see Armageddon face to face. The Third World War is about to start. This Third World War will end all wars because God intervenes at this time. We have a very serious job at a very serious time and we're just trying to get you some principles of conduct, understanding, direction and guidance in this *Brief Talk*.

Praise be to Allah. The Old World is going out and the New World is coming in. It's moving real fast. We have to get you qualified in a hurry. Allah gave Moses a helper in his brother Aaron. He also gave Moses a Staff and this Staff would work miracles. Moses gave the Staff to Aaron, Aaron is the Keeper of the Staff. Old World going out New World coming in. We must be qualified. The

KNOWLEDGE OF THE GODS

Staff is well on the way to completion. The New World is at its horizon, we are getting ready to take our throne of power. The Staff is being qualified. You are now being called upon to dedicate yourself to Allah and Muhammad because of what you know. Life or death, we must now bring the New World into existence and we must do this with our qualifications.

We must understand why we pray. Don't just pray to pray. You have to know why, so you have to study. You have to understand why we fast. What does fasting do? Get into those books. There are free libraries full of knowledge. Find out what fasting does to the system. Learn biology. Learn, study and qualify. We are doing this. I thank Allah for blessing me to do my work. I thank Allah for blessing you to do your work.

We are moving into a New World. The New World is coming on the scene. It is moving fast and the True Believers, the Staff, are being qualified. You are the people. You are given the credit for all the work that is being done right now. You are doing it. This is your Nation that you are bringing about. Your strength and dedication is to be copied by the masses that are getting ready to recognize us. Will we show them strength or weakness? Will we have knowledge to impart to them? Will we recite knowledge that we researched or studied? Or, will we paraphrase information that we heard? We are qualifying ourselves now and we are doing it right. With the guidance of Master Fard Muhammad, we will not fail. We will know nothing but success. Praise be to Allah.

In closing this chapter entitled, *Brief Talk*, We thank Allah for blessing us to love each other and to want to do righteousness in this day and time. We thank Allah for blessing our hands to fashion our Nation. This is a great day for us. This is Muhammad's Day and we are great people. We thank Allah. I would like to read Chapter 44 of **Our Saviour Has Arrived**. It's entitled *The Great Day*. Praise be To

A. M. Muhammad

Allah, the Lord of all the Worlds:

"We are living in a Great Day of God and Man. Allah (God) now desires to take the Reign for Himself, and over the nations of the earth. There are two Gods. One god is the god of evil and the other is the God of Righteousness and Justice. The nature of the two Gods is so much different from the other that it makes it impossible for one God to yield to the other God because of their nature. Unrighteousness and injustice have triumphed over the people for the past six thousand (6,000) years. The unjust god was not one to give up his place for the God of Justice.

Well, we cannot blame him since by nature he was made a god; a ruler. But his time is out and his rule is up. He is now in the time of the other God - the God of Righteousness, Freedom, Justice and Equality. So this is a Great Day - the passing away of one world and the coming in of another world. We have suffered under the evil that the devil was made for. Up until this very minute he wants to do all the evil that he can do regardless to the Bible and the Holy Qur'an teaching that Allah (God) will reward him and me for every act or good work. Everything is being changed from the old to a new thing. We Must Qualify For The New."

All Holy Praise is due to Allah, the Lord of all the Worlds. Yes, God is taking His Throne over all of the Muslims and we are His Staff. We are His people and we have so much to be thankful for. All the suffering, all the trials that we go through to learn our jobs brings us closer to Allah and Muhammad.

Follow the example that Allah has placed in your midst in Muhammad, for he has proven that He is with no one but Allah. He has proven this with His life. You must learn this from Muhammad. That nothing can come between you, Allah and Muhammad. That you are dedicated, that your life and your death is all for Allah and Muhammad.

KNOWLEDGE OF THE GODS

I thank Allah in the Person of Master Fard Muhammad, the Beneficent and Most Merciful Saviour. And in the Name of Our Father, the Most Honorable Mr. Elijah Muhammad to Whom we forever praise and love. I greet you my beloved beautiful black helpers, Brothers and Sisters, as I encourage you to carry on as we use to say in the old school, "Drive on cause We looking good. We the best in the West."

I greet you with the New World Nation of Islam's greetings of Peace in this world and Peace in the Hereafter . . .

Peace! Peace!

May Allah forever bless you with His richest blessings.

Chapter Eighteen
Home Coming

We thank Allah for Blessing us to be alive in this day and time. We thank Him for all of the work that He has given us to do. We thank Him for His Guidance, His Mercy and His Protection. We have so much to be thankful for. We are the inheritors of the Nation and all Nations thereafter, you and I, the most blessed people in the world, the absolute bottom of civilization. There are many people who claim our identity. There are those who claim to be the lost seed of Abraham, like the Jews. But the scriptures makes it absolutely plain that the lost seed of Abraham would be lost in a land that was not theirs, and they would be slaves for four hundred years. And they would be on the bottom according to the prophecy and that God would come to them. They would be a lost people. You can't find a nationality that would want to be a Negro rather than be what they are. The decision is unanimous all over the world, universally. All civilized people agree that the so-called American Negro is the Lost, the most Lost, and they are the bottom of the heap, the absolute bottom. No one wants to identify with this deaf, dumb and blind people who know not what they are or where they come from. We are the bottom and it's a distinction. We are the proof that Almighty God Allah is on time. We would have to be the first that He would come to. We are blessed and we thank Allah in the Person of Master Fard Muhammad. We forever praise and love Our Father, the Most Honorable Mr. Elijah Muhammad.

I want to bring you up to date concerning my coming home. We thank Almighty God Allah for those of you who have been striving

KNOWLEDGE OF THE GODS

hard and keeping the Ramadan. And we thank Allah for those of you who have been forced to break it. We thank Allah anyway. Allah Judges us by our intentions, and if we are trying to do good, Allah blesses us anyway, whether we succeed or not. Just keep the spirit of trying and eventually Allah will bless us with all that there is.

I had hoped that I could give you a more definite understanding of the exact time that I may be coming home, but as the situation stands right now the only definite thing is, it would be within the next three weeks. We'll see. So we leave that in the hands of Allah. There's nothing very much more that we can say about that. It's in Allah's hands.

But what we did want to talk to you about concerning your brother coming home is, just what does it mean to us? Of course, we will be happy. For after all of these years, Muhammad can do this work unhindered or hampered. Sure we are happy. We know the implications for such freedom, but we are a wise people. We know Muhammad's coming home will give some reason to rejoice and it will give some reason to be sad. Now you must prepare yourself so that Muhammad's coming home won't be a shock to you or catching you off guard. Sure you will be happy to see Brother Muhammad leave here tomorrow morning, come to your house, spend the day, have dinner and freely socialize with the family. Sure. But what about Muhammad coming to your door at three O'clock in the morning saying, "I seek refuge in Allah against the accursed Satan!" What would be your attitude then? Would you be willing to open the door? What would be your attitude if I said, at three O'clock in the morning, "Dear brother, dear sister, open your door! I have an injured brother. Let him stay here. Let him have sanctuary for a couple of days until we can move him." How will that affect your attitude in your readiness for Muhammad to come home?

We just want you to know that this is serious. Do you expect

A. M. Muhammad

Muhammad to come home and sit in the house all day? No! Muhammad is just like you. We are servants of Allah. We are on call 24 hours a day, especially the officers in the New World Nation of Islam. At any time we can be called upon to go somewhere and do some work for Allah and Muhammad. We are officers, our life is all for Allah and Muhammad. So we are on call 24 hours. No! Muhammad will not be able to sit down, He will have work to do. So you say," I will be happy for Muhammad to come home so that I can help him do his work." How will you feel in the middle of the night or early in the morning or whenever Muhammad calls and disrupts your plans so that you can come immediately to help him take care of some of the Nation's work? How will you feel then? How will you feel when we have to have some volunteers to be at our Mosque earlier than everyone else to make sure it's clean and proper to receive the people coming to hear our teachings and to socialize with us? Are you ready for the sacrifices? When Muhammad says, "Please show up and give me a helping hand for this occasion that we are having at the Mosque."

The sacrifices at this particular time that you make are all recorded. You are making history. You are making the history of those of you who help at a time when Muhammad is in danger. Such believers shall inherit Heaven, complete peace, no grief, all of their lives and mercy from Allah. Allah says, if you help one of my little ones I look upon it as you have helped all men. Now, how much more can a believer be blessed if he helps Muhammad in a time of danger? We thank Allah much.

Muhammad is coming home to a den of vipers; people who do not want to see us successful. Are we ready? Our sufferings in the beginning are like we said before; they are only trials to prove to ourselves, as well as to the world, that we are the qualified people to lead our Nation of Islam; That we are the Seed of Elijah; That we

KNOWLEDGE OF THE GODS

are the Original Nation of Islam. This is what's happening. You are actually learning at this particular time how to establish a Mosque, how to establish a Muslim Community, how the F.O.I. must be established, how the M.G.T. must be established. You are the ones whose hands are being used to fashion these things into shape at this time. As soon as we have experienced how to establish Mosque #25, the restaurant, the school and the clinic, then everyone of you will be qualified from your on-the-job training to go anywhere in the Nation and establish a Muslim Community. Allah is pairing you up now, you will soon be traveling in twos. Ministers and their wives, who will be the Captains of the M.G.T., who will go wherever Allah sends them, and they won't go poor. They will go with the National Treasury behind them, so that they can progress as fast as they can hear and obey. The trials that appear to be misfortunes to others are only demonstrating to the world, to all other wise people on the planet, that if we don't have Divine Guidance and Protection, we could not bring about the things that we are getting ready to bring about.

In order to prepare yourself for the home coming of Muhammad you must foster the idea in your mind that I am with Muhammad regardless to whom or what. My life, my death, all of my sacrifices are for Muhammad. I don't have to understand. All I want to know is, am I pleasing Allah and Muhammad. That will prepare you for our Homecoming. We are living a transitory life. Your homes, your property, all of this is the Nation's property. This is how it is with you and I, the first believers whose everything is the Nations. Such an attitude keeps you away from the pitfalls of this world, trying to hold on to a world on its way out. The joy that Allah has for you, once you have proven to the world that you are the ones who made the first sacrifices to help Muhammad establish Islam and to prepare our people for independence. You will be justified in living in the

A. M. Muhammad

Heaven that Allah will appoint for you. Can't you see that? And don't you see that we don't have much time to suffer? Which brings us to the next point of Poor Brother Ali's coming home.

You must know that Allah is not freeing Muhammad so that He will not be successful. Those of you who come forth to make the sacrifices when Muhammad is poor will not have to be contributing very long because history says that when this Muhammad comes on the scene, the Divine power that he is invested with will create immediately, a Heaven on earth. Those of you who Allah has blessed to be the sisters and brothers, companions, and family of Muhammad, you should be careful. You must keep in mind that the prophecy says, that the Prophet is respected everywhere but in His own Household. Keep this in mind, so that when you brothers, and family and companions see Muhammad being blessed, you should feel no jealousy. You must think about that. Go to your Qur'an and study the blessings that are promised to Muhammad. Never judge the blessings of Muhammad. Muhammad's being raised to greatness only means that this is the direction that you are following Him in. The water strikes the top of the mountain first. First Muhammad is blessed, then those of you who helped Muhammad before the victory you are the first ones to be pulled up into Heaven, for you helped Him when He had nothing. So Allah gives it all to you. You who struggle in the House of Muhammad to keep it clean and who share your bread so that the family can eat, you will soon live the life that you did not know existed. Such peace is promised to you; Heaven, Happiness, Security and a Long Life to serve Allah. You are those people in this position right now.

Look at the history of Prophet Muhammad of 1400 years ago, (May the Peace and Blessings of Allah forever be upon Him), you can see the history made by His followers when He left Mecca and went to Medina. And you can see as the history is recorded right on

KNOWLEDGE OF THE GODS

up until this very day, of what Islam has done in the Name of Muhammad. You, my brothers and sisters, who are on the scene right now, are the History Makers. Your relationship to Muhammad and the work that you help Him do is the history that is being made right now for all other nations and generations to follow and learn. How blessed you are! How great you are to be at this point! You must realize your blessing. Why you, to be the helpers of Muhammad? Surely Allah and His Power could remove you and replace you with someone else. Surely we are blessed. Allah has no need of any of us. He could easily reestablish or reproduce the creation. We are blessed to be in this position. Let us realize our position and take advantage of our position. So the history that we record at this particular time (when Muhammad comes home, in this serious time, that we are happy, but we are very wise, we are going to do everything that we can to help Muhammad, to comfort Muhammad) will show our wisdom. We thank Allah much, we have waited, the (Scientists) for more than 20 years for this day. If Muhammad touches your life in anyway, you are blessed. So if you comfort Muhammad in anyway, food, shelter, clothing, and you do this with a faithful heart, not seeking some kind of gain, Allah says you're saved. If they fight Muhammad and you help Muhammad fight, you are saved. If Muhammad is hungry and you feed Muhammad, you're saved. Just as long as you are doing it with a pure heart.

These are the words of the Lord to me. He has assured me that I have absolutely nothing to worry about concerning my life and my life's work. I will be with you so long, I think you'll be tired of me before I get tired of you. He says all I have to do is do my work. He said, just leave that devil up to Him. He says, "He got the devil, don't even worry about the devil, all He wants me to do is what He tells me to do. So we're not worried about anybody doing anything to

A. M. Muhammad

Muhammad or stopping this work, because Allah is behind this. We just want to make sure that because the history is getting ready to be recorded, by you, let's make it look good. Let's show that we knew what we were doing and we tried to do it the best we could.

When we give you these lessons, we don't just give you something to occupy your time, these lessons are the keys to your awakening. Every time you learn a lesson, study that lesson as we have directed you, you will come to the same doors that we've come to in the way or in levels of understanding, levels of awareness. When we tell you to study a certain lesson and commit it to memory, and you do this, you become aware of the same things that we became aware of when we trained. So your system changes to that degree of awareness.

If you don't follow these instructions, then you will not receive the keys and that particular awareness will not come to you. These lessons, and we thank Allah, they point you in the right direction. As you follow in that direction you are the one to discover the keys. As you become more and more aware, you begin to know all that's happening around you. You know how to relate to it and how it relates to you. You begin to see, you begin to hear and you know everything that's on the planet, because you have an idea of who you are and use yourself as a basis. You will know other people by the identity that has been established in you. This is important, that you get this through the lessons. As you become aware of certain things that are in the lessons it broadens your horizons. You're able to see more and know more each time one of those rusty locks are opened by the keys that we direct you to when we tell you about your lessons, about your diet, or about your prayers. All of these things are formulas, that if you walk on that path, you will discover the benefits of them. They will strengthen your mind and body so that you will be capable of seeing on a higher plane, hearing on a higher

KNOWLEDGE OF THE GODS

plane and knowing on a higher plane. Once you have practiced all of the rituals, all of the lesson plans that are given to you, you will then awaken on a level that you will know everything going on.

I remember years ago Brother Fard told us that the 24 Scientists will tune in on the planet every hour. Years ago, that was mysterious to us, so we just passed it on as word of mouth, which is a good point here. All of the lessons are not written down. Some could only be passed on by word of mouth. This is one of those lessons that was passed on by word of mouth. Brother Fard said that our Scientists (24 Scientists) would tune in on the planet every hour. That we would know what was going on, on the planet at all times. If anything happened anywhere on the planet, we would know it as soon as it happened. Years ago, we couldn't understand this. But let me show you how simple it is right now and how plain and simple the truth is so that you know. You can see it on a level that you're on right now.

The truth is infinite, and our government is infinite because we go on and on. Praise be to Allah. We are preparing ourselves to establish Allah in Muhammad Speaks. Allah in Muhammad Speaks will be something like, what happens when you turn on the news. You turn your television on and they give you what is happening all over the world. They do this by means of their contacts, their reporters, all over the world. Now, don't you see when Allah in Muhammad Speaks Newspaper is in production and available to the public, your Scientists will be keeping you aware of everything on every level of existence throughout this planet? And we're almost doing that now. That's the material side. Don't you know that all of this fasting and praying is for your spiritual growth and we are babies in knowledge? You are just beginning. You have wisdom, you have understanding and you have patience. All of that to go. So our First job is to get you all seeing the truth and knowing about Our

Father, and bring you up to the open door of Heaven so that you can see what our job is. Then we are as Gods. Because you know everything that you should and you know what we have to do to survive, and it's up to the power that is in our hands to do that. When we give you instructions, carry those instructions out. Don't try to judge Muhammad. He may not look like the folks to you, so Our Father says, but only Allah is able to decide in His choice of a Spokesman. We thank Allah.

Coming home means that all eyes are upon us. Coming home means the brothers have opened up their Mosque. That's Mosque #25. Look at those brothers and the way that they act, the way they talk and the way they walk. Look at those brothers and the way that they unify themselves and the way they go about their business in the community. It will be, look at those sisters. See what they're doing? See their relationship to their men and their relationship to their community? How they act at home and how they act abroad. How they are a people who do not practice the wickedness of the civilization we are coming up out of."

Our women do not hang around the street corners idling. They do not walk in a way that is masculine, lascivious, lustful or voluptuous. We don't do that. Our women don't do things like that to attract the attention of men. They go about their business in the market places. They'll watch us when they see the establishment of our House of Worship. The world watches to see if we're going to be good Muslims.

The world of Islam has been taught that the Mahdi will make His appearance in the West. The world is looking to us to see if we are the true people of Muhammad. They will bring the curtain up when Muhammad comes home. Will your attitude toward Muhammad be, "Well, how come you always ask me to do things? Can't you ask someone else?" Would your attitude be, "Well, why do we have to

KNOWLEDGE OF THE GODS

do this? Because Muhammad said we have to do this. Well, Brother Muhammad ought to tell somebody else. I'm not doing what Muhammad tells me to do. I'm going to do what I want to do." We are making the history and we can show the world what we want them to see of Muhammad's work and Muhammad's helpers at this particular time. We have prayed for it, so here it is. We thank Allah. We can't thank Allah enough.

There was a question about polygamy. Being that we have this opportunity to right a few things; we just want to say that our society and government will not be built on the principles of the societies of governments of worlds that we're coming out of. Polygamy is one of the necessary, basic things in the New World society or New World Civilization. One of its chief purposes is to weed out the weak and nurture the strong. In the Animal Kingdom, anytime they have one born deformed, retarded or not in a way he can benefit the species, the Animal Kingdom kills them, themselves. We are more civilized and are expected to show extreme mercy to our fellow man. But the principles remain the same. Our customs and traditions must weed out weaknesses and polygamy is one of the best institutions because of its rules and laws which govern it. You cannot be a weak or selfish person in a polygamous situation.

Our discipline as a society of people (as a family of people) we will have to learn by travel, by looking about, by studying the best customs, practices and traditions to incorporate in our society which gives us all kinds of opportunities to express discipline. It's the only way we can get things done. There is a principle here. Every individual has that positive and negative side. I call the negative side the devil. I usually identify him as the crooked-horned fellow. Whenever there is a suggestion to do a good deed, the devil, makes a suggestion and it says, "Well, you don't have to do that deed right now, you were lying down, lay down for a little while." You must understand that this process is a good process, it's not a bad process. This thinking process actually is the standard order of procedure in regards to the functioning of the mind and establishing of a strong will power. The minute you identify the negative thought (the devil's suggestion) suggesting that you go against righteous principles, then you can make yourself overcome the devil by being strong. Even if you have to call on Allah for the strength, which all Muslims do. All Praise is due to Allah. We thank Allah much.

You force the negative thought to assist in the righteous deed. The conflict comes when the two suggestions oppose each other. "Do this right deed," and then the negative suggestion comes up. The devil says, "No, you don't have to do that right now. Take your time and do something that will not amount to anything."

At that particular time you have to develop a will power to overcome the negative suggestion. You have to make yourself do this. At the beginning of this chapter, I was sitting there watching my notes, knowing that I had to go to work. But the thought kept saying, the crooked-horned devil kept saying, "Oh you got time. Sunday is a long way off." So I said, "I know I'm supposed to support the righteous thought." I then said, "Righteousness, why should I get up and start working on that chapter now?" And righteousness shows me all the reasons why Allah will be proud of me for doing a good deed. Then I said, "Yeah, well that's it! The arguments too good, is too strong. I have to start on this chapter right now." So I get up and force myself to start. And once I start, "In the Name of Allah", the work gets done. Do you see the discipline? Do you see that once you come into this knowledge that we are directing you, through the fasts, the prayers, through the Ramadan, through all the lessons, we bring you to this point of awareness where you are strong enough to do anything. To say, "Be and behold it is?"

KNOWLEDGE OF THE GODS

Well, this is what's happening with Muhammad's coming home. It is to clear the way so that there's an open territory wide open for us to build and establish a New World under the Guidance of Master Fard Muhammad, Our Saviour, Our Lord, and True King. We forever love and thank Our Father, the Most Honorable Mr. Elijah Muhammad. Allah has entrusted this Truth to Muhammad. We are just like you. We are a person, we are of you, we are from you, we are the same blood. Allah raised me from the bottom of the heap as proof that if He can raise Poor Brother Ali; If He can stand me up from my worthless state of affairs, then surely all of you can be saved. It is a sign that Allah raises One from every nation. He doesn't bring somebody different. If I was different from you, then that would be your beef to the Lord of the Worlds, that you had somebody you couldn't relate to. But because I am of you and are among you and not way up in some Whitehouse somewhere, but right here with you, you have no excuse for not recognizing the Guidance and following it. Allah has blessed me to be His Spokesman. The Words of Truth that I speak to you, this is a Life-Giving Truth. This Truth Resurrects the dead. It makes people who were unintelligent, wise, and it does it immediately. No one who comes in contact with the Words of Muhammad can leave Him being unchanged. Everyone bears witness to the Life-Giving Message that Muhammad has. That is miracle enough for any believer. I am the First one to bear witness to where this Truth comes from. Master Fard Muhammad, He is my Teacher. You may not know, but I do. Praise be to Allah.

What you have been given is getting ready to be the basis for the New Islam. They are going to call it a New Islam, but you can understand their mistaking this because we appear to be a New people. We actually are a New People because we are the ones who practice the principles of Elijah and have made the mental and physical changes that these principles bring about, so we are new. Just like He said, a New World is being established by Master Fard Muhammad but actually it is the same roots, the same Truth from before. Now, those believers coming to us in the companies as promised, as predicted, will automatically start learning the lessons; making the fasts, praying, following all of the customs or traditions. We have set-up the way by which they are to come and learn to be themselves, to reclaim their own. They will go further, open wider ways, and reveal many new things because of this doctrine. You will be the fastest growing New Way of Life known to this planet. We will be the most progressive people in the universe. We thank Allah so very much for blessing us to be His people, for giving us this opportunity to do His work.

Yes, it appears that Muhammad is coming home. We don't even have to worry about whether we will be successful. Just prepare yourself to help Muhammad when He comes home, on any level, at any time, regardless to whom or what. This is our day. No one today, who represents our people, or claims to represent our people, has the Life-Giving Message that we have. As Our Father predicted, the Children of Israel are now ready to learn what the teachers have to offer. Let us do right by this gift from Almighty God Allah and let us put forth the discipline to make ourselves be seen in the right light, as dedicated Muslims, who love each other, and who serve Allah and Muhammad. Praise be to Allah.

All Holy Praise is due to Allah, the Lord of all the Worlds. So in closing; and we pray to Allah that I'll be there with you soon, doing good work and that all of you will be my good helpers. I'll continue to pray for you. You must continue to pray for me. Thank Allah. Thank Allah.

I'd like to quote Section Two of the Chapter, "Muhammad." Chapter 47, Entitled:

KNOWLEDGE OF THE GODS

Oppressors Shall Be Brought Low

In the Name of Allah, the Beneficent, the Most Merciful

Surely Allah will make those who believe and do good enter gardens wherein flow rivers.

And those who disbelieve enjoy themselves and eat as the cattle eat, and the Fire is their abode.

And how many a town, more powerful than thy town which has driven thee out—We destroyed them, so there was no helper for them.

Is then he who has a clear argument from his Lord like him to whom his evil conduct is made fair seeming; and they follow their low desires.

A parable of the Garden which the dutiful are promised: Therein are rivers of water not altering for the worse, and rivers of milk whereof the taste changes not, and rivers of wine delicious to the drinkers, and rivers of honey clarified; and for them therein are all fruits and protection from their Lord. (Are these) like those who abide in the Fire and who are made to drink boiling water, so it rends their bowels asunder?

And there are those of them who seek to listen to thee, till, when they go forth from thee, they say to those who have been given knowledge: what was that he said just now?

These are they whose hearts Allah has sealed and they follow their low desires.

And those who follow guidance, He increases them in guidance and grants them their observance of duty.

Wait they for aught but the Hour that it should come upon them of a sudden?

A. M. Muhammad

Now tokens thereof have already come. But how will they have their reminder, when it comes on them?

So know that there is no God but Allah and ask protection for thy sin and for the believing men and the believing women. And Allah knows your moving about and your staying (in a place).

In the Most Holy Name of Allah, the Beneficent, the Most Merciful Saviour, Master of this day of Judgment We are now living. It is to Allah alone, Master Fard Muhammad, that I submit to and forever seek for help. We forever thank, We forever Praise, and We forever love Our Father, the Most Honorable Mr. Elijah Muhammad, the Last God of the Old World and the First God of the New World. I greet you my Beloved Black Brothers and Sisters in the New World Nation of Islam's greetings of Peace in this World and Peace in the Hereafter . . .

Peace! Peace!

Chapter Nineteen
Counsel To The Household of Brother Ali

This is poor Brother Ali, February 9, 1979. The title of this subject is, "Counsel to the Household of Brother Ali."

All praise is due to Allah. All Holy Praise is due to Allah, the Lord of all the Worlds. We forever thank Him in the Person of the Honorable Mr. Elijah Muhammad, for raising Him, teaching Him, guiding Him, and giving Him everything in black and white; so that you and I can be able to stand here in this day and time, doing this great work of resurrecting our people.

We can never stop praising Allah and Muhammad. The workings of Allah are wonderful. We have come a long way since opening our eyes, but still we must realize that you are babies in wisdom and understanding to Him. You cannot oppose Allah, you can only obey Him. We want to give Counsel to the Household of Brother Ali.

These are some of the hardest trials that we have ever encountered. These trials are put here to qualify you, to purge you and to train you to be the best. The great trial that now has us all in its grip asks, "Will you hold on to Poor Brother Ali regardless to whom or what?" This trial says to you, "Do you have any limitations? You mean, you will stay with Poor Brother Ali regardless? Does it mean that, you're with Brother Ali forever and ever?"

So many of you have said this. You've said this often to me. Just the other day I was listening to one of you saying this in a letter to

A. M. Muhammad

me. But didn't you think that you would be tried by what you say? Weren't you taught that word is bond? And that Allah gives you exactly what you ask for? So you asked for this. Now, who will stand? Which of you will still be with Brother Ali after this hard trial? How many will say, "I can't take no more of this here. So I am just going to have to turn this religious stuff a loose." How many will go that route?

The Counsel to the Household of Brother Ali. Don't you know that your Poor Brother Ali has met that fork in the road so many times. When the devil says, "What you gonna do man? Why don't you come this way because this is where everything is happening? You remember how you used to love the 38 Club!" But I know those days are gone forever. I know that the devil is offering a false dream, a false hope. But Allah says; "Brother, check out your wisdom. Didn't we give you lessons?" And I have to bear witness to the fact that I was ignorant and dead before being enlightened by Allah and Muhammad.

As I look a little further I see that the Lord has never let me down. He always gave me what I asked for, and I have to bear witness that I've dedicated myself to Allah and Muhammad. I don't care what happens. I don't care how poor I am, I don't care how rich I am, I'm with Allah and Muhammad and I don't care about nothing else. Trial or no trial, I'm with Allah and Muhammad. I've committed myself so many times in the past, meeting this particular fork in the road. But if I had not faced the fork in the road and took my stand; because every time you make a stand it gets easier. After a while the only thing that's left is the drink in the trial. That ends the trial when you get the drink. That's a fact. Once we've learned the trial we can pass the knowledge on to you.

Counseling. We just want to give you a little counseling. We don't want to get too far ahead of the subject here. Yes, we're still

KNOWLEDGE OF THE GODS

into counseling the Household of Poor Brother Ali.

After you go through trials, or after you reach that fork in the road, the trials get easier and easier. As you know, every time you get to that point where you rededicate yourself, you have to fight evil and go with Allah and each time, He elevates you higher and He gives you that which you have prayed for. Because the trial you have went through to dedicate yourself to Allah, proves you are worthy of the acceptance of His blessings. You are going through this experience right now. This experience will knock all the play out of you. This experience will bring your face smack down in the cold-blooded ground. This experience knocks all the foolishness out of you. It makes you realize that you have absolutely nothing but Allah and Muhammad. If you can hold on under these trying circumstances, then you qualify to be elevated into a heaven that you never imagined existed, and every trial here after will get easier.

The last counselling we gave you was to look for the drink in every trial. Once you see the drink it ceases to be a trial, it gets easier and easier. After a while, the only thing that's left in a trial for you and I is what your Poor Brother Ali is going through now. Now it is patience. You know that everything is alright after a while. When you start seeing things looking like they are going bad, you start feeling a little happy inside, because the completion of the trial is the measure of the blessing that Allah is going to give you. You have experienced it already. Once you go through what you are going through at this time, you'll see it. Many of you will cry when you see the blessings that Allah has for you. And you will feel so ashamed when you look back at how you even doubted Allah and Muhammad. You'll feel ashamed that you didn't just knock that devil down at the crossroads and keep running for Allah. You will be ashamed for the days when you were dragging your feet.

As you look for the lessons, and you'll get more lessons, you'll give your brother good news and you'll give your sister good news to try and elevate his or her spirits. Allah will bring it about, that the sister's spirits will elevate and she will elevate his or her spirits. This is what we have to do in hard times. What does a soldier have when he's out in the field and bombs are bursting all around him? Here he is a committed soldier, don't know when he's going to die. It could be the next minute! Don't know if he's going to pull through this or not, but both of you are soldiers. We have nothing but Allah and Muhammad. Things can't get no worse, but our purposes and aims remain firm.

You say you love Brother Ali. Don't you know that He tried Abraham and Lot? He tried all of the Prophets. Don't you know that we are going to be tried too? To the point, not only will we know that we can't stand it, but to the point others who see it will get mad with us too. Check out the history of the Prophets and the followers, where they would stone them from city to city, because they were doing so bad, they were so raggedy. People scorn us, they say "Oh man, them guys? They ain't nothing, they ain't got nothing." It's the same thing. It's in the history where they would scorn Jesus' followers, where they would scorn Moses' followers where they would scorn Abraham's followers. This is the same history, until the believers would say, "Oh Lord! Lord where's the help at?" And then, "Did you bring us this far, to let us die?"

What do you think about Prophet Muhammad of 1400 years ago (Peace and blessings of Allah be upon him) when He took refuge in the cave? And while he and Bakr were in the cave, the enemy came right up to the mouth of the cave. But in that little short space of time, a spider had weaved a web in the mouth of the cave and there was a dove's nest perched in the entrance. So when the enemy came to the mouth of the cave and saw the dove nesting and the spider's web, they figured that there was no way anybody could come through without disturbing the nest or the spider's web. So, the miracle in the lesson was that when Allah intends to protect you, or what Allah has for you, you got to get. It doesn't mean that Allah loves you more than He loves her. It simply means, you ask Him for what you want and your religion with your Lord should be a personal matter. It shouldn't involve other sisters and brothers, what you ask for in your dedication. That's your business. I'm with Allah and Muhammad. I don't know how far you are going to go with me Brothers and Sisters.

Counseling. I'm telling you what to do. These are hard times. Hold onto Allah and Muhammad with the firmest grip. Don't let nothing shake you, just hang in there and soon you'll see that to hang on in there gets easier and easier. In fact, just as soon as you make the commitment. Look how pitiful we have gotten. We don't have anything, and there's just a handful of us. What happened to all of the brothers and sisters? Don't you see? Don't you know everybody's just sitting back looking to see these last few just crumble? Which of you will trade in Allah and Muhammad for the devil's civilization? I say to you that this is the time to just swear your allegiance to Allah and Muhammad regardless to whom or what. That's what time it is. Hang in there. I'm talking about like there's nothing else to hang on to, because there is nothing. This is what I'm telling you. Don't even get into who Allah loves the most. Don't even think that Allah will promise you and deceive you.

There's no history where Allah has not answered prayer. Can you imagine that? Sometimes we get upset because we wonder about different things. All of the millions and millions of years, that Allah has been answering prayers; let's just take the last past thousand. Let's check His track record out. Have you ever heard of any Muslims; and there's some 800 million Muslims; have you ever heard of any Muslim who says Allah does not answer prayers? For the past 1000 years, just to give an indication, how is it that everybody, even you in your own experience, knows that Allah answers him who Praises Him?

You have to bear witness that Allah sure enough answers every sincere prayer that you made to Him. Everything you ask, He showed you some signs that He was quick in answering prayers. All Muslims experience this, all the time.

Think of what you ask Him for Brothers. You sisters, think of what you ask Him for. And you don't think the trials are going to be hard to prove who's going to hold on to Brother Ali regardless? I learned how to hold on to the Lord of the Worlds, and every time things would start shaking I just held on tighter, stopped worrying about it, paid it no mind. I knew there was going to be a blessing, all I had to do was hold on. So it has gotten to a point now that the only problem I have is waiting. Because once the trial starts, I know the blessing is coming. I get impatient. I have to fight to make myself be still. Because it's like as soon as things start going down and looking bad, I start knowing inside that, "Uh, oh Lord, what are you getting ready to do now. Because that last blessing was great, I know this one is going to be a miracle." You just get so impatient. You want it to come so fast. I told you last year, we are already a rich people. Our Father said He thanks Allah for such followers as us, and we are rich.

Praise be to Allah. See how on time Allah is? See how he shows you His signs so that you can recognize them? While I'm writing this chapter, and telling you how quick Allah is in answering prayers, a man just came in and told me that in today's Star-Ledger they're talking about the New World of Islam over in New York. There's a brother over there named Minister Eugene Graves, who has masterminded several bank robberies and netted over 80 thousand dollars, and they are supposed to be a branch of the New

KNOWLEDGE OF THE GODS

Jersey New World Nation of Islam. I was just mentioning to you, Revelations Chapter 12, of the Bible, the birth of the child and the great dragon casting out a flood of propaganda to try to destroy us. And that brings a sign of the end.

Allah cares for you or you wouldn't be here.

We are an infant Nation. Just at the time we are recognized as such, the dragon kicks out a flood of propaganda to keep everybody away from us. Just a week ago we were on National Television. Now they are talking about putting us on the Today Show. You see the publicity? You see the recognition of the infant organization? Everybody knows that this is the dragon, the old Satan called the devil. We know who is casting out a flood. The dragon kicks out a flood of propaganda trying to discredit us, trying to keep people away from us. However, the people aren't going to accept what the devil is putting out. They're trying to pass legislation right now to start cracking down hard on the religious cults.

These are the hardest of times and I'm telling you what to do! Hold onto Allah with both hands and don't turn loose. Praise be to Allah. I thank Allah for you, it's not going to be long now. Decide that you're going to be with Allah and Muhammad regardless to whom or what. Be at peace and do the best you can with what you have.

Brothers and Sisters, Muhammad has never lied to you. And Allah will answer your prayers as He has done before. So hang on in there and try to help each other out. These are the hardest trials because we're getting ready to come out of this with the greatest blessings. Like Our Father said, "May Allah's richest blessings forever be upon us."

In the Name of Allah, the Beneficent, the Most Merciful. In the Person of Master Fard Muhammad, the Great Mahdi. And in the

A. M. Muhammad

Name of Our Father, The Most Honorable Mr. Elijah Muhammad, to whom we Love and forever Praise. I greet you my Beloved Household, with the New World's greetings of Peace in this World and Peace in the Hereafter.

Peace! Peace!

KNOWLEDGE OF THE GODS

A.M. MUHAMMAD
Field Supreme Minister of The Honorable Elijah Muhammad

THE MUSLIM PROGRAM
WHAT THE MUSLIMS WANT

This is the question asked most frequently by both the whites and the blacks. The answers to this question I shall state as simply as possible.

1. **WE WANT freedom.** We want a full and complete freedom.

2. **WE WANT justice.** Equal justice under the law. We want justice applied equally to all, regardless of creed class or color.

3. **WE WANT equality of opportunity.** We want equal membership in society with the best in civilized society.

4. **WE WANT our people** in America whose parents or grandparents were descendants from slaves, to be allowed to establish a separate state or territory of their own - either on this continent or elsewhere. We believe that our former slave masters are obligated to provide such land and that the area must be fertile and minerally rich. We believe that our former slave masters are obligated to maintain and supply our needs in this separate territory for the next 20 to 25 years-until we are able to produce and supply our own needs.

   Since we cannot get along with them in peace and equality, after giving them 400 years of our sweat and blood and receiving in return some of the worst treatment human beings have ever experienced, we believe our contributions to this land and the suffering forced upon us by the white America, justifies our demand for complete separation in a state or territory of our own.

5. **WE WANT freedom** for all Believers of Islam now held in federal prisons. We want freedom for all black men and women now under death sentence in innumerable prisons in the North as well as the South. We want every black man and woman to have the freedom to accept or reject being separated from the slave master's children and establish a land of their own.

We know that the above plan for the solution of the black and white conflict is the best and only answer to the problem between two people.

6. **WE WANT an immediate end to the police brutality** and mob attacks against the so-called Negro throughout the United States. We believe that the Federal government should intercede to see that black men and women tried in white courts receive justice in accordance with the laws of the land or allow us to build a new nation for ourselves, dedicated to justice, freedom and liberty.

7. As long as we are not allowed to establish a state or territory of our own, we demand not only equal justice under the laws of the United States, but equal employment opportunities- NOW!

We do not believe that after 400 years of free or nearly free labor, sweat and blood, which has helped America to become rich and powerful, that so many thousands of black people should have to subsist on relief, charity or live in poor houses.

8. **WE WANT** the government of the United States to exempt our people from ALL taxation as long as we are deprived of equal justice under the laws of the land.

9. **WE WANT** equal education-but separate schools up to 16 for boys and 18 for girls on the condition that the girls are sent to women's colleges and universities. We want all black

children educated, taught and trained by their own teachers. Under such schooling system we believe we will make a better nation of people. The United States government should provide Free, all. Necessary textbooks and equipment, schools, colleges and buildings. The Muslim teachers shall be left free to teach and train their people in the way of righteousness, decency and self-respect.

10. **WE** believe that intermarriage or race mixing should be prohibited. We want the religion of Islam taught without hindrance or suppression.

These are some of the things that we, the Muslims, want for our people in North America.

THE MUSLIM PROGRAM
WHAT THE MUSLIMS BELIEVE

1. **WE BELIEVE** in the One God Whose proper Name is Allah.

2. **WE BELIEVE** in the Holy Qu-ran and in the Scriptures of all the Prophets of God.

3. **WE BELIEVE** in the truth of the Bible, but we believe that it has been tampered with and must be reinterpreted so that mankind will not be snared by the falsehoods that have been added to it.

4. **WE BELIEVE** in Allah's Prophets and the Scriptures they brought to the people.

5. **WE BELIEVE** in the resurrection of the dead--not in physical resurrection--but in mental resurrection. We believe that the so- called Negroes are most in need of mental resurrection; therefore, they will be resurrected first.
    Furthermore, we believe we are the people of God's choice, as it has been written, that God would choose the rejected and the despised. We can find no other persons fitting this description in these last days more than the so-called Negroes in America. We believe in the resurrection of the righteous.

6. **WE BELIEVE** in the judgment; we believe this first judgment will take place as God revealed, in America...

7. **WE BELIEVE** this is the time in history for the separation of the so-called Negroes and the so-called white Americans. We believe the Blackman should be freed in

name as well as in fact. By this we mean that he should be freed from the names imposed upon him by his former slave masters. Names, which identified him as being the slave master's slave. We believe that if we are free indeed, we should go in our own people's name-- the black people of the earth.

8. **WE BELIEVE** in justice for all, whether in God or not; we believe as others, that we are due equal justice as human beings. We believe in equality--as a nation--of equals. We do not believe that we are equal with our slave masters in the status of "freed slaves". We recognize and respect American citizens as independent peoples and we respect their laws, which govern this nation.

9. **WE BELIEVE** that the offer of integration is hypocritical and is made by those who are trying to deceive the black people into believing that their 400-year-old- open enemies of freedom justice and equality are, all of a sudden, their "friends". Furthermore, we believe that such deception is intended to prevent black people from realizing that the time in history has arrived for the separation from the whites in this nation.

If the white people are truthful about their professed friendship toward the so-called Negro, they can prove it by dividing up America with their slaves.

We do not believe that America will ever be able to furnish enough jobs for her own millions of unemployed, in addition to jobs for the 20,000,000 black people as well.

10. **WE BELIEVE** that we, who declared ourselves to be righteous Muslims, should not participate in wars, which take the lives of humans. We do not believe this nation should force us to take part in such wars, for we have nothing to gain from it unless America agrees to give us the necessary territory wherein we may have something to fight for.

11. **WE BELIEVE** our women should be respected and protected as the women of other nationalities are respected and protected.

12. **WE BELIEVE** that Allah (God) appeared in the Person of Master W. Ford Muhammad, July 1930; the long awaited "Messiah" of the Christians and the "Mahdi" of the Muslims.

We believe further and lastly that Allah is God and besides HIM there is no God and He will bring about a universal government of peace wherein we all can live in peace together.

COMING SOON BY:
ALI MAHDI MUHAMMAD:

Al Fard

Seven Steps to Allah God

English Lesson C-2

AVAILABLE NOW

Uncle Yah Yah $14.95

Uncle Yah Yah Pt 2 $19.95 (Hardcover)

S/H $4.25 for one book $7.00 for both

New World Nation of Islam
PO Box 8466
Newark, NJ 07108
www.newworldnationislam.com

email your sales questions to:
admin-order@newworldnationislam.com

A MUST READ!
The Future Master Fard Muhammad
By
The Most Hon. Elijah Muhammad

He, Elijah said, *"I have been made equal in knowledge with Allah. I control the winds and the seas. I have power over the sun, moon and stars. I have waited 379 years for this day."* -1960 Saviour's Day Speech (Chicago, Illinois)

Order Now!
New World Nation of Islam
PO BOX 8466
Newark, NJ 07108

$12.95 + $4.25 S/H +$1.00 Tracking Number = $18.20

The Future Master Fard Muhammad
By
The Most Hon. Elijah Muhammad

ON-DEMAND EPISODES

FEATURED SHOW

LISTEN TO THE LIFE SAVING TEACHINGS OF THE MOST HONORABLE ELIJAH MUHAMMAD AS TAUGHT BY THE NATIONAL SPOKESMAN OF THE NEW WORLD NATION OF ISLAM, MINISTER MUMIN ALLAH.

LISTEN LIVE EVERY FRIDAY FROM 6PM - 7PM
FOR QUESTIONS GO TO:
NWNOI.TALK@GMAIL.COM OR
VISIT: WWW.NEWWORLDNATIONISLAM.COM

LISTEN LIVE AT:
www.blogtalkradio.com/new-world-nation-of-islam

NWNOI NEWSLETTER
ALLAH IN MUHAMMAD SPEAKS

$12.00 DONATION

(1) YEAR SUBSCRIPTION:

NEW WORLD NATION OF ISLAM
PO BOX 8466
NEWARK, NJ 07108